Y0-CLC-694

DISCARDED

TEXAS IN CHILDREN'S BOOKS

TEXAS
in Children's Books
an Annotated Bibliography

REF
F
386.3
I48
1986

Barbara Immroth
with a foreword by A.C. Greene

LAMAR UNIVERSITY LIBRARY

Library Professional Publications
1986

© 1986 by Barbara Immroth. All rights reserved.
First published as a Library Professional Publication,
an imprint of The Shoe String Press, Inc.,
Hamden, Connecticut 06514

Printed in the United States of America

Library of Congress Cataloging-in-Publication Data

Immroth, Barbara Froling.
Texas in children's books.

Includes indexes.
1. Texas—Juvenile literature—Bibliography.
I. Title.
Z1339.I48   1986   [F386.3]   016.9764   86-10361
ISBN 0-208-02116-7
ISBN 0-208-02117-5 (pbk.)

This book is dedicated to soaring pioneer spirits
and to those who remember their history
and
in memory of

ROBERT OUTROM FROLING
and
SAM GERALD WHITTEN

CONTENTS

Foreword by A.C. Greene	ix
Preface	xv
Acknowledgments	xix
Annotated Bibliography	1
Subject Index	153
Title Index	171

FOREWORD

It is a romantic memory, I suppose, as sentimental, perhaps, as it is romantic, but it goes with me back to my earliest definition of the act of reading. When I hear the word itself, I cannot halt the sudden flow of recollection, cannot erase that image brought immediately to my mind.

That memory image is a building—a tall building of red brick, with wide eaves, a tile roof, and an inscription in classic Roman lettering chiseled over the front door: CARNEGIE PVBLIC LIBRARY. Trees line the perimeters of its grassy lawns: softly rustling trees (in my memory) of summer. The remembered weather is hot, of that you may be sure, for this tall brick building is in West Texas where summer is synonymous with *hot*—especially in those summers my image works with, because they were pre-air conditioning summers, and despite what the breezes sometimes did to papers and pages, the wide windows which line the library's south side must be kept raised.

The memory impulse is subtle, but strong and well-formed. I am opening the heavy front door to the small entryway; I am entering the main reading room and going slightly to my right; then I am climbing the stairs, trying hard, in my eagerness, not to take them two at a time, my young heart working faster as I reach the first turn and head for the second floor landing. Then, on the second floor, I push open another door —or, being summer, this door is probably propped open already—and enter my private domain of reading: the children's library.

There were no playthings in this children's library; no stuffed animals or brightly colored slides and mazes. It was for *reading*... at least, by the time I started visiting it almost daily, that was the use most of its clients were putting it to. I'm sure there were books for little non-readers, picture books and ABCs, but I was beyond that. I wanted as much excitement and discovery of what life was going to be like as I could find. I was not interested in instruction *per se*: no do-it-yourself stuff. If I wanted do-it-yourself instructions I could go downstairs to the adult library and study the *Popular Mechanics* magazines. But I wanted well-crafted exposure to life: adventure and history. I wanted something that would tell me about things; what had happened around me; or what I could expect to happen to me when I "grew up." I read frantically, furiously, trying to discover more of the world's life. I took reading seriously, exultant that I could do it well enough to challenge everything I saw around me — although that leaves too dour a picture of the boy I was. And if these sound like too-adult thoughts, remember, children are becoming adults every day of their lives and their interests are becoming remarkably similar to those of adults at that same rate — only an arbitrary assignment of age separates the two classifications.

Although my grandmother was the head librarian of the Abilene Carnegie Library, which is where I spent my youth, the children's department was autonomous, and I was forced to abide by rules which even today I cannot see the sense of. The rule under which I and dozens of Abilene youngsters chafed the most was the regulation that young readers could check out only two books per day. Some of us were reading that many in a morning.

I became wrapped up in the various series books for boys, the Hardy Boys, the Boy Allies, Tom Swift, and so on through the dozen or more such series then offered young readers. Any boy who couldn't handle at least three of these marvelous assembly-line opuses shouldn't have been allowed to clutter up the library in the first place. But rules were rules, even before I knew what bureaucracy meant. Pleas for leniency to my grandmother fell on deaf ears; Mrs. S. was, after all, the children's librarian and she ran her section the way she wanted to. I can't help, even now, contrasting the two women as librarians. My grandmother's job, she felt, was to put the reader with the right book; Mrs. S. was there to see that the rules were enforced. I've wondered (and this is the basis for this little outburst) how many young would-be readers she turned into radio-listeners, and how many like her today create television-watchers? She made her young clients feel as if they were troublesome when they asked questions. Her attitude was that of guardian, there to protect the books, not to feed curiosities. Children tend to fear places presided over by adults, and she did nothing to dispel this fear. So my first impression of children's literature was darkened by the shade of unease that enveloped me when I faced the restrictions of the upstairs. But I persisted, reading at the prescribed rate of two per day. I adopted the camouflage of the casual patron. I never stopped by her desk and chatted with Mrs. S. as I did the librarians who worked downstairs at the main desk. I slipped quietly around one corner of the L-shaped room and sped through whatever sequence in the parade of books was on hand. When time came to leave, I never asked anything, but simply checked out my two-book allowable.

Because of my unique situation, with someone near and dear in a position to overcome the damage, the problems of the children's library had less effect than they might have had on my continued reading. But this rambling on about it is evidence that there were scars from the experience; and if this happened to me, one of the lucky ones, what about the hundreds of other children who had no recourse other than up those stairs and into the lion's den?

I remain an advocate of what I call open reading. I have read thousands of books, I have sold books, edited books, and written books — but first there must be reading. When I was a bookseller, parents approached me fearful that little Joe or Jane was spending too much time ("wasting her time," was how it was usually put) reading something like the books I have talked about here, or pursuing mystery stories, or ghost stories, or circus stories . . . and my advice was then and remains: let 'em read. First, last, and always. The kind of readers that libraries and the book world need are those driven souls who, if nothing else is at hand, must consume the backs and side panels of cereal boxes, who still lament, thirty years later, the demise of the Burma-Shave "poetry" signs along the roadsides. Anything to read, read, read. Anywhere. Anything is better than being denied.

Education is reading. You can train a horse, for example, to do marvelous tricks, and I have seen performing dogs who might hold their own at a good many roundtables if the thing called for is trained response. But a horse, no matter how well trained, a dog, no matter how full of tricks, can't set its own course. Animals have only instincts they must obey. Mankind can make choices, and reading is the best invention, to date, to help that process along in the quickest, most personal, and efficient manner.

Now, you may be asking, what has all this to do with a bibliography of children's books about Texas? Everything. If a book cannot help you locate yourself some way, be it emotionally, vocationally, philosophically, or geographically, then writing has no purpose. And while discussing the region of Texas, let's define region so that it becomes a sphere of activities and interests, not just a geographical area. Yes, regionalism can involve the focusing of attention on specific spots for specific purposes. The young reader in Texas is, happily, given greater opportunities in this respect than are most other young readers for a number of reasons. First, the unquestionable aspect of size. Texas is large enough to offer a reader such a variety of stories, whether they be ethnic, historical, or vocational (there are lots more Texas workers than just cowboys and oilmen) that, as a Texas author once wrote, it is a world in itself.

Putting the child with the right book at just the right time is probably the biggest single goal any children's librarian should strive for. As the twig is bent, the tree's inclined. If you have an avid young reader you don't have to worry about the adult reader, and in — what, eighty or ninety per cent of the cases? — if he's not been a child reader you will never have an adult library user. I am suspicious of the children's librarian who tries to keep a child from doing what the "children's section" is meant to do — push one ahead. Competition for the young mind is fierce, and much better financed than you are: television, cartoons, feature movie, and MTV producers; toy and cereal manufacturers; sports equipment makers; the list against the child reader stacks higher and higher every year. Unless the librarian, the bookseller, the author, know about and learn to encourage these green, potential readers, users, and buyers, there is little future for their product.

But I must not make it sound like only a fiscal fight. The advantage that visual entertainment enjoys is just the tip of the iceberg labeled "unread" — the iceberg that can sink even a talented *Titanic*. Make no mistake. We, whether parents or producers, yea, even librarians, must recognize the value and need for entertainment. We avail ourselves of it in many forms (including reading) and we cannot deny it to our children. But, like the beautiful iceberg seen above the water, the danger lies in its deeper significance. No one would pit visual stimulation, for instance, against the tougher, more demanding skill of reading without taking into account the uses of each. Visual and sensual stimulation will win every time unless the receptive mind has begun to grasp the true excitement of understanding achieved on one's own, without the intervention of outside processing. The entertainment iceberg itself, so innocent-appearing but deceptively hidden under education's dangerous waves, is all the more alarming because it usually seems so effective (don't tell me the picture book won't grab first attention every time!). But unguarded against, the picture book will rip the bottom out of thought. Reading remains the foundation of modern knowledge, despite electronic marvels and advances — and I am not against electronic advances, since this is being written on a word processor. But the spirit of achievement that accompanies reading contributes more to knowledge than does the reception of visual stimulation alone. Reading makes a lasting impression on minds, just as printing makes an impression on paper. The television tube, which exhibits thousands of pictures per hour, retains none of them once the power is turned off.

I must admit, this piece has begun to pick up tones of crusading, and that is not my purpose and I hope has not shaped my message, although I am not opposed to crusading for reading (children's or adults')

Foreword   xiii

at any time. In those formative childhood years I have described, I read for pleasure, not to increase knowledge or inflate wisdom. I might have bucked if I had been told otherwise. And my morality was strictly black and white. There were good guys and bad guys and I knew precisely which had been which when I finished a book. Children generally do not discern shades of gray. That's why children sometimes horrify sensitive adults by feeling good when the billy goat butts the nasty troll off the bridge into the foaming rapids. But because children tend to have this wonderful naïve approach to stories, it is even more incumbent on the children's librarian to keep them satisfied. Point them but do not shove. If they drop off the recommended list to pursue a butterfly — or a mosquito — stand by ready to help them continue their journey to reading maturity but without rules. And please, don't let age become too big a factor in reading. I'm old-fashioned perhaps, but I do not believe in "aging" books. Yes, I know; as a bookseller I silently thanked the publishers many times for that discreet little "Ages 3-8" notice on the flap. It saved me lots of discussion with some parents: "It says Ages 8 up; therefore, it's safe for Betty, or Joey." On the other hand, how much more grateful was I for those people who bought the book because, like my grandmother the librarian, they wanted to put the reader with the right book, not the book for a specific age. Oh, there are limits. My enlightened grandmother would let me read everything (as I got older) but *God's Little Acre*, so I waited until I had joined the U.S. Navy to do so. But her denial served a purpose, even if that was not the basis for it. I was able to grasp the book's fuller meaning when I read it as an adult; a meaning I am certain would have floated past my big, round eyes had I perused it as a youngster.

Make use of this book, Texas librarians, or librarians wherever you might be. Capture minds with its net. Stir the interest of these minds and do not, for one afternoon, pin them to a "recommended" board like so many beautiful but unfortunate specimens, no matter how it goes against what you were taught in some class or other on the way to the L.S. degree. And speaking of degrees, apply this bibliography for uses broader than theses and dissertations. You might even read a few hitherto unknown titles yourself.

This book is a wide net, but no wider than you will be able to make use of most of the time. As a musician once told me, a good chord has to capture some tones both above and below the human ear's capability of hearing for the right sound to come through. Study the terrain of Texas as it is pictured and described by books on this list. Are these books all great literature? Of course not. Some of them, I might even say with a pompous lift of my mature, well-informed chin, are awkward and clumsy

— but if they touch a nerve, create a tingle of response or the bite of curiosity in a young reader who is not yet as well-informed, mature — and pompous! — as we are (Ahem!), then the purpose of the bibliography and of the librarian has been fully and wonderfully met.

— A.C. Greene
Dallas, October 1985

PREFACE

This bibliography was begun in the spring of 1981 as a University of Texas at Austin Centennial Programs grant project sponsored by the Graduate School of Library and Information Science. Centennial Programs funding provided a research associate, Barbara DeCoster, and clerical assistance. The goal was to produce a comprehensive, historical, annotated bibliography of children's books about Texas for the benefit of book collectors, boooksellers, children's librarians in public and school libraries, students and researchers in children's literature, parents interested in providing books about Texas for their children, and teachers of Texas history. Children's books are defined as books that match the reading ability level and interests of children from preschool through the eighth grade.

A number of sources were consulted in compiling the bibliography. Four previously published selective lists, limited to titles that were in print or readily available and thus covering shorter time spans, were consulted and compared. These lists are the "Texas" section of *The Southwest in Children's Books*, edited by Mildred P. Harrington (Baton Rouge: Louisiana State University Press, 1952): *Texas in Children's Books* by Kay Pinckney Braziel and Dorothy Brand Smith (Austin: Graduate School of Library Science, University of Texas, 1974); *A Selective Buying Guide to In-Print Children's Books about the Southwest*, edited by Will Howard, "Texas" section by Shirley Lukenbill, Dorothy Smith, and Kay Braziel (Denton: Southwestern Library Association, 1977): and *Reading for Young People: The Southwest*, Jean Greenlaw, state editor (Chicago: American Library Association, 1972). Numerous typescript lists prepared by public and school librarians over the years were also collected and consulted.

Searches in seventy-nine subjects were made in the *National Union Catalog*, the databases of the Online Computer Library Center (OCLC) and the Washington Library Network (WLN), and the catalogs of the Barker Texas History Center and the Perry Castañeda Library at the University of Texas at Austin and the Austin and Dallas Public Libraries. Over 1,600 titles were identified for examination and possible inclusion.

Each title included has been determined by examination to meet two criteria: (1) it was written and published for children preschool through grade eight, or is a classic commonly found in children's collections, and (2) it has an identifiable Texas focus or setting. Titles were excluded if they fell into any one of the following categories:

1. Titles with a broad geographical scope inclusive of Texas, such as the Southwest or the West, but without sufficiently identifiable Texas setting or focus.

2. Most titles written for adults, even though of interest to children and written within their reading capability, with the exception of classics commonly found in children's collections. It was reasoned that there are other sources for these titles, such as the Texas Library Association's *Texas Reference Sources: A Selection Guide* (1978 edition and 1984 supplement) and the Texas State Historical Association's *Texas History Teacher's Guide to Supplementary Materials and Professional Bibliography* (1985 edition).

3. Textbooks, for which there are state adoption listings.

4. Ephemera, such as toy books and most coloring books, which would not be found in library collections.

For titles published in more than one edition, the first edition is the one listed, if bibliographical data for it were available. Many later editions, especially reprints, are omitted or noted briefly in the annotation unless there has been a title change, in which case there is an entry for each title. The latest date for titles listed is 1984.

A detailed subject index developed by Barbara DeCoster, with the assistance of Heartsill Young, identifies places by city, county, or region as specifically as possible. The subject index may be used by librarians as a guide in expanding subject access to their Texana collections because it is an extension of the *Library of Congress Guide to Subject Headings*. This subject access should be useful in the study of local history mandated as an essential element by the Texas Education Agency. The subject index should also be useful to publishers and writers in identifying gaps in coverage in biographical, geographical, and historical subjects. Much has been written about the Revolution and cowboys, for instance, but little is available about the development of the oil fields and the urbanization of Texas.

It is the author's hope that the bibliography will be used as a tool to recognize and preserve children's literature of the state and to share the amazing variety of literature about Texas with children everywhere.

It is my hope that users will call attention to appropriate titles which have not been listed, perhaps reported by those checking their collections against the list. It is apparent that many new titles are being written for the sesquicentennial year; they, with others identified, might be considered for inclusion in a future revision of this effort to identify Texas in children's literature.

ACKNOWLEDGMENTS

Support for this project was furnished by two University of Texas at Austin grants, the Centennial Programs grant and the University Reseach Institute, Summer Research Award. Dean C. Glenn Sparks and Dean Ronald E. Wyllys of the Graduate School of Library and Information Science (GSLIS) have provided continuing support. Members of the GSLIS faculty afforded intellectual interest. Sam Whitten, GSLIS faculty member, who suggested that the project be undertaken, shared his expertise and love of Texana, as well as his ardent opinions about the subject. A native Texan, born on Texas Independence Day, Heartsill Young shared a wealth of insight and knowledge it would have been impossible to gain in other ways. His positive encouragement during the course of the project was of major assistance in its completion.

Mary Beth Fleischer of the Barker Texas History Center has unstintingly shared her expertise and experience, easing the burden of research. Dr. May Boyvey, Texas Education Agency, who suggested to The Shoe String Press that the bibliography be published is truly the godmother of the project. Virginia H. Mathews has been a kindly and wise editor. Barbara DeCoster, first as research associate, and more recently as an interested contributor, has maintained sustained involvement and contributed much through the creation of the subject index, undoubtedly the most detailed index available for juvenile Texana. Christopher Immroth volunteered numerous hours devoted to data entry and searching for elusive volumes in various libraries.

GSLIS students who performed data entry in an efficient and timely manner were Vicki Ash-Geisler, Ling-Hwey Jeng, and He-Ting Shin. Students in the "Practicum in Libraries and Other Information Agencies" class searched the Austin Independent School District (ISD) collections for copies of books, in a massive treasure hunt. Librarians at the Barker Texas

xx Acknowledgments

History Center, the Inter-Library Service of the Perry Castañeda Library, the Austin Public Library, Austin ISD, and at Toad Hall Children's Books have provided invaluable assistance in locating needed titles.

Librarians around the state who have provided encouragement and suggestions for titles include: Jo Ann Bell, Richardson ISD; Catherine Conger and Sue White, Houston ISD; Ida Courtney, Elizabeth Polk, Charles Griggs, Carolyn Hart, Jackie Kraal, Lynn McCree, Judy Rhinehart, Terry Rodriguez and Dorothy Smith, Austin ISD; Mary Lankford, Irving ISD; Patsy Weeks, Bangs ISD; Dona Weisman, Dallas Public Library; Christina Woll, El Paso ISD; and James Thomas, Texas Woman's University.

Lawrence Kreitzer, computer specialist, has cheerfully assisted at each stage of the long process.

Gratitude and thanks are due in large measure to each of these people who have contributed to the completion of this bibliography. The compiler extends her heartfelt appreciation to each of them for their assistance.

ANNOTATED BIBLIOGRAPHY

1   Abernethy, Francis Edward. **HOW THE CRITTERS CREATED TEXAS**. Illustrated by Ben Sargent. Austin. Ellen C. Temple. 1982. 1 v. (unpaged)   **(P I)**

   Sargent's humorous drawings of familiar Texas animals populate this version of the creation story adapted from that of the Alabama-Coushatta Indians, as contained in Howard Martin's **Myths and Folktales of the Alabama-Coushatta Indians of Texas**.

2   Adams, Andy. **LOG OF A COWBOY : A NARRATIVE OF THE OLD TRAIL DAYS**. Illustrated by E. Boyd Smith. Boston. Houghton Mifflin. 1903. 387 p.   **(J)**

   A fictional account of a five-month cattle drive from Brownsville to Yellowstone in 1882, written by a real cowboy from his own experiences. Joys and hazards of the trail, both natural and human, are recorded in episodes of daily occurrences. A vivid picture of trail driving at its height, this classic work was first published in 1903, and has had many later editions, including Time-Life, 1981.

3   Adams, Andy. **TRAIL DRIVE : A TRUE NARRATIVE OF COWBOY LIFE FROM ANDY ADAMS' LOG OF A COWBOY..** Illustrated by Glen Rounds. New York. Holiday House. 1965. 250 p.   **(I J)**

   Rounds, who was a working cowboy, has illustrated the trail episodes from Andy Adams's 1903 classic about the great cattle trail drives, **Log of a Cowboy**. The text of this edition includes approximately three-fourths of the original.

4   Adams, Andy. **WHY THE CHISHOLM TRAIL FORKS : AND OTHER TALES OF THE CATTLE COUNTRY**. Illustrated by Malcolm Thurgood. Austin. University of Texas Press 1956. 296 p.   **(J)**

This collection of campfire stories was selected from Adams's **Log of a Cowboy, A Texas Matchmaker, The Outlet**, and **Cattle Brands**. The folklore of the cowboy, his adventures and hardships, are captured in idiomatic language. Wilson M. Hudson's introduction provides detailed background information. Reprinted by the University of Nebraska Press, 1976.

5   Adams, Audrey. **KARANKAWA BOY**. San Antonio. Naylor. 1965. 70 p.   **(P I)**

Kwash, son of Hosko, chief of the Karankawa Indians, tells of the difficult life of the tribe. The early-19th-century story is set along the Gulf Coast between the Trinity and Nueces Rivers.

6   Adams, Carolyn H. **STARS OVER TEXAS**. Illustrated by Donald M. Yena. San Antonio. Naylor. 1969. 122 p.   **(I)**

This historical reader depicts pioneer life and the positive impact on Texan culture of ethnic groups whose transplanted customs and skills nurtured the development of the state's resources. Exercises in vocabulary, history, and crossword puzzles are included at the end of each brief chapter. A revised edition was published by Eakin in 1983.

7   Adams, Willena Casey. **FIFTY-NINE FOR FREEDOM : THE TEXAS SIGNERS**. Austin. Graphic Ideas. 1970. 127 p.   **(I J)**

Brief biographies of the fifty-nine signers of the Texas Declaration of Independence include birth, arrival in Texas, and personal and political life. Maps of land grants and counties, a list by delegation, and a copy of the Declaration help make this a useful reference source.

8   Adler, Larry. **THE TEXAS RANGERS**. New York. McKay. 1979. 56 p.   **(I)**

This brief historical overview written for the younger reader discusses the origins of the Rangers during the Texas Revolution; famous leaders Col. Jack Hays and Major John B. Jones; battles with Mexicans, Indians, and outlaws; and their current duties and status. An impressive variety of excellent black-and-white illustrations, photographs, and famous paintings expand the text.

9   Alexander, Frances. **CHOC, THE CHACHALACA**. Austin. Von Boeckmann-Jones Co. 1969. 20 p.   **(I)**

A charming story about a South Texas ranch couple's experience with a chachalaca (ortalis vetula vetula), based on daily notes of observation. Lee and Clo Dickinson brought eggs from Mexico to their ranch, where an old hen hatched Choc. The bird soon grew to be two feet long and took an active interest in all aspects of ranch life.

10   Alexander, Frances, ed. **MOTHER GOOSE ON THE RIO GRANDE : RIMAS SIN TON NI SON**. Illustrated by Charlotte Baker. Dallas. Banks Upshaw. 1944. 101 p.   **(P)**

Mexican nursery rhymes and games, collected from young and old in the Rio Grande Valley. Spanish verses, illustrated with colorful drawings and accompanied by English translations, are an introduction to Mexican American folklore for children.

11   Alexander, Frances. **ORPHANS ON THE GUADALUPE**. Illustrated by Lucille Alexander. Wichita Falls, Tex. Nortex. 1971. 88 p. (Stories for Young Americans)   **(J)**

A warm story of survival, living close to nature, Indians, carrying on ethnic traditions, and learning to love the new homeland, as told through Erich, one of nineteen orphans among the German settlers in New Braunfels who were cared for by Pastor and Mrs. Ervenberg. Erich is a likable teenager who matures in his efforts to assist his family of orphans.

12   Alford, Sara C. **THRILLS ON A TEXAS RANCH**. San Antonio. Naylor. 1938. 263 p.   **(J)**

Two recent Vassar graduates spend an adventurous time on the Allen ranch near Del Rio in 1880. After experiencing the Western ranch excitement, the girls, in the melodramatic plot, travel to New Orleans, where they find their real father, and discover they are twin sisters.

13   Allen, Allyn. **LONE STAR TOMBOY**. Illustrated by Jane Castle. New York. Watts. 1951. 235 p.   **(I J)**

Blonde, blue-eyed Francie Lou loves life on her family's ranch. In 1907 she is sent to San Antonio to live with friends and learn to be more ladylike.

14 Allen, Allyn. **THE REAL BOOK ABOUT THE TEXAS RANGERS.** Illustrated by F. Watts. 1952. 192 p. (Real Books)   **(I J)**

A history of the Rangers from a daring rescue of a three-year-old Hibbons boy from the Indians in 1836 through battles with Indians, Mexicans, and outlaws, to the 1935 reorganization of the Texas Ranger Service. Vignettes of conditions of pioneer lawlessness and the brave men who brought law and order to the frontier.

15 Allen, Charles Fletcher. **DAVID CROCKETT : SCOUT, SMALL BOY, PILGRIM, MOUNTAINEER.** Illustrated by Frank McKernan. Philadelphia. Lippincott. 1911. 308 p. (The American Trail Blazers)   **(J)**

A fictional biography of Crockett, this narrative includes the well-known legends of his life highlighted by lines of poetry. The Battle of the Alamo is briefly described, then romanticized. There is a description of the state of the Alamo museum in 1911 at the end of the volume.

16 Allen, Edward. **HEROES OF TEXAS.** Illustrated by Paul Frame. New York. Messner. 1970. 94 p.   **(I)**

Brief, readable biographies of the founding fathers show the historical importance and personality of Moses and Stephen Austin, Bowie, Crockett, Travis, Houston, and Lamar.

17 Allen, Edward. **SAM RAYBURN : LEADING THE LAWMAKERS.** Chicago. Encyclopaedia Britannica. 1963. 191 p. (Britannica Book Shelf--Great Lives)   **(J)**

A comprehensive biography of a poor farm boy from Bonham who was elected twenty-five consecutive times, 1913-1961, to the U.S. House of Representatives, becoming Speaker of the House, a respected and powerful position. Rayburn's sense of his roots and vision of his goals in life are shown, as is his impact on American life.

18 Allen, Jeffrey. **BONZINI! THE TATTOOED MAN.** Illustrated by James Marshall. Boston. Little, Brown. 1976. 40 p.   **(P)**

This picture book fantasy, set in the desert town of Kazoo, Texas, features Bonzini, who comes to town after getting lost in a dust storm on his way to join the circus. After a long absence, Bonzini returns as promised with the whole circus. Merry drawings by James Marshall bring the story to life.

19   Allen, Winnie and Allen, Corrie Walker. **PIONEERING IN TEXAS : TRUE STORIES OF THE EARLY DAYS**. Illustrated by Pauline Batchelder Adams. Dallas. Southern Pub. Co. 1935. 286 p.   **(I J)**

Twenty-three stories, taken from pioneer diaries and journals, recount how well-known figures such as Jane Long, David Crockett, and Big Foot Wallace, and lesser known persons such as Gideon Lincecum, Josiah Whipple, and the SMS kid, met practical problems of daily life. Each story is written in the style of frontier time; the language is not simplified, but a pronunciation guide is included.

20   Alter, Judy. **AFTER PA WAS SHOT**. New York. Morrow. 1978. 189 p.   **(J)**

After Ellsbeth James's father is killed in the line of duty as acting sheriff of Center, the twelve-year-old girl assumes the responsibilities of caring for her widowed mother and family, runs a boardinghouse, and finally escapes from her evil stepfather who has kidnapped her. Alter paints a warm picture of small-town East Texas life in 1904, an extended family, and a memorable heroine in the style of Patricia Beatty.

21   Alter, Judy. **LUKE AND THE VAN ZANDT COUNTY WAR**. Fort Worth. Texas Christian University/Sundance. 1984. 131 p.   **(I J)**

Dr. Burford and his fourteen-year-old daughter Theo move to Canton, Van Zandt County, in 1867 for a fresh start after the Civil War. Young, feisty Luke Widman, whose father has abandoned him, apprentices himself to the doctor and moves in. When local leaders raise a militia to protect themselves from the Ku Klux Klan and the Reconstruction forces, Dr. Burford and Luke disagree on the issue of secession and fighting for their rights. Illustrated with pen-and-ink drawings, the story told by Theo is rich in history and local flavor.

22   Alter, Judy. **THE TEXAS ABC BOOK**. Illustrated by Sally Jackson. Fort Worth. Picnic Press. 1981. 53 p.   **(P I)**

In this all-ages alphabet book printed on brown paper, bold, black letters and pictures correspond with the informative, conversational text. The entry words pertain to the history or some distinguishing feature of the state. For example, A is for Alamo; B is for Bluebonnet; U is for Unique; W is for Wild West.

23   Alter, Robert Edmond. **TWO SIEGES OF THE ALAMO**. Illustrated by Albert Orbaan. New York. Putnam. 1965. 192 p. **(J)**

Francis Tackett, a cub pilot on the Mississippi River, goes with three others to join the Texas revolt in San Antonio. After a number of dramatic, unlikely experiences, he participates in the Battle of the Alamo. The fictionalized view of the end of the battle is seen through the eyes of Henry Warnell, possible lone survivor.

24   Altsheler, Joseph Alexander. **THE QUEST OF THE FOUR : A STORY OF THE COMANCHES AND BUENA VISTA**. New York. Appleton. 1911. 385 p.   **(J)**

Philip Bedford, who hopes to search for his brother in a Mexican prison, and three of his friends join General Taylor's army on the Rio Grande and fight against Santa Anna at the battle of Buena Vista. This adventure story with fictional characters is set in the border region at the time of the Mexican War, the late 1840s. The prolific author of boys' books includes historical detail about the war, Indian attacks, and the search for gold.

25   Altsheler, Joseph Alexander. **TEXAN SCOUTS : A STORY OF THE ALAMO AND OF GOLIAD**. New York. Appleton. 1913. 355 p.   **(I J)**

This second volume in the Texas Revolution trilogy, following **Texan Star** and preceding **Texan Triumph**, continues the adventures of Ned Fulton and his friends during the period of the battles at the Alamo and Goliad. The fictitious characters perform unbelievable feats against the background of historical events.

26   Altsheler, Joseph Alexander. **TEXAN STAR : THE STORY OF A GREAT FIGHT FOR LIBERTY**. New York. Appleton. 1912. 372 p. **(I J)**

The exciting adventures of Ned Fulton are begun with his escape from a Mexican prison, where he had been held with Austin, and his return to

Texas to participate in the Revolution. The fictitious hero meets all of the historical characters during events leading to the Battle of the Alamo in this first volume of a trilogy including **Texan Scouts** and **Texan Triumph**.

27 Altsheler, Joseph Alexander. **TEXAN TRIUMPH : A ROMANCE OF THE SAN JACINTO CAMPAIGN.** New York. Appleton. 1913. 356 p. **(I J)**

The third volume in the Texas Revolution trilogy, following **Texan Star** and **Texan Scouts**, concludes the heroic adventures of fictitious characters Ned Fulton and his friends at the time of the Battle of San Jacinto.

28 Ames, Joseph Bushnell. **CURLY OF THE CIRCLE BAR.** Illustrated by Clyde Forsythe. New York. Century. 1919. 263 p. **(J)**

Curly, a young cowboy, seeks work at the LS Ranch in Randall County after his guardian is shot for stealing cattle. He meets Dorothy Graham, a beautiful young orphan who comes to the ranch with her uncle, the owner. After a series of accidents intended to injure him, Curly leaves the ranch in search of a member of Dandy Jim's gang. With the assistance of a Galveston lawyer, Curly and Dorothy discover that they are siblings and owners of their beloved ranch. This Western adventure story was approved by the Boy Scouts of America.

29 Ames, Joseph Bushnell. **PETE, COW-PUNCHER : A STORY OF THE TEXAS PLAINS** Illustrated by Victor Perard. New York. Holt. 1908. 324 p. **(J)**

In this boys' adventure story, Donald Harrington rebels against his New York father's plans for his career, arrives in the Panhandle, and takes the name Pete. The tenderfoot survives hazing, horse thieves, and prairie fire to become a cowboy respected by his peers and his father, who encourages him to go into the ranching business. Reprinted by Grosset & Dunlap, 1920.

30 Anderson, LaVere. **QUANAH PARKER : INDIAN WARRIOR FOR PEACE.** Illustrated by Russell Hoover. Champaign, Ill. Garrard. 1970. 96 p. (Americans All)   **(P I)**

A biography of the last great Comanche chief, who fought confinement on the reservation and then helped the tribe benefit from the new way of life. The easy-to-read text is illustrated with drawings and photographs.

31 Anderson, Ruth Love. **LOST HILL**. Illustrated by Dorothy Love Evans. Manhattan Beach, Calif. Child Focus Co. 1975. 87 p. **(I)**

A nostalgic picture of the simple pleasures of family life is depicted in the Derby family's move from Austin to a run-down farm house in Central Texas. The parents and their five children live without running water or electricity while repairing their house, attend church socials and the country school, and celebrate holidays with the neighbors.

32 Andrus, Pearl. **JUANA : A SPANISH GIRL IN CENTRAL TEXAS**. Burnet, Tex. Eakin. 1982. 135 p. (Stories for Young Americans)   **(J)**

In 1843 Juana Cavazos is captured by Comanches near Matamoros. The eighteen-year-old daughter of Spanish landowners survives and learns Indian ways. In 1848 she is ransomed, marries Charles Barnard, a Yankee trader, and lives as a respected member of the community in Central Texas.

33 Aronson, Howard Stanley. **ZEB PIKE**. Illustrated by Fred Darge. San Antonio. Naylor. 1963. 47 p. (American Heroes: Explorers of the Western Territories)   **(I J)**

In 1806 Pike and his party were arrested by a Spanish posse and taken first to Santa Fe, then through El Paso to Chihuahua and back through San Antonio to Nacogdoches. Pike's detailed description of his journey, published in his memoirs, contributed to the colonization of Spanish Texas by informing the English-speaking world of its riches.

34 Ashley, Carlos C. **THAT SPOTTED SOW : AND OTHER HILL COUNTRY BALLADS**. Illustrated by Harold D. Bugbee. Austin. Steck. 1949. 63 p.   **(I J)**

Ashley's collection of ballads flows from his San Saba childhood and his poetic ability to capture the spirit of West Texans. The people's speech and humor, their thoughts and possessions, form a lifestyle pictured in verse and Bugbee's illustrations. Reprinted by Shoal Creek Publishers, 1975.

35 Bachmann, Evelyn Trent. **TRESSA**. Illustrated by Lorence F. Bjorklund. New York. Viking. 1966. 155 p.   **(P I)**

Ten-year-old Tressa experiences the hardships of West Texas ranch life in 1926 as she endures rattlesnakes, dust, hail storms, and a house fire. She enjoys the friendliness of neighbors at gatherings at the crossroads school and in helping out in time of need. The novel written by a resident of the area rings true.

36 Bailey, Bernadine Freeman. **PICTURE BOOK OF TEXAS.** Illustrated by Kurt Wiese. Chicago. Whitman. 1950. 28 p. **(P I)**

An introduction to Texas history, geography, customs, and economy, illustrated with colorful drawings. A revised edition was published by Whitman in 1964.

37 Baker, Betty. **WALK THE WORLD'S RIM.** New York. Harper & Row. 1965. 169 p. **(I J)**

In 1527 Cabeza de Vaca, black slave Esteban, and two others of a six-hundred-member expedition to Florida were the sole survivors of a shipwreck near Galveston and then spent seven years with Indians tribes. Chakoh, a young Avavore Indian, joined the four as they set out for Mexico City. Chakoh matured as he struggled with traditional values and with harsh natural and human realities, came to accept Esteban's friendship, and recognized the true honor of his life.

38 Baker, Charlotte. **THE BEST OF FRIENDS.** Illustrated by the author. New York. McKay. 1966. 152 p. **(I)**

Finding Rachel, a homeless dog, is the impetus for a group of young friends to undertake the care of unwanted animals. The children in a 1960s small East Texas town form a kindness club to learn how to be "the best of friends" to animals. **The Kittens and the Cardinals** is a sequel.

39 Baker, Charlotte. **THE KITTENS AND THE CARDINALS.** Illustrated by the author. New York. McKay. 1969. 150 p. **(I)**

Children in Mission Springs, Texas, circa 1960, form kindness clubs to care for animals. The Kittens (girls) and Cardinals (boys) are involved in fund raising, rescuing injured animals, changing the school curriculum, and providing care and homes for animals. The pleasant, if somewhat didactic, story is a sequel to **The Best of Friends.**

40 Baker, Charlotte. **MAGIC FOR MARY M.** New York. McKay. 1953. 148 p.   **(P I)**

The discovery of oil brings excitement to Buckner, a turn- of-the-century East Texas village, and unwanted boarders to Gran'ma Higgins. Mary M. Higgins and the three Allbright children enjoy the boom, especially when a well comes in at the farm of Flora, the black cook. Baker portrays a happy childhood time in this novel.

41 Baker, Charlotte. **NECESSARY NELLIE.** Illustrated by the author. New York. Coward-McCann. 1945. 89 p.   **(P I)**

A Mexican American grandfather cares for his five lively grandchildren in their home near a San Antonio mission. Nellie, a stray dog they have adopted, becomes a heroine when she locates the long lost mission bell.

42 Baker, Charlotte. **NELLIE AND THE MAYOR'S HAT.** Illustrated by the author. New York. Coward-McCann. 1947. 96 p.   **(P I)**

In this sequel to **Necessary Nellie**, the five children seek a good home for Nellie's puppies. The mayor adopts them after Nellie rescues his beautiful white hat, a gift from the mayor of Monterrey, at the Founders' Day parade in San Antonio.

43 Baker, Elizabeth Whitemore. **SONNY-BOY SIM.** Illustrated by Susanne Suba. Chicago. Rand McNally. 1948. 31 p.   **(P I)**

The flavor of backwoods language heightens the atmosphere of this folktale-style story about a boy and his dog who live in a little log house in the piney woods. Suba's gentle illustrations of Grandma, Grandpappy, Sonny-Boy, Homer, and all the wild creatures enhance the simple folk tale.

44 Baker, Elizabeth Whitemore. **STOCKY : BOY OF WEST TEXAS.** Illustrated by Charles Hargens. Philadelphia. Winston. 1945. 188 p.   **(J)**

John McDowell, a buffalo hunter on the Brazos River near Fort Griffin in 1878, finds orphaned Stocky on the plains and takes him to his ranch. Stocky becomes part of the pioneer family and by his loyalty and honesty wins his way. Many Western cliches are contained in the story of the boy's adventures with Indians, campfires, cattle and horse thieves, outlaws, Spanish gold, and rattlesnakes.

45 Baker, Karle Wilson. **TEXAS FLAG PRIMER**. Illustrated by Rodney Thomson. Yonkers-on-Hudson, N.Y. World Book. 1925. 124 p.   **(P)**

Ted and Jenny explore their East Texas farm home and travel to visit relatives at a West Texas ranch in this 300-word primer. Grandfather tells stories about Texas history which interest the children in collecting the six flags that have flown over Texas.

46 Baker, Karle Wilson. **TWO LITTLE TEXANS**. Illustrated by Rodney Thomson. Yonkers-on-Hudson, N.Y. World Book. 1931. 160 p.   **(P)**

Ted and Jenny learn about Texas history and nature at their East Texas farm and a relative's West Texas ranch. Text and illustrations were used in **Texas Flag Primer**, 1925, and show a comfortable lifestyle of that period.

47 Baker, Nina Brown. **TEXAS YANKEE : THE STORY OF GAIL BORDEN**. Illustrated by Alan Moyler. New York. Harcourt, Brace. 1955. 129 p.   **(J)**

Gail Borden, inventor of the process for producing commercial condensed milk, moved to Texas in 1829 and began a ranch with his father-in-law. Editor of **The Telegraph and Texas Register** until Santa Anna's troops destroyed the press, Borden became the collector of customs at Galveston after the Texas Revolution. This is a readable biography of a complex man.

48 Balch, Glenn. **INDIAN SADDLE-UP**. Illustrated by Robert Frankenberg. New York. Crowell. 1953. 210 p.   **(I J)**

In 1715 on the Staked Plains, Twisted Foot, a crippled young Comanche, captures two stray Spanish horses and learns to control and ride them. He has heard from Old Man Crazy, the oldest Indian in Kills Something's band, about men whose skin is white and their big, strong animals. The virtues of risk taking, bravery, and prevailing over a disability are portrayed in a sympathetic picture of Indian life.

49 Balch, Glenn. **LITTLE HAWK AND THE FREE HORSES**. Illustrated by Ezra Jack Keats. New York. Crowell. 1957. 180 p.   **(I J)**

Little Hawk was a late-17th-century Comanche boy whose tribe was beginning to hunt horses. In this realistic tale of his adventures, Little Hawk shot a bear, raced an enemy warrior to save a friend, and rescued his father in a daring raid on an Apache camp with the help of Shy Girl. Keats's line drawings add movement to an exciting Indian horse story.

50 Baldwin, Gordon Cortis. **INDIANS OF THE SOUTHWEST**. New York. Putnam. 1970. 192 p. (An American Indians Then & Now Book) **(I J)**

The Lipan Apaches of the Texas Panhandle are one group described in this ethnologic examination of Apache history and culture from their arrival in the Southwest to 1970. The readable text is supported by scholarly research and is illustrated by numerous black-and-white drawings and photographs. A bibliography and index are appended.

51 Ball, Zachary. **NORTH TO ABILENE**. New York. Holiday House. 1960. 190 p. **(I)**

Orphaned in an Apache raid, Seth Hartley and his prize bull, Crockett, are adopted by Amos Keedy, a tough cattleman, who teaches Seth to ride, rope, shoot, and herd for the Circle K Ranch. On a trail drive to Abilene, Seth courageously fights Comanche raiders, bandits, and stampedes, and falls in love with a young pioneer woman. This is a pleasant story about a boy growing up by testing himself against man and nature.

52 Bannon, Laura. **THE FAMOUS BABY-SITTER**. Illustrated by the author. Chicago. Whitman. 1960. 47 p. **(P)**

While the Gamio family prepares for the San Jacinto Fiesta in San Antonio by building floats for the parades, Johnny is left to baby-sit little sister Rosa. In the amusing picture story Johnny takes Rosa fishing, finds a hundred-year-old kit of eating utensils in the San Antonio River, and learns a bit of San Antonio history.

53 Bard, Bernard. **LBJ : THE PICTURE STORY OF LYNDON BAINES JOHNSON**. New York. Lion Press. 1966. 90 p. **(I)**

This photographic essay of Johnson's family background, childhood, and political career illustrates the thirty-sixth president's enormous energy, populist understanding, and political skill.

54 Barker, Eugene Campbell. **FATHER OF TEXAS**. Indianapolis. Bobbs-Merrill. 1935. 248 p.   **(I J)**

Written for young people by the preeminent Austin scholar in observance of the Texas Centennial, this book is the definitive juvenile biography of the Father of Texas. The lucid text gives a clear picture of the character of the man and of the historical events in which he took part. An excellent index facilitates use as a reference tool.

55 Barron, Edna. **A CHILD'S HISTORY OF TEXAS**. San Antonio. Naylor. 1936. 59 p.   **(I)**

This broad overview was advertised as a "complete, condensed history." The simplistic text, a third of which is devoted to the Revolution, is confusing because few dates are given. Blue-and-black drawings illustrate the text written by a Houston teacher.

56 Barton, Florence. **A TRIP THROUGH THE MAGIC VALLEY OF TEXAS**. Illustrated by the author. Austin. Eakin. 1983. 46 p. (Stories for Young Americans)   **(P)**

The reader is taken on an imaginary bus trip through the Lower Rio Grande Valley from Padre Island to Roma. Highlights of each town along the way are presented, including brief bits of history, folklore, commerce, agriculture, architecture, and geography. The text refers the reader to a centerfold map drawn by the author, as are black-and-white sketches decorating each page.

57 Barton, Thomas Frank. **LYNDON B. JOHNSON : YOUNG TEXAN**. Illustrated by Fred M. Irvin. Indianapolis. Bobbs-Merrill. 1973. 200 p. (Childhood of Famous Americans)   **(P I)**

This biography of Johnson follows its series format of emphasizing the subject's early life. The influences of grandfather and parents, small-town and family activities, pranks, and visits to the Alamo and the State Legislature are followed by his many adult achievements.

58 Baylor, Byrd. **THE BEST TOWN IN THE WORLD**. Illustrated by Ronald Himler. New York. Scribner. 1983. 30 p.   **(P I J)**

A father's memories of his Texas Hill Country youth, as retold by his child, include the best country store candy, longer summer days, taller wildflowers, better cooks, and the smartest people in the world. Himler's impressionistic full-color, full-page watercolors glow with the warmth of color and of the relations of people to one another and to nature, in emotions ranging from contentment to total happiness.

59 Baylor, Byrd. **IF YOU ARE A HUNTER OF FOSSILS.** Illustrated by Peter Parnall. New York. Scribner. 1980. 26 p.   **(P I)**

A contemporary hunter of fossils on the side of a West Texas mountain uses a poetic narrative to describe the landscape and its geologic history. Dramatic, colorful illustrations portray the sweeping passage of time.

60 Baylor, Byrd. **THEY PUT ON MASKS.** Illustrated by Jerry Ingram. New York. Scribner. 1974. 46 p.   **(P I)**

The narrative text, integrated with several drawings of masks on each page, presents a variety of Native American masks and their importance in religious ceremonies. The inclusion of Apaches is of special interest to Texas historians.

61 Baylor, Frances Courtenay. **JUAN AND JUANITA.** Illustrated by Henry Sandham. Boston. Houghton Mifflin. 1886. 276 p. (The Riverside Literature Series)   **(I J)**

Two young Mexican children, captured by Comanches, live among the Indians on the Llano Estacado for four years until they escape, making their way home alone across the wilderness. The Mexicans are portrayed as quaint and picturesque, the Indians as noble savages, the children as wise in nature lore and survival skills. First published in **St. Nicholas Magazine**; subsequently published in several editions by various publishers.

62 Beals, Frank Lee. **DAVY CROCKETT.** Illustrated by Jack Merryweather. Chicago. Wheeler. 1941. 252 p. (The American Adventure Series)   **(I J)**

Crockett's exploits as Indian hunter, woodsman, and member of Congress are told in fast-moving style. The hero is courageous, loyal, and honorable to the death as a defender of the Alamo.

63 Beamer, Charles; and Cox, Bertha Mae; and Frantz, Joe B. **THE**

TEXANS ! TEJAS TO TODAY. Austin. Graphic Ideas. 1972. 288 p. (A Graphic Ideas Book)   **(I)**

Colorful illustrations, maps, and photographs enliven this supplementary reader with thirty-three stories about Texas from the legend of the bluebonnet to 2023 A.D. pioneers. Study aids include introductory information with each story, discussion questions, vocabulary words, and activities. Contributions of various ethnic groups are recognized.

64 Beasley, Fred. **FIRST ACROSS NORTH AMERICA : THE JOURNEYS OF CABEZA DE VACA AND ESTEVANICO THE BLACK.** Austin. Graphic Ideas. 1974. 63 p.   **(I)**

A dramatic picture-book presentation of the incredible journeys across Texas of Cabeza de Vaca and the black slave Estevan, who, along with two others, survived the shipwreck near Galveston of an expedition to Spanish Florida in 1527. Bold, colorful drawings illustrate the brief, clear text.

65 Beatty, Patricia. **BILLY BEDAMNED, LONG GONE BY.** New York. Morrow. 1977. 223 p.   **(I J)**

On a trip in a 1923 Studebaker driven by their mother and grandmother, Merle and Graham Tucker unexpectedly meet their great-uncle at his small-town Texas home. Rudd Quiney's explanations of how he lost the bottom part of his left ear are Texas tall tales in cowboy dialect about Civil War battles, terrible weather, and frontier and Indian life. This family of droll characters acts out another humorous Beatty story.

66 Beatty, Patricia. **HOW MANY MILES TO SUNDOWN.** New York. Morrow. 1974. 222 p.   **(I J)**

Beulah Land (Beeler) Quiney, accompanied by Travis, her twelve-hundred-pound pet steer, pursues her brother Leo, who has stolen her horse Jinglebob. They go off to help Nate Graber search across Texas and the New Mexico and Arizona territories for his father in 1881. The thirteen-year-old tomboy proves she is the equal of anyone in meeting a series of adventures with picturesque characters, outlaws, and circus performers. This companion piece to **A Long Way to Whiskey Creek** continues the humorous Quiney family saga.

67 Beatty, Patricia. **A LONG WAY TO WHISKEY CREEK.** New York. Morrow. 1971. 224 p.   **(I J)**

In 1879, thirteen-year-old Parker Quiney sets out with a coffin in the back of his wagon to bring home the body of his older brother Jess for proper burial. On the 400-mile journey across Texas with friend Nat and J.E.B. Stuart, his dog, Parker meets a number of amusing characters, including a lady blacksmith and her evangelist husband, a witch from Chihuahua, a medicine showman, and an old outlaw, the Tonkawa Kid. Beatty combines historical fact, strong feelings about the Civil War, and gunplay of the Old West with her usual humor in this delightful story.

68 Beatty, Patricia. **THAT'S ONE ORNERY ORPHAN**. New York. Morrow. 1980. 216 p.   **(I J)**

In 1889, adoption placements put willful thirteen-year-old Hallie Lee Baker into the care of a hellfire-and-brimstone preacher, a country doctor, and a traveling actress before she is picked as a daughter by a loving family. Beatty's accurate portrayal of the historical period serves as a setting for the fine characterization of a spunky young woman.

69 Beatty, Patricia. **WAIT FOR ME, WATCH FOR ME, EULA BEE**. New York. Morrow. 1978. 221 p.   **(J)**

While his father and brother are fighting for the Confederates, thirteen-year-old Lewallen Collier and his little red-headed sister Eula Bee are captured by Comanches. Lewallen escapes to Fort Belknap and joins with a Comanchero to rescue his sister. A realistic picture of West Texas life in the 1860s and of conflicts among the Anglo settlers, Indians, Mexicans, Yankees, and Confederates unfolds in a historically accurate, exciting story.

70 Benedict, Rex. **THE BALLAD OF CACTUS JACK**. New York. Pantheon. 1975. 136 p.   **(I J)**

Cactus Jack, leader of the notorious Pecos Gang, circulates a rumor that he is carrying a fortune in gold. The sheriff of Medicine Creek, Texas, and grandson of Cactus Jack's lifelong adversary, Deppity Sagebrush Sheridan the Third, forms a posse of wayward boys to chase the criminals. The series of hilarious, improbable situations form a sequel to Benedict's **Goodbye to the Purple Sage**.

71 Benedict, Rex. **GOOD LUCK ARIZONA MAN**. New York. Pantheon. 1972. 168 p.   **(I J)**

A half-breed Apache named Good Luck Arizona Man searches for his origins and hidden gold in the Guadalupe Mountains of Texas. He finds the mountains infested with eccentric varmints shooting at each other. In order to avoid the curse of dying upon finding the gold, he returns to Chief Old Wickiup's tribe empty-handed. The witty use of Western motifs will amuse those fond of black humor.

72 Benedict, Rex. **GOODBYE TO THE PURPLE SAGE : THE LAST GREAT RIDE OF THE SHERIFF OF MEDICINE CREEK.** New York. Pantheon. 1973. 120 p.   **(I J)**

Sagebrush Sheridan I, sheriff of Medicine Creek, Texas, pursues Cactus Jack and the Pecos Gang--Cold Eyed Luke, Memphis Bill, Dalhart Ike, Three Finger Doc, and Sanatone Rose--through West Texas in a playful Western novel narrated by the Deppity. The characters attempt to recreate the poetry and romance of the old "Code of the West" in a lifelong game.

73 Benner, Judith Ann. **LONE STAR REBEL.** Illustrated by R.B. Dance. Winston-Salem. J.F. Blair. 1971. 232 p.   **(J)**

In 1862 fourteen-year-old "Rooster" Crawford rides his mustang 800 miles to join his older brother in the Sixth Texas Cavalry and becomes an aide to Colonel Lawrence Sullivan Ross. This suspenseful adventure story of the Civil War period climaxes in a confrontation with counterfeiters.

74 Bishop, Curtis Kent. **BANJO HITTER.** Austin. Steck. 1951. 204 p.   **(I)**

Ricky Scott, college baseball star, signs a professional contract with the Comets, owned and managed by his wife's grandfather. Settings include University of Texas and Alice Aces bush league ball games and work on an oil pipeline.

75 Bishop, Curtis Kent. **THE BIG GAME.** Austin. Steck. 1963. 156 p.   **(I J)**

Twelve-year-old George Dawson joins the Atlas Giants team of the West Austin Little league after intense coaching from his father. Manager Tracy moves George from pitcher to catcher for the team's benefit, but against Mr. Dawson's wishes. Detailed descriptions of baseball games form a background from which George overcomes his problems and those of his father in this typical boys' sports story.

76 Bishop, Curtis Kent. **FAST BREAK.** New York. Lippincott. 1967. 185 p.   **(I J)**

Sam Daley is named to the Riverside High basketball team because of his friendship with Rene, recently arrived from Mexico. Much basketball action provides the setting for Sam's struggle and growth. The locale is Central Texas.

77 Bishop, Curtis Kent. **FIELD GOAL**. Philadelphia. Lippincott. 1964. 187 p. **(I J)**

Tom Farrell of Austin loses thirty pounds and impresses the new coach with his unconventional method of barefoot kicking to win a place on the Belmont High football team.

78 Bishop, Curtis Kent. **FIGHTING QUARTERBACK**. Austin. Steck. 1954. 208 p. **(I J)**

By lying about his age, Jim Corson joined the Marines to fight in the Korean War. After his discharge, he attended Belmont High to complete his senior year and play football under Coach Edmund. Overcoming all obstacles, Jim won a football scholarship to Staunton University.

79 Bishop, Curtis Kent. **THE FIRST TEXAS RANGER, JACK HAYS**. New York. Messner. 1959. 192 p. **(I J)**

Jack Hays earned a reputation as a frontier fighter and leader of the Texas Rangers, the most effective law enforcement body in the West against raiding Indians and Mexicans. Nineteen-year-old Hays volunteered in the Texas Army after the Battle of San Jacinto, worked as a surveyor, and married Susan Calvert, a Seguin judge's daughter. This biography of a legendary frontier personality explores his contributions to Texas.

80 Bishop, Curtis Kent. **FOOTBALL FEVER**. Austin. Steck. 1952. 206 p. **(I J)**

Thomas Baldridge, wealthy oilman, contributes Baldridge Fellowships for petroleum engineering to Belmont College, where his son is captain of the football team and president of a fraternity. The social structure of this fictional post-World War II Texas college is rearranged when the younger Baldridge must work with junior college transfer students to win a football game.

81 Bishop, Curtis Kent. **GOAL TO GO**. Austin. Steck. 1955. 202 p. **(I J)**

Jim Milner moved to Belmont High as a senior. Although his older brother was a former all-state quarterback who had been paralyzed from a game injury, Jim won a place on the team through his own efforts and with the encouragement of family, new friends, and the coach.

82 Bishop, Curtis Kent. **GRIDIRON GLORY**. Philadelphia. Lippincott. 1966. 175 p.   **(I J)**

Bozo Brocks, a high school dropout who has been driving trucks for his brother, returns to Riverside High to play football and graduate. A wise English teacher and a bright student, Jane Winthrop, show Bozo he can achieve academically, as well as in Texas football.

83 Bishop, Curtis Kent. **HACKBERRY JONES, SPLIT END**. Philadelphia. Lippincott. 1968. 174 p.   **(I J)**

Hackberry Jones, a new boy at Riverside High who could rope calves and ride wild horses, had learned to be a pass receiver by watching goats. Senior football star Jim Carter learned to share the glory with Hackberry and and won a scholarship to the University of Texas.

84 Bishop, Curtis Kent. **HALF-TIME HERO**. Austin. Steck. 1956. 183 p.   **(I J)**

Hal Conroy quits the Melville High football team to work in his uncle's garage after his best friend, quarterback Bob Nelson, suddenly moves away. Charley Kirk, the new quarterback, changes his attitude toward Hal after he has an auto accident from which Hal helps him to recover. In the familiar Bishop pattern, Hal overcomes his problems to help his team win the championship game.

85 Bishop, Curtis Kent. **LANK OF THE LITTLE LEAGUE**. Philadelphia. Lippincott. 1958. 190 p.   **(I J)**

Jim Holland befriends Lank and persuades him to try out for the West Austin Little League. Lank lives on a houseboat on the river and works at a boathouse to support himself. Miss Cartwright, a rich old woman whose elegant house is modeled after the Pease mansion in Austin, rescues Lank from being placed in an institution by adopting him.

86 Bishop, Curtis Kent. **LARRY COMES HOME**. Austin. Steck. 1955. 202 p.   **(I J)**

Twelve-year-old Larry Scott's third year in Little League leads to a championship after several unexpected occurrences. Mr. Tracy, beloved manager, shares the coaching with Miss Sara Milton, a summer visitor from Williamsport. This is a sequel to **Larry of Little League** and **Larry Leads Off**.

87 Bishop, Curtis Kent. **LARRY LEADS OFF**. Austin. Steck. 1954. 149 p.   (I J)

In Larry Scott's second year on the Calumet Little League team, Coach Tracy moves him to the catcher position, making him the lead batter. Tommy Millican, son of a jet pilot and Korean War POW, joins the team and helps win the championship game, which his father returns in time to see. This story, set in 1953, is second in a series about Larry's Little League experiences.

88 Bishop, Curtis Kent. **LARRY OF LITTLE LEAGUE**. Austin. Steck. 1953. 161 p.   (I J)

Not quite ten years old and small for his age, Larry Scott is chosen by Coach Tracy to play on the Calumet Little League team. Although he does not play in a single game, Larry cheers his team on to the championship and wins a bicycle for showing the best team spirit. This story is first in a series about Larry's experiences in the Little League.

89 Bishop, Curtis Kent. **THE LAST OUTLAW**. Nashville. Broadman. 1967. 144 p.   (I J)

In 1882, thirteen-year-old Jeb Allen moves from Chicago to the XIT Ranch in West Texas, where his father is superintendent of the five-million-acre spread. Jeb witnesses one of the most bitter feuds in the West over water rights and fencing the open range. He is befriended by an old pioneer blacksmith and taken on a wild mustang hunt. The Allens help the small farmers and in turn are accepted by the community.

90 Bishop, Curtis Kent. **LITTLE LEAGUE AMIGO**. Philadelphia. Lippincott. 1964. 187 p.   (I J)

Carlos Galvez, new member of the West Austin Little League Atlas Giants team, had learned baseball in Havana. The Cuban refugee overcame his fear of humiliation and learned to pitch in this baseball story.

91 Bishop, Curtis Kent. **LITTLE LEAGUE DOUBLE PLAY.** Philadelphia. Lippincott. 1962. 189 p.   **(I J)**

Ronnie Marlowe, student at St. Stephen's Academy and orphan who lives with his Aunt Susan, earns a place on the West Austin Little League Giants with the help of Susan's fiance. Ronnie and Julian Vega, son of a bracero bootmaker, lead the team to a championship.

92 Bishop, Curtis Kent. **LITTLE LEAGUE HEROES.** Philadelphia. Lippincott. 1960. 190 p.   **(I J)**

Joel Carroll won a place on the West Austin Little League even though he realized that some boys did not want a black player on the team. Joel saved the team equipment when a disgruntled player set fire to the clubhouse, and won respect from the whole community.

93 Bishop, Curtis Kent. **LITTLE LEAGUE LITTLE BROTHER.** Philadelphia. Lippincott. 1968. 185 p.   **(I J)**

Jesse Kenton, crippled from a burn accident, played for the Giants of the West Austin Little League. Jesse and his brother Duane were trained to play baseball by their father, who hoped for a battery with Duane as pitcher and Jesse as catcher. Two years after Duane started with the Giants, Jesse became a take-charge boy.

94 Bishop, Curtis Kent. **LITTLE LEAGUE STEPSON.** Philadelphia. Lippincott. 1965. 154 p.   **(I J)**

Robin Scott's mother married Chase Alloway, manager of one of the West Austin Little League teams. Robin wanted to move from the minors on his own, instead of being automatically picked for his stepfather's team. Chase helped Robin overcome the handicap of a weak leg while developing a loving relationship with his new stepson. Traditional sex roles date this warm family-oriented sports story.

95 Bishop, Curtis Kent. **LITTLE LEAGUE VICTORY.** Philadelphia. Lippincott. 1967. 187 p.   **(I J)**

Ed Bogart, known for his uncontrollable temper which was being treated by a psychologist, was chosen to be a team member of the Atlas Giants for the West Austin Little League. Ed began as an outsider, but became a winning pitcher and was accepted by his teammates.

96 Bishop, Curtis Kent. **LITTLE LEAGUE VISITOR**. Philadelphia. Lippincott. 1966. 192 p.   **(I J)**

When Sonny Barton, a well-known rock 'n' roll singer, performed in Austin, his younger brother Tom met members of the West Austin Little League. Tom joined the Atlas Giants and became their most valuable player in a close season.

97 Bishop, Curtis Kent. **THE LITTLE LEAGUE WAY**. Austin. Steck. 1957. 159 p.   **(I J)**

Overweight Dave "Ducky" Owen tries to lose weight to earn a place on the Belmont Little League Atlas team and is hospitalized because of it. With the assistance of a new boy in town, Dave becomes a catcher and plays baseball.

98 Bishop, Curtis Kent. **LITTLE LEAGUER**. Austin. Steck. 1956. 172 p.   **(I J)**

When Kerry Burk set fire to the Belmont Little League clubhouse after being suspended from the team, Coach Sneaker Kane came to Kerry's rescue by becoming the orphan's guardian. This is another of Bishop's novels about baseball and hard work shaping a boy's character.

99 Bishop, Curtis Kent. **LONE STAR LEADER : SAM HOUSTON**. New York. Messner. 1961. 192 p.   **(I J)**

This biography traces the events of Houston's life from early years through the political and military achievements which led to his success as the winning general at San Jacinto and later to the first presidency of Texas. Houston is portrayed as a passionate patriot who thrived on danger. A list of further readings and an index are included.

100 Bishop, Curtis Kent. **LONESOME END**. Philadelphia. Lippincott. 1963. 188 p.   **(I J)**

Jim Osborne enters Belmont High, where his father had been the popular football coach. Returning from the State School for Boys, where he had been sent after his father's disappearance, Jim overcomes his feelings of estrangement by helping the team win two key games.

101 Bishop, Curtis Kent. **THE LOST ELEVEN**. Austin. Steck. 1950. 213 p.   **(J I)**

Staunton University alumni showed their determination to have a winning football team in 1947 by renewing Coach Jim Sheldon's contract and scouring the entire Southwest for likely talent. Football action and team spirit led to a Sugar Bowl bid for the post-war team. The story was copyrighted in 1942 by Love Romances Publishing.

102 Bishop, Curtis Kent. **THE PLAYMAKER**. Austin. Steck. 1960. 200 p. **(I J)**

Craig Townsend works from scholastic probation to the honor roll and a key position on the Belmont Junior College basketball team. After two years in the Air Corps, orphaned Craig seeks a scholarship from a top Southwestern university to advance his career.

103 Bishop, Curtis Kent. **REBOUND**. Philadelphia. Lippincott. 1962. 157 p. **(I J)**

When Rob Hudson transferred from Round Rock to a larger school, he was too small to play center on the varsity basketball team. After much hard work and with the support of his best friend, the coach, and a pretty girl, Rob rebounded to championship.

104 Bishop, Curtis Kent. **SAN JACINTO**. Illustrated by Elizabeth Rice. Austin. Steck. 1957. 185 p. **(I J)**

A fictional account of how the two cannons called the "Twin Sisters" reached General Sam Houston just in time for their use as the only artillery pieces in the Battle of San Jacinto. Two sheltered New Orleans teenagers, Sally and Dick Darrow, have an adventurous journey accompanying the cannons on their way to Houston in 1836.

105 Bishop, Curtis Kent. **SATURDAY HEROES**. Austin. Steck. 1951. 217 p. **(I J)**

Larry Baker, star college and professional football player, makes the transition to coach. The rich, powerful Governor of Texas, Lucky Larkin, wants his team to be invited to the Rose Bowl. Sports action is overlaid by a clash of values.

106 Bishop, Curtis Kent. **SIDELINE PASS**. Philadelphia. Lippincott. 1965. 190 p. **(I J)**

In spite of his stern father's opposition because of an older son's injury, Jim Kemp wins permission to play football at Belmont High and has a winning season.

107 Bishop, Curtis Kent and Bishop, Grace. **STOUT RIDER.** Illustrated by M.J. Davis. Austin. Steck. 1953. 104 p.   **(P I)**

The account of ten-year-old Bobby Slaughter's 365-mile ride from Dallas to the Long S Ranch describes Bobby's mission to regain his father's ranch, which had been sold to renegade Englishmen. The story is fiction, based on a historical incident which occurred in the 1880s.

108 Bishop, Curtis Kent. **TEAMWORK.** Illustrated by Elizabeth Rice. Austin. Steck. 1942. 326 p.   **(I J)**

This collection of five short stories about sports extols the virtues of hard work and selflessness. The Southwest Conference and a small college conference are featured in the title story. A selfish, talented young player moves to a small school with a losing team for his own glory and in a sudden change of heart helps save the college by winning a bowl game.

109 Bishop, Curtis Kent; and Bishop, Grace; and Martin, Clyde Inez. **TRAILS TO TEXAS.** Illustrated by Watt Harris. Austin. W.S.Benson. 1965. 320 p. (Adventure Trails to Reading)   **(I J)**

A supplementary reader covering two centuries of Texas history, the text is divided into nine sections. The trail theme is carried out in the title of each section and in a map showing trails across Texas for explorers, Comanches, cattle, and oil. Drawings illustrate each reading, and study questions are included.

110 Blair, Walter. **DAVY CROCKETT, FRONTIER HERO : THE TRUTH AS HE TOLD IT, THE LEGEND AS FRIENDS BUILT IT.** Illustrated by Richard Powers. New York. Coward-McCann. 1955. 215 p.   **(I J)**

This tall-tale style biography uses folklore, songs, and ballads of the period within the text and humorous black-and-white drawings to portray the hero's life. After a matter-of-fact account of the Battle of the Alamo, stories about Crockett's death and life as a living legend conclude the volume. A chronology, 1786-1836, and a bibliography of reference sources are useful aids.

111 Blassingame, Wyatt. **PECOS BILL AND THE WONDERFUL CLOTHESLINE SNAKE.** Illustrated by Herman Vestal. Champaign, Ill. Garrard. 1978. 40 p. (American Folktales Series) **(P)**

Pecos Bill and Slue-Foot Sue search Snake Canyon, where they find hoop snakes, saddle snakes, glass snakes, pancake snakes, and finally a young clothesline snake to take home. Modern-style Western cartoon drawings illustrate the easy-to-read tale.

112 Blassingame, Wyatt. **PECOS BILL CATCHES A HIDEBEHIND.** Illustrated by Herman Vestal. Scarsdale, N.Y. Garrard. 1977. 40 p. (American Folktales Series) **(P I)**

Fantastic creatures, including the shy hidebehind, on Pecos Bill and Slue-Foot Sue's ranch attract an eastern zoo manager looking for an addition to his zoo. The updated characters have lost the colorful flavor of the tall tale in the easy-to-read story.

113 Blassingame, Wyatt. **PECOS BILL RIDES A TORNADO.** Illustrated by Ted Schroeder. Champaign, Ill. Garrard. 1973. 30 p. **(P)**

An easy-to-read version of the tall tale in which Pecos Bill rides the back of a tornado as he would a wild horse until he tames it and it becomes a gentle spring breeze, which Slue-Foot Sue decides to keep on the ranch.

114 Bolton, Herbert Eugene and Barker, Eugene Campbell. **WITH THE MAKERS OF TEXAS : A SOURCE READER IN TEXAS HISTORY.** Austin. Gammel-Statesman. 1904. 316 p. **(I J)**

Ninety-one selections from original sources, spanning Texas history from Spanish sovereignty through statehood, were chosen to be used as a supplement to the state-adopted text by Barker, Potts, and Ramsdell. The carefully designed book contains bibliographic references, marginal notes, poetry, music, and illustrations.

115 Bonehill, Ralph. **FOR THE LIBERTY OF TEXAS.** Illustrated by Louis Meynelle. Boston. Dana Estes. 1900. 298 p. (His Mexican War Series, 1) **(J)**

Ralph and Dan Radbury, pioneer boys living on their father's ranch near Gonzales in 1835, become involved in the Texas Revolution, as the book's title, the battle cry used at Gonzales, reveals. Their father, Amos Radbury, is a lieutenant in the Texas volunteers and fights at Gonzales, Concepcion, San Antonio, and San Jacinto. Dan and his friend, Poke Stover, fight at the Alamo and after the battle escape through a secret tunnel. This historically based but improbable adventure, the first of three volumes in the author's Mexican War series, sets the stage for the territorial controversy which led to the war with Mexico.

116 Bonehill, Ralph. **WITH TAYLOR ON THE RIO GRANDE**.
Illustrated by J.W. Kennedy. Boston. Dana Estes. 1901. 287 p.
(His Mexican War Series, 2)   **(J)**

This sequel to **For the Liberty of Texas** covers the further adventures of the Radburys from the end of the Texas Revolution through the beginning of the Mexican War. Dan, Ralph, and Poke Stover, their old frontiersman friend, leave the family ranch near Gonzales to join General Taylor's campaign on the Rio Grande at the battles of Palo Alto, Rescaca de la Palma, and Matamoros, and in the interior of Mexico at Monterrey and Buena Vista. A new villain, Juan the Giant, unsuccessfully attempts to thwart the young Texans. The third adventure in this series is **Under Scott in Mexico**.

117 THE BOOK OF KNOWLEDGE, VOL. 21: THE BOOK OF TEXAS. Dallas. The Grolier Society. 1929. 384 p.   **(I J)**

Volume 21 of the 1929 edition of **The Book of Knowledge** consists entirely of twenty-one chapters about Texas in a comprehensive treatment of history, industry, education, commerce, literature, and the arts. Articles are illustrated with black-and-white photographs of the period, and an index provides easy reference access.

118 Borg, Jack. **THE TRAIL DRIVERS**. London. Childrens Press. 1966. 188 p.   **(I J)**

Fourteen-year-old Tim Bryant from McMullen County goes on a trail drive to Dodge in the late 1870s. Tim and his best friend encounter three outlaws, are captured by the Comanche Chief Coup-Counter, and experience a stampede and the drowning of a friend. The narrative, written in a mixture of cowboy dialect and colloquial British English, creates a Western adventure story told by an outsider.

119 Bosworth, Allan R. **LADD OF THE LONE STAR**. Illustrated by George A. Malik. New York. Aladdin. 1952. 192 p. (American Heritage) **(J)**

Fourteen-year-old Ladd Merrill from Tennessee arrives in Texas in 1835 in search of his brother. In the tradition of boys' adventure stories, the fictional character Ladd meets Deaf Smith at the Red River and in series of improbable adventures takes part in the battles of Gonzales, Concepcion, San Antonio, the Alamo, and San Jacinto.

120 Bosworth, Allan R. **SANCHO OF THE LONG, LONG HORNS**. Illustrated by Robert Frankenburg. Garden City, N.Y. Doubleday. 1947. 206 p. **(I J)**

Sancho, an intelligent, bell-wearing longhorn, leads cattle up the trail from South Texas to Dodge City, proving himself so valuable that he is brought back to Texas for another trail drive. Chapo and Tomasina, grandchildren of Old Juan, the trail cook, treat Sancho as the family pet and continue to hope for his return. This is a humorous, touching treatment of a folk tale recorded by J. Frank Dobie and also used as the basis of Latham's **Lonesome Longhorn**.

121 Bowman, James Cloyd. **PECOS BILL : THE GREATEST COWBOY OF ALL TIME**. Illustrated by Laura Bannon. Chicago. Whitman. 1937. 296 p. (Junior Press Books) **(I J)**

The American cowboy tall-tale hero Pecos Bill was formed around Western campfires during the last three decades of the 19th century, according to the scholarly author of this ample collection. The adventures are arranged chronologically in four sections: Pecos Bill becomes a cowboy; modern cowpunching is invented and developed; Pecos Bill roams the Southwest; the passing of Pecos Bill. Told with humor and in the dialect of the cowboy, this volume is a rich source for reading aloud and storytelling. Bannon's brilliantly colored and black-and-white illustrations supply vivid images of the folk characters.

122 Boyce, Myrtle. **SAND IN MY HAND**. Illustrated by Janice Palmer. Austin. Steck-Vaughn. 1965. 47 p. **(P)**

Colorful drawings and brief text present a pastoral family holiday on the Gulf Coast. From their cabin on stilts two children hurry to the beach, where they find shells, birds, crabs, and a picnic.

123 Bracken, Dorothy Kendall. **DOAK WALKER : THREE TIME ALL-AMERICAN**. Austin. Steck. 1950. 258 p.   **(J)**

Walker is a Texas sports hero who played football for Southern Methodist University and won the Maxwell Award and Heisman Trophy in 1948. This biography begins with his early training from his coach father, continues with play-by-play descriptions of games and his sportsmanlike conduct through Highland Park High School and S.M.U., and ends with his signing a Detroit Lions contract.

124 Brim, Burl and Brim, Mary. **THE MAGIC TRAIN AT SAD MONKEY**. Illustrated by the authors. Amarillo. La Casa Verde Pub. 1968. 53 p.   **(P)**

A picture story of the tourist train ride from Sad Monkey, Texas, through the Palo Duro Canyon describes the local natural history. Black-and-white drawings show rock formations, juniper trees, and wild animals near the smallest town in the world.

125 Bryan, George Sands. **SAM HOUSTON**. New York. Macmillan. 1917. 183 p. (True Stories of Great Americans)   **(J)**

This biography sketches Houston's early life, then gives a detailed historical background of events in Texas in which Houston participated. Personal traits are discussed in the final chapter, "Houston the Man." Black-and-white photographs illustrate the political world of early Texas.

126 Buck, Ray. **DANNY WHITE : THE KICKING QUARTERBACK**. Chicago. Childrens Press. 1983. 48 p. (Sports Stars)   **(I)**

This brief biography of the Dallas Cowboys quarterback and 1982 Dallas Father of the Year emphasizes the personal qualities and values which have formed White's successful career and family life. Black-and-white sports action photographs illustrate the easy-to-read text.

127 Buffler, Esther. **RODRIGO AND ROSALITA**. Illustrated by Elizabeth Rice. Austin. Steck. 1949. 64 p.   **(P I)**

Rodrigo and Rosalita help their father, a sick artist, become nationally recognized by encouraging him to paint and selling his work. Set in Palos, a Rio Grande Valley village in the 1940s, this simple story is illustrated with realistic pastels.

128 Burchard, S.H. **EARL CAMPBELL.** New York. Harcourt, Brace, Jovanovich. 1980. 63 p. (Sports Star Series)   **(I)**

This simple biography of Campbell, Houston Oilers superstar and 1977 Heisman Trophy winner, will appeal to young football fans.

129 Burk, Bernadine. **SWEET THANG IS MY BLOODHOUND.** Illustrated by Omar Davis. New York. Exposition Press. 1965. 31 p.   **(P)**

A gentle old bloodhound, Sweet Thang, greets five-year-old Cindy when she visits her grandparents' ranch, El Loco Rancho, in East Texas. Girl and dog explore and play together in this contemporary picture story illustrated with line drawings.

130 Burleson, Adele Steiner. **TOUGHEY : CHILDHOOD ADVENTURES ON A TEXAS RANCH.** Illustrated by Elizabeth Rice. Austin. Steck. 1950. 119 p.   **(I J)**

The rural vacation experiences of the author's three daughters on the Texas family ranch in the summer of 1900 are presented in a fictional manner. The girls meet the prison trusties who work the farm and an elderly Mexican goatherd. The adventures of the upper-class children of Congressman A.C. Burleson include a possum hunt and securing the release of a man wrongly imprisoned.

131 Burleson, Elizabeth Morris. **A MAN OF THE FAMILY.** Chicago. Follett. 1965. 289 p.   **(I J)**

Speck, the baby of a loving family, turns thirteen and strives to be a man like his father and older brothers. Living on a High Divide country ranch in 1920, he survives personal and natural hardships as he learns the difficult work of horse breaking, sheep and goat herding, and the value of a town school education. Strong values of family loyalty, hard work, and honesty are expressed.

132 Burleson, Elizabeth Morris. **MIDDL'UN.** Illustrated by George Roth. Chicago. Follett. 1968. 192 p.   **(P I)**

Thirteen-year-old Hannah Worth learns that courage is a quality a young woman can possess. Growing up on a Hill Country ranch at the turn of the century, Hannah has the experiences of catching cattle rustlers and adjusting to her father's illness. In the process she matures from a tomboy to a young lady.

133 Burt, Olive Woolley. **CAMEL EXPRESS : A STORY OF THE JEFF DAVIS EXPERIMENT.** Illustrated by Joseph C. Camana. Philadelphia. Winston. 1954. 178 p. (Winston Adventure Books) **(I J)**

In 1855 Congress appropriated funds to carry out Secretary of War Jefferson Davis's plan to bring seventy-five camels to the desert Southwest. Young Obed Green traveled as veterinary assistant to the Middle East and back through Matagorda Bay across Texas. Texans and soldiers scorned the exotic camels until they proved their worth. Encounters with camel drivers, Comanches, belligerent soldiers, and hardships of the trail provide an exciting story.

134 Byars, Betsy. **THE WINGED COLT OF CASA MIA.** Illustrated by Richard Cuffari. New York. Viking. 1973. 128 p. **(I J)**

Uncle Coot, an eccentric, retired movie stunt man, lives on a ranch near Marfa, where he raises horses. Young Charles, who has read all about horses, is sent to stay with his uncle while his mother recovers from an injury. In a series of humorous interchanges, Mrs. Minney expresses her anger when a horse purchased from Uncle Coot gives birth to a fantastic winged colt. Understanding and trust develop between Coot and Charles as they search for and make a dramatic rescue of the colt. The contemporary Texas setting is captured in the black-and-white drawings.

135 Callihan, D. Jeanne. **OUR MEXICAN ANCESTORS, VOL. 1.** Illustrated by Thom Ricks. San Antonio. Institute of Texan Cultures. 1981. 124 p. (Stories for Young Readers)   **(I)**

A history of the Mexican Texans from the time of the Aztecs to the Texas Revolution is told in twenty-seven brief, readable chapters, heavily illustrated with drawings and reproductions of period art. Contributions of Mexican Texans to the cause of independence are highlighted in this appealing work.

136 Campbell, Camilla. **BARTLETTS OF BOX B RANCH.** Illustrated by Glenn Chesnut. New York. Whittlesey House. 1949. 256 p. **(I J)**

The Bartletts work hard to succeed on the West Texas family ranch. Grandfather and grandson lead a trail drive from near Lone Cow Creek, the site of the lost Bowie silver mine, to a ranch in South Texas. The family story gives the flavor of ranch work and lifestyle in the 1940s.

137 Campbell, Camilla. **GALLEONS SAIL WESTWARD.** Illustrated by Ena McKinney. Dallas. Mathis, Van Nort. 1939. 326 p.   **(I J)**

This fictionalized retelling of Cabeza de Vaca's journey across America in the 16th century is based on his diary as translated by F.W. Hodge. The account includes details of his Texas experiences from the time he and three other shipwrecked members of a Spanish expedition landed on the Gulf Coast near Galveston through their life among Texas Indians, first as slaves and then as medicine men.

138 Campbell, Wanda Jay. **THE MUSEUM MYSTERY.** Illustrated by Charles Geer. New York. Dutton. 1957. 191 p.   **(P I)**

While his father paints diorama backgrounds for the Texas Panhandle Historical Museum, Lance Michelson hunts for buried treasure in Palo Duro Canyon one 1950s summer. Lance and his teenage friends find clues in the Museum to solve the mystery of money buried with a curse in 1896.

139 Campbell, Wanda Jay. **THE MYSTERY OF MCCLELLAN CREEK.** Illustrated by Everett Raymond Kinsiler. New York. Dutton. 1958. 191 p.   **(I)**

Three boy friends and an unwelcome girl solve a robbery and cattle theft during a summer vacation in the Panhandle near Mobeetie. The author of **The Museum Mystery** weaves in historical events and local legends to create the atmosphere for the mystery.

140 Campbell, Wanda Jay. **MYSTERY OF OLD MOBEETIE.** Illustrated by Charles Smith. New York. Dutton. 1960. 191 p.   **(I J)**

Old Mobeetie, one of the oldest towns in the Panhandle, is the setting for a 1950s mystery story involving Scott McFarland, his two sisters, and their widowed mother. Bad fortune befalls them when they return to the mother's family home and begin to run a small store. Their barn mysteriously burns, the roof of their house is blown off in a storm, and the store is burglarized. While Scott searches for the arsonist and burglar, the small town neighbors rally around, offering protection and assistance.

141 Campbell, Wanda Jay. **TEN COUSINS.** Illustrated by Leonard Shortall. New York. Dutton. 1963. 191 p.   **(P I)**

Carrie Lawson, one of ten children, is not pleased when prim, prissy Cousin Josephine comes to stay awhile. The two girls become friends as they solve household mysteries of the theft of the children's cotton picking money, and the disappearance of the eldest son's horse and father's gamecock. This warm family story is set on an 1880s Texas farm in Bosque County.

142 Cardenas, Leo. **RETURN TO RAMOS.** Illustrated by Nilo Santiago. New York. Hill and Wang. 1970. 54 p. (A Challenger Book)   **(J)**

A poor migrant family returns from cotton picking in West Texas to their small South Texas home. The eldest daughter is leading a student boycott of high school classes to protest discrimination of Mexican Americans. The social climate of the early 1970s is accurately portrayed in high/low text.

143 Carmer, Elizabeth Black and Carmer, Carl Lamson. **PECOS BILL AND THE LONG LASSO.** Illustrated by Mimi Korach. Champaign, Ill. Garrard. 1968. 31 p.   **(P)**

In this easy-to-read version of the tall tale, Pecos Bill catches Slue-Foot Sue with the longest lasso in the world after she bounces off Widow-Maker. Four-color drawings illustrate the story.

144 Carpenter, John Allan. **TEXAS : FROM ITS GLORIOUS PAST TO THE PRESENT.** Illustrated by Roger Herrington. Chicago. Childrens Press. 1965. 95 p. (Enchantment of America)   **(P I)**

The history, geography, and natural and human resources of the state are presented in an attractive format which can be read straight through or used as a reference tool. In the 1978 revised edition, out-of-date material has been removed and photographs replace the illustrative drawings, but very little new material has been added.

145 Carter, Kathryn Turner. **AT THE BATTLE OF SAN JACINTO**

WITH RIP CAVITT. Austin. Eakin. 1983. 52 p. (Stories for Young Americans)   **(I)**

Eleven-year-old Ripley Morris Cavitt and others of his family are forced to join the flight of Texas colonists from the path of the oncoming Mexican army, known as the Runaway Scrape, shortly after his father has left to join General Sam Houston's army. Rip participates in the Battle of San Jacinto as a waterboy and returns home to find his family intact. Carter includes details of everyday life in 1836 along with the story of the decisive battle.

146 Casad, Mary Brooke. **BLUEBONNET AT THE ALAMO.** Illustrated by Pat Binder. Austin. Eakin. 1984. 40 p. (Stories for Young Americans)   **(P)**

Bluebonnet, a Hill Country armadillo, visits the Alamo, where she meets Digger Diller. Full-page, cartoon-style illustrations by Pat Binder facing each page of text show the story of the two armadillos attempting to return Jim Bowie's knife to the Alamo museum.

147 Casad, Mary Brooke. **BLUEBONNET OF THE HILL COUNTRY.** Illustrated by Pat Binder. Austin. Eakin. 1983. 38 p. (Stories for Young Americans)   **(P)**

Bluebonnet, an anthropomorphic armadillo named for the Texas state flower, disrupts life at a Hill Country camp, then becomes a heroine by saving campers from a flash flood on the Guadalupe. Full-page, cartoon-style illustrations by Pat Binder face each page of text.

148 Castor, Henry. **THE FIRST BOOK OF THE WAR WITH MEXICO.** Illustrated by Albert Micale. New York. Watts. 1964. 87 p.   **(I)**

This Watts "The First Book of" outlines the Mexican War from General Zachary Taylor's arrival at Point Isabel and shedding of American blood on American soil to the Treaty of Guadalupe Hidalgo. Clear explanations of military and political events and their implications are illustrated with black-and-white drawings. A chart of important dates, 1845-1848, has a Texas section.

149 Catlin, Wynelle. **OLD WATTLES.** Illustrated by Ron Kuriloff. Garden City, N.Y. Doubleday. 1975. 92 p.   **(P I)**

The youngest child in a frontier farm family, nine-year- old Eleanore has to follow the turkey hen to find her nest and gather the eggs. After a series of distracting adventures with ants, a rattlesnake, a bull, and a rock, she locates the eggs. Butter churning, yard sweeping, and other activities of daily life are shown in this gentle picture book.

150 Chadwick, Joseph. **COWBOYS AND CATTLE DRIVES**. Illustrated by William Moyers. New York. Hawthorn Books. 1967. 127 p.
   (I)

Twelve chapters about the cowboy way of life, some narrative, some factual, primarily about the time of the trail drives and the dangers of the trail. A map of twelve trails is included in this interesting Texas potpourri.

151 Chapman, Iva. **TWELVE LEGENDARY STORIES OF TEXAS**. Illustrated by Warren Hunter. San Antonio. Naylor. 1940. 79 p.
   (I)

Variants of material in publications of J. Frank Dobie and the Texas Folklore Society, these retellings of legends about Indians, Spaniards, and settlers were prepared for children and evoke people from the past in exciting situations. Specific place references are given in each story.

152 Charnley, Mitchell Vaughn. **JEAN LAFITTE : GENTLEMAN SMUGGLER**. Illustrated by Jay Van Everen. New York. Viking. 1934. 240 p.   **(J)**

Jean Lafitte's privateering community established at Galveston on the Texas Gulf Coast following expulsion from Louisiana after the Battle of New Orleans in 1815 is described in detail. This biography explores Lafitte's complicated character, love of an elegant lifestyle, and political intrigue. The book was a Junior Literary Guild selection at publication.

153 Chastain, Madye Lee. **LOBLOLLY FARM**. Illustrated by the author. New York. Harcourt, Brace. 1950. 227 p.   **(I J)**

A charming family story about Melinda's visit to her grandparents' East Texas farm in the early 1900s. The narrative evokes the native landscape of pine, sweet gum, and Cape jasmine and familiar community activities of the period, such as a group sing and a house raising for a poor family followed by a square dance.

154 Christian, Mary Blount. **THE MYSTERY OF THE DOUBLE DOUBLE CROSS.** Illustrated by Marie De John. Chicago. Whitman. 1982. 127 p.   **(I)**

Sixteen-year-old Jeff Tyler takes over his sick older brother's job, driving a limousine for a wealthy oilman attending a cartel meeting in Houston. A mystery develops when Mr. Grossmark and Jess are kidnapped and held in a beach house in Galveston during Hurricane Bernice. Their escape during the storm and revelation of the real villain add excitement to a mystery with Gulf Coast flavor.

155 Clark, Idena McFadin. **LITTLE DUDE.** Illustrated by Matt Duncan. New York. Ariel. 1952. 186 p.   **(I)**

Jim MacFarlane, Little Dude, lives on a farm near Jacksboro with his large family in 1872. He experiences the excitement of a country school opening, community celebrations, and a Comanche raid on Star Valley School in which the teacher is killed and he accepts responsibility for the younger children's safety. A pleasant story about family frontier life is told by Clark.

156 Clark, Margaret Goff. **WHO STOLE KATHY YOUNG.** New York. Dodd, Mead. 1980. 191 p.   **(I)**

Two unusual looking tourists attract the attention of Meg Carberry and Kathy Young, school girls on vacation in their Gulf Coast hometown. Then Meg sees her deaf friend Kathy being kidnapped. The search for her involves shrimp boats, abandoned oil fields, the local sheriff, an out-of-state private detective, and the Texas Rangers. Insights into Kathy's adjustment to her hearing loss are realistically portrayed.

157 Coerr, Eleanor. **WAZA WINS AT WINDY GULCH.** Illustrated by Janet McCaffery. New York. Putnam. 1977. 44 p. (A See and Read Storybook)   **(P)**

Waza, a white camel, and a lively driver, Hi Jolly, are the central figures in a humorous, easy-to-read story based on the historical arrival of the Army Camel Corps in Texas in the 1850s. Dirtyshirt Dan, the chief mule driver, tries to disgrace Waza because of his jealousy and dislike for the camels but fails in his mean attempts.

158 Cohen, Peter Zachary. **THE GREAT RED RIVER RAFT.** Illustrated by James Watling. Niles, Ill. Whitman. 1984. 40 p.   **(I)**

A poetically written biography of Henry Shreve and his success in clearing the Red River of a centuries old, two-hundred-mile logjam, thus opening Texas to river trade in the 1830s. The hardship, year of persistent efforts, and excitement of man and machine conquering nature are portrayed in brown- and-white drawings.

159 Colbert, Edwin Harris. **THE YEAR OF THE DINOSAUR.** Illustrated by Margaret Colbert. New York. Scribner. 1977. 171 p.   **(J)**

In the Mesozoic Era dinosaurs roamed in a tropical land bordering a sea southwest of Dallas near Glen Rose and Bandera City. From research on footprints found in the area in the 1930s, vertebrate paleontologists have reconstructed the behavior patterns of the ancient reptiles, including their search for food, mating, nesting, and fights with enemies. The fascinating text alternates a conjectural account of a year in the life of a brontosaur living 150 million years ago with the scientific information about its behavior which was used as evidence. Black-and-white sketches, notes, a selected and annotated bibliography, and an index add to the value of the book.

160 Collins, David R. **SUPER CHAMP! THE STORY OF BABE DIDRIKSON ZAHARIAS.** Austin. Eakin. 1982. 77 p. (Stories for Young Americans)   **(I)**

Babe Didrikson Zaharias is portrayed as a fun-loving, hard-working, courageous woman in this fast-paced, highly readable biography. This story of the outstanding athlete from Beaumont covers her early years; her many victories--amateur, professional, and Olympic; and her fight against cancer. Her lifetime record from **Who's Who in Sports** and a note about her memorial in Beaumont are included after the text.

161 Collins, Michael. **FLYING TO THE MOON AND OTHER STRANGE PLACES.** New York. Farrar. 1976. 159 p.   **(I J)**

An inside look at the training and work of an astronaut and at the NASA Johnson Space Center near Houston is provided in the autobiography of Texan Collins. After years of preparation, he participated in the first lunar landing in 1969 and then returned to a hardworking career on the ground.

162 Conner, John Edwin; and Conner, Jack Edward; and Harper, Robbie C. **THE FLAGS OF TEXAS.** Norman, Okla. Harlow. 1964. 270 p.   **(J)**

Flags, symbols of "man's glory, and memory and hope," are used as the theme of this supplementary reader. Selections for reading compose a brief history of Texas, illustrated with colorful drawings of flags. Learning activities are listed after each chapter.

163 Conrad, Dick. **TONY DORSETT : FROM HEISMAN TO SUPERBOWL IN ONE YEAR.** Chicago. Childrens Press. 1979. 42 p. (Sports Stars Series)   **(I)**

This easy-to-read biography of the Heisman trophy winner, with emphasis on his transition from college player to Dallas Cowboy player and 1977 NFL Rookie of the Year, is heavily illustrated with photographs.

164 Cook, James Henry. **LONGHORN COWBOY.** Illustrated by Herbert Morton Stoops. New York. Putnam. 1942. 241 p.   **(I J)**

This is a lively first-person narrative of the adventures of a young man who came to Texas in the early 1870s. Cook rode the Chisholm Trail, met Big Foot Wallace, worked on the Slaughter ranch, learned the ways of the vaqueros and cowboys, and survived to tell about it in his old age. The tales of "brush poppers," longhorns, outlaws, and Indians are illustrated with realistic black-and-white drawings.

165 Corby, Jane. **THE STORY OF DAVID CROCKETT.** New York. Barse & Hopkins. 1922. 182 p. (Famous Americans for Young Readers)   **(I)**

This fast-paced biography incorporates episodes common to the Crockett legend, such as his killing a panther with a knife, being championed by Comanches for his bravery, and fighting to the death at the Alamo. The narrative provides more insights into the hardships of Crockett's youth than some biographies. Numerous ethnic slurs, common to the language of the 1920s, are found within the dialogue.

166 Cosner, Shaaron. **AMERICAN COWGIRLS : YESTERDAY AND TODAY.** New York. McKay. 1978. 54 p.   **(I)**

This history of cowgirls describes the working women of the West on ranches and in rodeos and Wild West shows. The evolution of clothing and equipment is described, and the importance of each item is explained. Several tempting chuck wagon recipes are included.

167 Cousins, Margaret. **THE BOY IN THE ALAMO**. Illustrated by Nicholas Eggenhofer. San Antonio. Corona. 1983. 180 p. (We Were There Books, 18)   **(I)**

The twenty-fifth anniversary reprint of **We Were There at the Battle of the Alamo**, published by Grosset & Dunlap in 1958.

168 Cousins, Margaret. **WE WERE THERE AT THE BATTLE OF THE ALAMO**. Illustrated by Nicholas Eggenhofer. New York. Grosset & Dunlap. 1958. 180 p. (We Were There Books, 18)   **(I J)**

Will Campbell stows away on a stagecoach from Nacogdoches in time to join his older brother in the famous battle. After traveling around for three months and witnessing battles at the Alamo and San Jacinto, the young boy returns to live with his aunt and uncle. Black-and-white drawings illustrate details of the historic events. The twenty-fifth anniversary reprint in 1983 is entitled **The Boy in the Alamo**.

169 Coy, Harold. **CHICANO ROOTS GO DEEP**. New York. Dodd, Mead. 1975. 210 p.   **(J)**

This lively narrative of Chicano history and culture presents the Chicano point of view in the struggle for dignity and the freedom to retain important cultural values in an Anglo society. Coy traces the roots of one family back five generations. Spanish, Mexican, and Indian influence in exploration, mining, water rights, and cowboy lore are discussed.

170 Crosby, Alexander L. **THE RIO GRANDE : LIFE FOR THE DESERT**. Champaign, Ill. Garrard. 1966. 96 p. (Rivers of the World, W-15)   **(I J)**

The historical and geographical significance of the Rio Grande from Creede, Colorado, to the Gulf of Mexico is shown through descriptions gathered during an automobile tour. Wildlife, natural beauty, and present conditions are illustrated with black-and-white drawings and photographs.

171 Crownfield, Gertrude. **LONE STAR RISING**. Illustrated by Lydia Parmelee. New York. Crowell. 1940. 338 p.   **(I J)**

Nancy Raymond, fifteen-year-old daughter of a San Antonio merchant, witnesses the siege of the Alamo and the Battle of San Jacinto in the Texas Revolution. Owen Dunbar, a handsome young freedom fighter, provides a touch of romance as he conveys information about the

Revolution to the Raymonds. Details of colonial and Spanish customs form the background for this heroic adventure novel.

172 Cumming, Marian. **ALL ABOUT MARJORY**. Illustrated by David Stone Martin. New York. Harcourt, Brace. 1950. 148 p. **(P I J)**

In this charming story, Marjory spends a happy year in 1904 growing up in Bayou City (Houston). Picnicking in the park, partying with friends, making mud pies, getting a doll house, watching Christmas fireworks, traveling to New Orleans by train for Mardi Gras, having a ride in an automobile, and taking part in her Sunday School teacher's wedding fill the seven-year-old's days.

173 Cumming, Marian. **CLAN TEXAS**. Illustrated by Peter Burchard. New York. Harcourt, Brace. 1955. 117 p. **(I)**

Schoolboy Karl Zorn, of an immigrant German family, is embarrassed to wear a Scottish Glengarry cap until Jock Gordon tells him of its origin in the brave history of the Highland soldiers. In 1873 the Gordon family has recently immigrated from Scotland to the Zorn farm near Brenham, where Jock and Karl become friends and form Clan Texas, a boys' club. The adjustment of different ethnic groups to life in a new land is portrayed in a positive story.

174 Cumming, Marian. **JUST LIKE NANCY**. Illustrated by Edward Sweet. New York. Harcourt, Brace. 1953. 174 p. **(P I)**

This sequel to **All about Marjory** portrays the Cameron sisters of Bayou City (Houston) growing up in 1906. Nancy's calm personality develops within a warm, loving family. Customs of the period add flavor to the story.

175 Cumming, Marie. **VALENTINE FOR CANDY**. Illustrated by Susanne Suba. New York. Harcourt, Brace. 1959. 160 p. **(P I)**

Ten-year-old Candace Fulton spends 1894 in Bayou City (Houston) with her aunt and uncle while others of her family are in Germany. The Massachusetts girl goes crayfishing, joins the Bayou City Lyceum, collects books and money for the children's library, and enjoys the new town as she learns the customs and speech of the South. The book is dedicated to Frances Clarke Sayers.

176 Daffan, Katie. **TEXAS HEROES : A READER FOR SCHOOLS**. Boston. Sanborn. 1912. 165 p. **(I J)**

Brief biographies of persons of importance in early Texas history are contained in eighteen chapters of this supplementary reader. Three groups--mission priests, Indians, and Confederates--are included, with individual sketches of Lafitte, Jane Long, La Salle, Austin, Bowie, Milam, Bonham, Crockett, Fannin, Travis, Houston, A.S. Johnston, Sul Ross, and John Reagan. The readable text is illustrated with black-and-white plates and portraits.

177 Daniel, Doris Temple. **PAULINE AND THE PEACOCK**. Illustrated by Barbara Brown Schoenewolf. Diboll, Tex. Ellen C. Temple. 1980. 55 p. **(P)**

The author's experience of raising peafowl on her East Texas farm near Nacogdoches has been infused into a picture-book story. Pauline, the peahen with blue-green feathers, grows up; Beau Brummell, the peacock, arrives; and soon after five chicks appear. A love of animals is displayed in a charming story of caring for exotic birds.

178 Darling, Kathy. **PECOS BILL FINDS A HORSE**. Illustrated by Lou Cunette. Champaign, Ill. Garrard. 1979. 40 p. (American Folktales Series) **(P)**

In need of a mount, Pecos Bill tries a mountain lion, lightning, and a bear before finding the perfect golden mustang. This easy-to-read tall tale explains how Bill invented rodeo riding.

179 Davis, Anne Pence. **THE TOP HAND OF LONE TREE RANCH**. Illustrated by Sam Savitt. New York. Crowell. 1960. 81 p. **(P I)**

Paddy Pence's desire for a calf to raise, thwarted when he fails in the local calf scramble, is fulfilled when he finds a calf accidentally left on his grandfather's North Texas ranch. Paddy matures as he secretly raises Tiny Miss and struggles to follow grandfather's advice to always tell the truth.

180 Davis, Hazel H. **DAVY CROCKETT**. Illustrated by William Moyers. New York. Random House. 1955. 64 p. **(P)**

This picture-book biography of Crockett alternates colored and black-and-white double-page illustrations of important events in his life, concluding with his stand at the Alamo in 1836. Legendary and human characteristics of the folk hero are combined in this book.

181 Davis, Mary Evelyn Moore. **UNDER SIX FLAGS : THE STORY OF TEXAS**. Boston. Ginn. 1897. 187 p.   **(I J)**

The story of the colonization of the vast territory of Texas is explored in ten sections in this history: Fort St. Louis, San Antonio, Nacogdoches, San Felipe de Austin, Goliad, Houston, Austin, Galveston, Thirty Years, Texas from French Exploration to the Turn of the Century. The fast-paced, readable text is illustrated with fascinating old maps and black-and-white illustrations. A facsimile edition of the 1897 volume was published for the Texas Centennial.

182 Dawson, Everett T. **TEXAS WILDLIFE**. Illustrated by Orville Rice. Dallas. Banks Upshaw. 1955. 174 p.   **(I J)**

This supplementary reader, written to teach a "wholesome respect for wildlife and conservation," presents long units about birds and mammals and shorter units about fishes, reptiles, amphibians, and conservation. Each animal is represented by four pages of text and a full-page color drawing, which provide information about habits and identification.

183 Dee, M.M. **THE ADVENTURES OF L.A**. Illustrated by Donna Newsom. Dallas. Hendrick-Long. 1983. 48 p.   **(P)**

In easy-to-read style, Little Armadillo's first exposure to the outside world is told. He leaves the burrow, digs for bugs, is warned about enemies, and returns home. Realistic black-and-white drawings illustrate the text.

184 Dengler, Sandy. **THE HORSE WHO LOVED PICNICS**. Chicago. Moody. 1980. 123 p. (Pioneer Family Adventures, 3)   **(I)**

Daniel Tremain lives on his family homestead near Springer in 1882. The West Texas youth applies Christian teaching to his problems of losing a friend and wanting a horse in this didactic novel.

185 De Paola, Tomie. **THE LEGEND OF THE BLUEBONNET : AN OLD TALE OF TEXAS**. Illustrated by the author. New York. Putnam. 1983. 28 p.   **(P I)**

The Comanche legend explaining the origin of the Texas state flower is the story of a young girl who sacrifices a doll, her most valued possession, to appease the Great Spirits and end the drought. De Paola's double-page, full-color illustrations portray the bleak drought, the night of sacrifice, and the glorious return of spring rains and fields of bluebonnets. An author's note gives background of the legend and the creation of the book.

186 Dewey, Ariane. **PECOS BILL**. Illustrated by the author. New York. Greenwillow. 1983. 56 p.   **(P)**

The legends of Pecos Bill in easy-to-read language show the hero inventing ranching, courting Slue-Foot Sue, riding a tornado, and sliding down lightning. Cheerful, full-color illustrations by the author extend across the pages.

187 Dill, Minnie G. **FOOT PRINTS OF TEXAS HISTORY**. Austin. B.C.Jones. 1901. 105 p.   **(P I)**

This collection of short historical stories was written for second and third grade children to form their character. Stories cover the period from the early Indians until the death of Albert Sidney Johnston in 1862. The small book went through six editions between 1901 and 1916.

188 Dill, Minnie G. **LITTLE ANDIRONS : OR, SCENES FROM TEXAS HISTORY**. Austin. 1893. 12 p.   **(P I)**

This charming book for reading to young children contains a short story about twin brothers, Andy and Ira, who lived in Goliad during the Revolution. Their adventures around San Antonio, the Alamo, and San Jacinto were used in Dill's later book, **Foot Prints of Texas History**.

189 Dill, Minnie G. and Dill, Elma. **TEXAS STORIES FOR READING AND ACTING**. Austin. 1925. 22 p.   **(P I)**

Brief selections about the Capitol, the Texas seal, the bluebonnet, and the pecan, accompanied by dramatic presentations of the fall of the Alamo and the Battle of San Jacinto, were written for school children by an educator from Pease School, Austin.

190 Dines, Glen. **SUN, SAND AND STEEL : COSTUMES AND EQUIPMENT OF THE SPANISH-MEXICAN SOUTHWEST**. New York. Putnam. 1972. 62 p.   **(I J)**

Detailed descriptions of costumes worn by explorers, priests, rancheros, soldiers, and civilians in the Southwestern area, 1540-1850, are given in words and in full-color illustrations, redrawn from historical paintings and sketches. This material gives an added dimension to regional history.

191 Disney (Walt) Productions. **WALT DISNEY'S OLD YELLER.** New York. Simon and Schuster. 1957. 1 v. (unpaged) (Little Golden Book)   **(P)**

This brightly colored Little Golden Book contains a few incidents from the Disney film based on Fred Gipson's classic novel about a boy and his dog. Intended for younger children, the brief story, in picture-book format, tells how Arliss acquired the dog from Mr. Sanderson in exchange for a meal and how Old Yeller saved Arliss from a bear. This is an appetizer, but the main course is missing.

192 Dobie, James Frank. **CORONADO'S CHILDREN : TALES OF LOST MINES AND BURIED TREASURES OF THE SOUTHWEST.** Illustrated by Ben Carlton Mead. Dallas. Southwest Press. 1930. 367 p.   **(J)**

Coronado rode in search of a dream of great wealth, and the mirage has never faded. According to Dobie, Coronado's children are inheritors and possessors of the imagination necessary to dream of the wealth of secret mines and hidden treasures. These nineteen chapters are topical groupings, a rich collection of history and related legends about rumored treasure and tales of those who sought it over the years. This delightful mixture of Spanish, Indian, and Anglo folklore and stories with Texas settings is illustrated with diagrams, maps, and a code of symbols developed by the Spaniards to indicate buried treasures. The University of Texas Press published hardback and paperback editions in 1978 with illustrations by Charles Shaw.

193 Dobie, James Frank. **ON THE OPEN RANGE.** Illustrated by Ben Carlton Mead. Dallas. Southwest Press. 1931. 312 p.   **(I J)**

Dobie, the noted Texas folklorist, wrote this book for children "to deliver them something that is theirs by right of inheritance." These stories of the open range make history come alive in fourteen chapters brimming over with the traditions of the range, wildlife, "bars," longhorns, mustangs, horses and riders, cowboys, brands, Indian captives, place names, buried treasures, and lost mines. Color plates and black-and-white drawings by Ben Carlton Mead enhance the Texas flavor. A bibliography and glossary of range words, names, and phrases add to the value of the work.

194 Dolan, Edward R. and Lyttle, Richard B. **KYLE ROTE, JR. : AMERICAN-BORN SOCCER STAR.** Garden City, N.Y. Doubleday. 1975. 87 p.   **(I J)**

Dallas-born Rote was graduated from Highland Park High School and faced the choice of playing football or soccer. The outstanding athlete chose to play professional soccer for the Dallas Tornado and the Houston Hurricanes. His life story is told in this simple sports biography.

195 Downey, Fairfax Davis. **CAVALRY MOUNT.** Illustrated by Paul Brown. New York. Dodd, Mead. 1946. 227 p.   **(J)**

The Texas Panhandle in the 1870s is the setting for a fictional story based on historical sources of a Morgan horse, a small black gelding with five gaits, and the Fourth Cavalry's campaigns against Indians and Comancheros. Historical characters include Quanah Parker, General Mackenzie, Lt. Robert G. Carter, and Sergeant Charlton. Black-and-white drawings and appropriate bugle calls heading each chapter illustrate the book.

196 Downey, Fairfax Davis. **TEXAS AND THE WAR WITH MEXICO.** New York. American Heritage Pub. Co. 1961. 153 P. (American Heritage Junior Library)   **(I J)**

The importance of Texas in the political and military history of the War with Mexico, 1845-1848, is explained in this clearly written work. An accurate account and analysis of the political situation and the rationale for the military policies are given. Outstanding illustrations, typical of the American Heritage series, include paintings, prints, drawings, maps, and photographs of the period.

197 Driggs, Howard Roscoe and King, Sarah Smith. **RISE OF THE LONE STAR.** Illustrated by Edwin W. Deming. New York. Stokes. 1936. 438 p.   **(I J)**

This series of stories collected directly from pioneers makes the dramatic history of the rise of Texas come alive. The flavor of early Texas is explored in two parts: "Texas in the Making" and "Pioneers Bring Back Heroic Days." Sarah King, daughter of pioneer parents, was principal of Bowie School in San Antonio at the time of publication during the Texas Centennial. The partiotic, readable text is illustrated with black-and-white drawings and eight color plates. Some stories are used without citing sources.

198 Driskill, Frank A. **DAVY CROCKETT : THE UNTOLD STORY.** Burnet, Tex. Eakin. 1981. 56 p. (Stories for Young Americans) **(I J)**

Crockett's journey to join Sam Houston in the battle for freedom and his adventures on the way to the Alamo are based on unpublished sources. This biography emphasizes Crockett's Texas connections.

199 DuBois, William Pene. **OTTO IN TEXAS : THE ADVENTURES OF OTTO.** Illustrated by the author. New York. Viking. 1959. 45 p. **(P I)**

Otto, the giant dog, captures cattle thieves Frank Dregs, Jasper Dregs, and Billy the Brat while visiting Texas tycoon Sam Hill at his ranch and receives a gigantic medal for his work. This lively, bright, humorous picture book by a noted author-illustrator is one of several stories about Otto's adventures.

200 Dunn, Mary Lois and Mayhar, Ardath. **THE ABSOLUTELY PERFECT HORSE.** New York. Harper & Row. 1983. 186 p. **(I J)**

The Braeden family move to their mother's farm in contemporary East Texas, where their disabled veteran father begins raising cattle. Annie attempts to buy the horse of her dreams and comes home with an ancient Indian pony nicknamed Dogmeat. The characters and setting come alive in this story of friendship, courage, and strong family ties while the young people grow and develop sound values.

201 Duval, John Crittenden. **EARLY TIMES IN TEXAS.** Austin. H.P.N. Gammel. 1892. 253 p. **(I J)**

Duval, the descendant of a distinguished Southern family, kept a journal while a soldier in the Texas Revolution. In this account of his military experiences, written fifty-six years later from the perspective of an old man looking back, the style is grand, the language elaborate. The first eight chapters tell the story of the ill-fated Fannin expedition, which ended on Palm Sunday, 1836, at Goliad. The amazing adventures of the young survivor of the massacre, who avoided Mexicans, Indians, and wild animals to rejoin the victorious Texas Army, constitute the remainder of the lively narrative. Reprinted by Steck in 1935 and by Tardy Publishing Company in 1936.

202 Eberle, Irmengarde. **LISTEN TO THE MOCKINGBIRD**. Illustrated by Sabra Mallett Kimball. New York. Whittlesey House. 1949. 64 p. (I)

Two Texas mockingbirds select a young pecan tree in a friendly yard, build a nest, and raise four young birds. Young Janie Harper and neighbor Bob watch the birds and protect them from the gray cat. The habitat and habits of the state bird, noted for its unusual ability to imitate the calls of other birds, are described and illustrated in sketches. The anthropomorphic perspective of the narrative removes it from the nature book catagory.

203 Eberle, Irmengarde. **LONE STAR FIGHT**. Illustrated by Lee Townsend. New York. Dodd, Mead. 1954. 292 p. (J)

This heroic story of the Texas Revolution focuses on twelve-year-old Alton Jameson and his San Antonio friends. They witness the actions of Texas heroes Travis, Crockett, Bonham, Milam, Bowie, and Deaf Smith during the siege and fall of the Alamo. A fictional scout, Steve Martin, and a beloved horse add to the excitement of the story.

204 Eberle, Irmengarde. **MUSTANG ON THE PRAIRIE**. Illustrated by Joseph Cellini. Garden City, N.Y. Doubleday. 1968. 89 p. (I)

While his older brother is fighting with General Sam Houston at San Jacinto, ten-year-old Andrew Dennon captures a wild bay stallion and mare on the family homestead near San Antonio, then hides them during a Comanche raid. Andy is the only well-developed character in this novel, which gives a clear picture of the settler's life in the period of the Texas Revolution.

205 Eberle, Irmengarde. **VERY GOOD NEIGHBORS**. Illustrated by Flora Nash DeMuth. Philadelphia. Lippincott. 1945. 95 p. (I)

In this story set in the 1940s in San Antonio, a Mexican family builds a house of tin cans and odds and ends. The story revolves around the family's struggle to maintain their home and warm family life while continuing Mexican customs but adding newly learned ways. A dated, condescending attitude of Anglos toward poor Mexicans is balanced by the presence of kindly neighbors. Four- color drawings by DeMuth illustrate the story.

206 Erdman, Loula Grace. **THE GOOD LAND**. New York. Dodd, Mead. 1959. 182 p. (I J)

Carolyn Pierce, youngest daughter of a Texas Panhandle pioneer ranching family, is fifteen in 1904. She attempts to befriend a poor, hard-luck family new to the neighborhood, assists as her sister Katie marries, attends high school in Amarillo, and falls in love with Jim Foster, who shares her love of the region. Dramatic events, such as a prairie fire, and the community spirit and neighborliness necessary for survival provide a sense of place in this third novel in a trilogy which includes **The Wind Blows Free** and **The Wide Horizon**.

207 Erdman, Loula Grace. **ROOM TO GROW**. New York. Dodd, Mead. 1962. 242 p.   **(I J)**

French immigrants Celeste and Pierre Danton arrive in New Orleans in 1901 on their way to settle at Marcy in the Texas Panhandle. The atmosphere of the small town on the railroad, with its board sidewalk, general store, boarding house, and local cowboys from the Big W Ranch who befriend the family and teach them Western customs, gives an authentic regional flavor.

208 Erdman, Loula Grace. **WIDE HORIZON : A STORY OF THE TEXAS PANHANDLE**. New York. Dodd, Mead. 1956. 245 p. **(I J)**

Fifteen-year-old Katie Pierce, middle daughter of a Panhandle pioneer family, matures when she is given the responsibility of caring for younger siblings while her mother is away. Katie overcomes her shyness and fear of making decisions. She saves some younger children stranded in a schoolhouse during a blizzard, begins to fall in love, and is sent to an academy for young ladies in East Texas. One of a trilogy which includes **The Wind Blows Free** and **The Good Land**.

209 Erdman, Loula Grace. **THE WIND BLOWS FREE**. New York. Dodd, Mead. 1952. 242 p.   **(I J)**

Melinda Pierce moves from East Texas to her family's Panhandle claim near Amarillo in 1893. The family lives in a one-room dugout with the wind always blowing while they establish themselves. The hardships of the settlers, the nostalgic details of family life, a young woman's coming of age, and growing love of the region are portrayed in this story written from "left over" notes of Erdman's **The Edge of Time**, an adult novel. **The Wide Horizon** and **The Good Land** are sequels of this winner of the American Girl-Dodd Mead Prize Competition.

210 Erickson, John R. **THE FURTHER ADVENTURES OF HANK THE COWDOG**. Illustrated by Gerald L. Holmes. Perryton, Tex. Maverick Books. 1983. 92 p. **(I J)**

In a series of humorous misadventures, Hank is stricken with eye-crosserosis, humiliated by a mean doberman, and bewitched by a little owl, Madame Moonshine. Erickson's tall tale storytelling includes wordplay, doggerel, and crafty tricks which will appeal to young readers.

211 Erickson, John R. **HANK THE COWDOG**. Illustrated by Gerald L. Holmes. Perryton, Tex. Maverick Books. 1983. 87 p. **(I J)**

The misadventures of Hank, head of ranch security, and his sidekick Drover, who try to protect their master and his wife, provide a light, humorous look at Panhandle ranch life told in cowboy dialect. Falsely accused of chicken killing, Hank leaves home to become an outlaw and takes up with two buzzards and a pack of coyotes who show him their wild, freewheeling lifestyle. Holmes's amusing drawings illustrate the text.

212 Erickson, John R. **HANK THE COWDOG, IT'S A DOG'S LIFE**. Illustrated by Gerald L. Holmes. Perryton, Tex. Maverick Books. 1984. 93 p. **(I J)**

In a series of misadventures, Hank the cowdog solves the mystery of an end-of-the-world rumor, visits his sister in town, teaches his nieces and nephews some low-down tricks, is captured by the dog catcher, is suspected of having hydrophobia, and escapes from the pound to return to his old ranch. Again Erickson uses cowboy language and playground doggerel, while Holmes's drawings illustrate Hank's inept activities.

213 Evans, May. **MY PARDNER**. Illustrated by Lorence Bjorklund. Boston. Houghton Mifflin. 1972. 106 p. **(I J)**

During the 1929 depression, twelve-year-old Dan drives a string of horses from Texas to Oklahoma for his father. Accompanied by a charming but deceitful cowboy named Boggs, who teaches him to live by his wits, Dan survives the Panhandle drought and learns the value of imagination. The characterizations of Boggs and Dan are delightfully humorous.

214 Evey, Ethel L. **STOWAWAY TO TEXAS**. Houston. Larksdale. 1984. 201 p. **(I)**

After his father is unjustly imprisoned, thirteen-year-old Allen Dupree flees New Orleans in 1837 by stowing away on a ship bound for Texas. He meets a series of rough and kind characters on the frontier while seeking aid for his father. A historically accurate picture of a sailing trip to Galveston and of crossing frontier East Texas, the novel has a happy ending.

215 Fall, Thomas. **EDDIE NO-NAME**. Illustrated by Ray Prohaska. New York. Pantheon. 1963. 45 p.   **(P I)**

Eddie is an orphan who yearns to be adopted. The strong fear that Jonah and Cora Whalen, prospective parents, will not adopt him leads to blundering behavior. Despite Eddie's mistakes, the Whalens finally accept him as a member of the family. The simple story is illustrated with watercolor drawings.

216 Fall, Thomas. **WILD BOY**. Illustrated by Henry C. Pitz. New York. Dial. 1965. 105 p.   **(P I)**

On the Wild Horse Desert of West Texas in 1870 Roberto de Alverez Jones decides to follow in his father's work as a mustanger. Because his father was killed while attempting to capture the powerful stallion Diablo Blanco, Roberto turns first to his frail grandfather and then to old Comanche chief Leaning Rock for help. He is sent for training in horsemanship and warfare with a hundred Comanche braves, surviving the instructor's hatred of whites to become a skilled and courageous young man. This suspensefully constructed story, with colorful sensory descriptions of the Texas landscapes, sensitively portrays the conflict of one caught between two cultures.

217 Felton, Harold W. **COWBOY JAMBOREE : WESTERN SONGS AND LORE**. Illustrated by Aldren A. Watson. New York. Knopf. 1951. 107 p. (Borzoi Books for Young People)   **(I J)**

Twenty cowboy songs are individually introduced with appropriate stories of cowboy life and explanations of unusual vocabulary. The text and songs provide valuable background about the cowboy as well as being a source of entertainment. Humorous, strong drawings by Aldren A. Watson illustrate the text. Simplified musical arrangements were written by Edward S. Breck.

218 Felton, Harold W. **NAT LOVE, NEGRO COWBOY**. Illustrated by David Hodges. New York. Dodd, Mead. 1969. 93 p.   **(P I)**

An adventure-filled biography of a black man who was superb at breaking horses, shooting .45s and rifles, mustang roping, and Indian fighting. Born a slave, Nat Love made his way West at age fifteen and through his skill and determination won a place in cowboy mythology as "Deadwood Dick," champion cowboy. After twenty exciting years as a cowboy, he saw the changes brought about by the railroad and became a Pullman porter. Felton used material from Love's autobiography, **The Life and Adventures of Nat Love: Better Known in Cattle Country as "Deadwood Dick" -- By Himself**.

219 Felton, Harold W. **NEW TALL TALES OF PECOS BILL**.
Illustrated by William Moyers. Englewood Cliffs, N.J. Prentice Hall. 1958. 164 p. **(P I)**

Thirteen stories created by a master storyteller about Texas' own folk hero reveal previously unknown incidents in the life of Pecos Bill. Three-Fingered Ike, another colorful character, appears in several of the stories.

220 Felton, Harold W. **PECOS BILL AND THE MUSTANG**. Illustrated by Leonard Shortall. Englewood Cliffs, N.J. Prentice Hall. 1965. 1 v. (unpaged) **(P)**

This simple retelling of the legend explains how Pecos Bill captures the famous pacing mustang with a coat the color of a newly minted gold coin and becomes the first cowboy. Yellow and pink drawings illustrate the picture book.

221 Felton, Harold W. **PECOS BILL, TEXAS COWPUNCHER**.
Illustrated by Aldren A. Watson. New York. Knopf. 1949. 177 p. **(I J)**

Twelve delightful tall tales tell about the cowboy folk hero's early life and coyote upbringing, his achievements as a cowboy with the Hell's Gate Gulch outfit and the great pacing white mustang, and his romance with Slue-Foot Sue. The final chapter defends his true character and explains his disappearance. The humorous narrative is colloquial, with dialogue in cowboy dialect. The extensive bibliography includes books, articles, poetry, drama, music, and art about Pecos Bill, from Dobie's 1926 article through 1949.

222 Flynn, Jean. **REMEMBER GOLIAD : JAMES W. FANNIN**.
Illustrated by G.E. Mullan. Austin. Eakin. 1984. 53 p. (Stories for Young Americans) **(I)**

As a leader of the troops massacred at Goliad, Fannin is remembered as a martyr of the Texas Revolution. His ill-fated life is accurately portrayed, from his birth as the illegitimate son of a Georgia plantation owner, his departure from West Point without graduating, and his engagement in illegal slave trade to support his family to his death at age thirty-one. Flynn's carefully researched text is supplemented by notes, a bibliography, and drawings by G.E. Mullan.

223 Flynn, Jean. **STEPHEN F. AUSTIN : THE FATHER OF TEXAS.** Burnet, Tex. Eakin. 1981. 49 p. (Stories for Young Americans) **(I J)**

A biography of the "Father of Texas" which portrays the significance of Austin's career but also reveals his human foibles.

224 Flynn, Jean. **WILLIAM BARRET TRAVIS : VICTORY OR DEATH.** Illustrated by G.E. Mullan. Austin. Eakin. 1983. 63 p. (Stories for Young Americans) **(I)**

A carefully resarched, honest portrayal of the Texas hero who led the Texans in the Battle of the Alamo. Information about Travis's marital difficulties are included along with his political activities. Black-and-white drawings and a bibliography of source materials enhance the volume.

225 Ford, Anne. **DAVY CROCKETT.** Illustrated by Leonard Vosburgh. New York. Putnam. 1961. 45 p. (A See and Read Biography) **(P)**

This easy-to-read biography of the legendary David Crockett, hero of the Alamo, is illustrated with black-and-green sketches of scenes from his life.

226 Foster, Ed. **TEJANOS.** Illustrated by Bill Negron. New York. Hill and Wang; distributed by Random House. 1970. 48 p. (A Challenger Book. La Raza Series) **(I J)**

Eleven-year-old Enrique Esparza's account of his father Gregorio's fighting and dying with the Texian forces at the Alamo while his Uncle Pancho fights with Santa Anna shows the horror of war. Adapted from a source in the Bexar County Archives, the easy-to-read text with Spanish phrases explains the perspective of the Tejano during the Texas Revolution.

227 Fowler, Frank. **THE BRONCHO RIDER BOYS WITH THE TEXAS RANGERS : OR, THE CAPTURE OF THE SMUGGLERS ON THE RIO GRANDE**. New York. Burt. 1915. 249 p. (The Broncho Rider Boys Series)   **(I J)**

Broncho Billie Stonewall Jackson Winkle and two young friends meet Captain June Peak, Texas Ranger, in El Paso. Pancho Villa appears during the boys' adventures on both sides of the border as they capture horse thieves and foil gunrunners to the Mexican revolutionaries. One of a series of stories for boys, the book uses current events as background for the action.

228 Fowler, Zinita. **GHOST STORIES OF OLD TEXAS**. Austin. Eakin. 1983. 61 p. (Stories for Young Americans)   **(I)**

Twenty-seven ghost stories are retold in exciting storytelling versions by a winner of the Siddie Joe Johnson Award for excellence in children's librarianship. Stories of lost mines and buried treasure, familiar from Dobie sources, and of spirits, wraiths, ghosts, and visions, some in ballad form, are told with great good humor.

229 Fox, Vivian. **THE WINDING TRAIL : THE ALABAMA-COUSHATTA INDIANS OF TEXAS**. Austin. Eakin. 1983. 99 p. (Stories for Young Americans)   **(I)**

The history and customs of the Alabama-Coushatta Indians from prehistoric times to 1983, with traditional and modern lifestyles compared. Life on the only Indian reservation presently in Texas is described and illustrated in black-and-white photographs.

230 Fradin, Dennis B. **TEXAS IN WORDS AND PICTURES**. Illustrated by Richard Wahl. Chicago. Childrens Press. 1981. 46 p.   **(P)**

This well-written, easy-to-read presentation of Texas geography, history, and economic conditions, with a section on famous Texans, was written by a second grade teacher. Colorful photographs illustrate the text. Reference aids include maps, a page of facts about Texas, a brief timeline, and an index.

231 Frank, Jeannie MacCallum. **HISTORY OF THE SOUTHWEST : AN ELEMENTARY HISTORY OF THE MEXICAN BORDER**. El Paso. El Paso Schools. 1922. 110 p.   **(I J)**

This history of the El Paso area from prehistoric times to 1932 was written by an English teacher to be used as a supplementary grade school text. Bits of folklore and local residents' memories of earlier times enliven the history of the important border region. Republished in 1947 under the title **History of the District of El Paso in Texas and New Mexico.**

232 Frankel, Haskel. **RODEO ROUNDUP.** Illustrated by Lorence F. Bjorklund. Garden City, N.Y. Doubleday. 1962. 144 p. **(I J)**

Dan Pearson, son of a successful rancher, makes friends and enemies when he and his palomino, Crown, join the rodeo circuit. During forty-eight hours he meets a rodeo clown, a brave bareback rider, a rodeo doctor with a secret about rodeo life, and two unscrupulous rodeo regulars who care only for the winning money. Seventeen-year-old Dan's experiences with riding in a small West Texas rodeo lead him to career decisions.

233 Fulle, Suzanne G. **LANTERNS FOR FIESTA.** Philadelphia. Macrae Smith. 1973. 134 p. **(I J)**

Juanita, twelve-year-old daughter of a cotton picker, lives in the poor section of Lamar in East Texas where families use a communal water faucet and helps her grandfather sell tamales from a cart. A special school for the children organized by the parish priest opens new horizons for Juanita and brings hope to the whole community.

234 Gaither, Frances Ormond. **THE SCARLET COAT.** Illustrated by Harve Stein. New York. Macmillan. 1934. 205 p. **(J)**

Pierre Rolland, a young French colonist from Fort St. Louis, traveled with La Salle, witnessing his murder. Pierre's captivity, first by the Cenis Indians and then by Spanish soldiers, and his reunion with his brothers and sisters in an Indian camp on the Gulf Coast provide an adventure tale about the early exploration of Texas by Europeans.

235 Garst, Doris Shannon. **BIG FOOT WALLACE OF THE TEXAS RANGERS.** Illustrated by Lee Ames. New York. Messner. 1951. 188 p. **(J)**

This biography of a Texas folk hero combines historical fact with the myths that have grown up around his extraordinary deeds. Wallace came to Texas to avenge his brother's death at Goliad. He became a Texas Ranger, a member of the Mier Expedition, and later a San Antonio-El Paso stagecoach driver. Garst has captured his human qualities as well as his outstanding achievements. Useful reference tools are a chronology, a bibliography, and an index.

236 Garst, Doris Shannon and Garst, Warren Edward. **COWBOYS AND CATTLE TRAILS**. Illustrated by Jack Merryweather. Chicago. Wheeler. 1948. 252 p. (The American Adventure Series) **(I)**

Stampedes, Indians, floods, drought, dust, and the exhilaration of outdoor life of a Texas cowboy compose the fictionalized biography of John Benjamin Kendrick, who rode the Chisholm Trail to Wyoming, where he later became governor.

237 Garst, Doris Shannon. **JAMES BOWIE AND HIS FAMOUS KNIFE**. New York. Messner. 1955. 192 p. **(J)**

All of Bowie's adventurous exploits are recounted in this readable biography. Bowie met with Lafitte while participating in the slave trade; traveled to Texas, where he married the Mexican Vice-Governor's daughter; fought knife duels and invented the bowie knife; searched for the lost silver mines of San Saba; and died in the Battle of the Alamo. Useful reference aids include a 1796-1836 chronology and a bibliography.

238 Garst, Warren Edward. **TEXAS TRAIL DRIVE**. Illustrated by Joshua Tolford. New York. Ariel. 1952. 214 p. **(J)**

The Walters family's West Texas ranch near Terlingua Creek undergoes difficult times during the Civil War when the men of the family are away fighting and cattle prices drop. Twelve-year-old Dave captures and trains a magnificent mustang, Duster, and learns roping and riding skills from a trusted old hand. Thus prepared, he persuades his strict father to allow him to be a trail hand on a cattle drive to Abilene immediately after the war. In the face of enormous adversity, Dave displays bravery and loyalty, saving the ranch by getting the cattle through to the buyer.

239 Gartman, Louise. **KENSIL TAKES OVER**. Philadelphia. Westminster. 1964. 176 p. **(I J)**

Sixteen-year-old Kensil Drake, the ugly-duckling, younger daughter of a wealthy family, grows up in an early-1960s suburban community where social life centers around the Sycamore Hills Club. Kensil befriends and tutors Cuban refugee Ana Avelina Montejo and begins to date Bart Jerrold when he is not chauffering his stepsisters. The girls spend a great deal of time considering boys and clothes but also focus on studies and the Cuban missile situation.

240 Gilbert, Minnie. **SUNRISE SONG**. Illustrated by Marilyn Moseley. Austin. Eakin. 1984. 114 p. (Stories for Young Americans) **(I J)**

Rosita's fifteenth year, September 15, 1910, to September 15, 1911, culminating in her quinceanera, is filled with the excitement of the Rio Grande Valley during the Mexican Revolution. Mexican customs, folklore, and holiday celebrations are explained to Helen, Rosita's Anglo friend. Marilyn Moseley's black-and-white drawings are a charming addition to the story.

241 Gillett, James B. **THE TEXAS RANGER : A STORY OF THE SOUTHWESTERN FRONTIER**. Illustrated by Herbert M. Stoops. Chicago. World Book. 1927. 218 p. (Pioneer Life Series) **(I J)**

This first-hand account of the life of Captain James Gillett (1856-1937) of the Texas Rangers gives a picture of Texas from frontier times to the 1930s. Gillett fought Indians, Mexicans, and outlaws as a member of the Frontier Battalion and later as a marshall of Old El Paso. The book was formerly adopted as a supplementary seventh-grade reader.

242 Gilstrap, Robert L. **TEN TEXAS TALES**. Illustrated by Betsy Warren. Austin. Steck. 1963. 142 p. **(P I)**

Lively, simple retellings of stories from written and oral sources cover episodes in Texas history from ancient Indian legend to a 20th-century oil discovery. Each story is introduced by a brief background note and illustrated with a black-and-white drawing.

243 Gipson, Frederick Benjamin. **CURLY AND THE WILD BOAR**. Illustrated by Ronald Himler. New York. Harper & Row. 1979. 88 p. **(I)**

Twelve-year-old, motherless Curly Waggoner seeks revenge on the wild boar who smashed the prize watermelon he had grown for the county fair. A strong sense of the local color of Mason County, Texas, is given through Gipson's storytelling style and finely drawn characters.

244 Gipson, Frederick Benjamin. **LITTLE ARLISS.** Illustrated by Ronald Himler. New York. Harper & Row. 1978. 83 p.   **(I J)**

Travis's younger brother Arliss is twelve years old, small for his age, and determined to prove himself in this story set seven years after **Old Yeller**. The men laugh at him when he asks to go along to capture an outlaw horse; Arliss responds by throwing rocks at them. He plays hooky and manages to catch and ride the wild stallion but is promised another horse instead of being allowed to keep the outlaw. In this late work, published posthumously, Gipson's distinctive storytelling qualities evoke rural life in the Texas Hill Country.

245 Gipson, Frederick Benjamin. **OLD YELLER.** New York. Harper & Row. 1956. 158 p.   **(I J)**

Fourteen-year-old Travis acts as the man of the family while his father trails cattle to Abilene, Kansas, in the late 1860s. Besides caring for his mother and his five-year-old brother Little Arliss at their log cabin on Birdsong Creek in the Hill Country, Travis must tend the corn, chop wood, hunt for meat, and mark wild hogs. At first unwanted, the dingy yellow dog becomes his companion, fighting off wild animals, hunting, and finally performing heroic feats to save lives. Gipson's unique storytelling brings alive Texas pioneer life in this popular modern classic, which has been translated into several languages and made into a movie.

246 Gipson, Frederick Benjamin. **RECOLLECTION CREEK.** Illustrated by Carl Burger. New York. Harper & Row. 1959. 248 p.   **(I J)**

First published in 1955, this book was revised for young people by the author in 1959. Hopper Creech's golden memories of his ninth year, 1908--the people he knew, the pranks he and his cousin played, the excitement of exploring the Central Texas countryside--provide a humorous portrait of an old-fashioned rural boyhood.

247 Gipson, Frederick Benjamin. **SAVAGE SAM.** New York. Harper & Row. 1962. 214 p.   **(P I)**

Sam, son of Old Yeller, rescues Travis, Little Arliss, and Lisbeth from a band of Apaches. The setting is the Hill Country in the 1870s. This sequel to **Old Yeller** was also made into a popular movie.

248 Gipson, Frederick Benjamin. **THE TRAIL-DRIVING ROOSTER.** New York. Harper & Row. 1955. 79 p.   **(P I)**

This delightful tall tale about a scrawny rooster on an 1881 cattle drive from Texas to Dodge City is Gipson's first book for children. Dick "crowed the bunch out of bed" and won his way into the cowboys' hearts, not their stomachs, by his entertaining antics.

249 Gold, Herbert. **THE YOUNG PRINCE AND THE MAGIC CONE.** Illustrated by Julie Brinckloe. Garden City, N.Y. Doubleday. 1973. 68 p.   **(I)**

In this fantasy based on the stereotype of the rich, materialistic Texan, the Prince of North Texas, a poor little rich boy, has all the possessions he can dream of asking for, but no friends. With the help of a magic ice cream cone he learns that he must first love himself.

250 Gonzalez, Catherine Troxell. **CYNTHIA ANN PARKER : INDIAN CAPTIVE.** Illustrated by Virginia Scott Gholson. Burnet, Tex. Eakin. 1980. 69 p. (Stories for Young Americans)   **(I J)**

Cynthia Ann, abducted by Comanches in 1836 during the Fort Parker massacre and recovered with her daughter Prairie Flower in 1860, became the best known Texas Indian captive. Quanah Parker, last of the Comanche chiefs, was her son.

251 Gonzalez, Catherine Troxell. **JANE LONG : THE MOTHER OF TEXAS.** Burnet, Tex. Eakin. 1982. 57 p. (Stories for Young Americans)   **(I J)**

Jane Long, "The Mother of Texas," followed her husband, Dr. James Long, on an unsuccessful expedition to free Texas from Spain. During the winter of 1821-1822 she lived on Bolivar Point near Galveston, fought off Karankawa Indians, and survived cruel hardships, leaving only after learning of her husband's death in Mexico, where he had been imprisoned. Later she settled in Brazoria as an active member of Austin's colony.

252 Gonzalez, Catherine Troxell. **LAFITTE : THE TERROR OF THE GULF.** Burnet, Tex. Eakin. 1981. 69 p. (Stories for Young Americans)   **(I J)**

In 1817 Jean Lafitte established Campeche, his pirate headquarters, at Galveston, where he built a fine home and lived until 1821 when ordered to leave by the United States government. This biography emphasizes the adventurous role Lafitte played in Texas history.

253 Gonzalez, Catherine Troxell. **SAM HOUSTON : HERO OF SAN JACINTO.** Austin Eakin. 1983. 80 p. (Stories for Young Americans)   **(I)**

Houston's life from his boyhood to his death, including his political career before he came to Texas and the influential role he played in Texas history, is told in this biography. Three portraits of Houston at different ages, a letter from U.S. President Andrew Jackson to Houston (January 19, 1844), and a bibliography are included.

254 Gorsline, Marie and Gorsline, Douglas. **COWBOYS.** Illustrated by the authors. New York. Random House. 1978. 32 p. (A Random House Picture Book)   **(P)**

This cheerful, lively picture-book introduction to the post-Civil War cowboy is illustrated with colorful drawings inspired by the paintings of Charles Russell. Double-page montages showing details of clothes, equipment, ranch work, the dangers of the trail drives, activities at the end of the trail, and famous people give a vivid picture of a late-19th-century Texas lifestyle.

255 Grant, Bruce. **THE COWBOY ENCYCLOPEDIA : THE OLD AND THE NEW WEST FROM THE OPEN RANGE TO THE DUDE RANCH..** Illustrated by Jackie Mastri and Fiore Mastri. Chicago. Rand McNally. 1951. 160 p.   **(I J)**

Factual information about the cattle industry and cowboys arranged in alphabetical order includes topics of biography, activities, equipment, language, history, and traditions. Black-and-white drawings and diagrams present important visual information about such things as animals, brands and equipment. While the coverage is broader than Texas, this volume is especially useful for quick reference about cowboy terms.

256 Grant, Bruce. **CYCLONE.** Cleveland. World Pub. Co. 1959. 190 p.   **(I J)**

Cyclone, a paint mule, is owned by and owns Ward Hampton. Hampton becomes a member of Capt. Randolph Marcy's contingent of soldiers assigned to inform the southern Comanches of the reservation in Texas where the government plans to send them. Ward accompanies a wagon train to the frontier west of Gainesville, where his father is a storekeeper.

257 Grant, Bruce. **DAVY CROCKETT : AMERICAN HERO**. Illustrated by William Timmins. Chicago. Rand McNally. 1955. 1 v. (unpaged) (A Rand McNally Giant Book)   **(P)**

This large-size, full-color picture biography with simple text presents a brief sketch of the legendary deeds of a Texas hero.

258 Grant, Bruce. **LEOPARD HORSE CANYON : THE STORY OF THE LOST APPALOOSAS**. Cleveland. World Pub. Co. 1957. 221 p.   **(J)**

Ted Holliday lives on the Lazy Leopard Spot Ranch in Fisher County, Texas, at the turn of the century. As he solves the mystery of a strange Indian picture map inherited from his Uncle Theodore, Ted meets cattle thieves; Squinch Owl Sam, an old Indian; and the prize Appaloosa breed of wild ponies. In a story of adventure and reconciliation of Indian and white man, Chief Joseph, a famous Nez Perce, and President William McKinley each aid in saving the special breed of ponies.

259 Grant, Bruce. **LONGHORN : A STORY OF THE CHISHOLM TRAIL**. Illustrated by Herman D. Giesen. Cleveland. World Pub. Co. 1956. 215 p.   **(J)**

Nineteen-year-old Sul Burnet, Texas Ranger Brick's younger brother, obtains a job as a cowboy to herd on the Chisholm Trail in 1879. Sul and Juan, a Mexican whose pet longhorn, El Diablo, leads the herd, become friends while experiencing the dangers of the trail, rustlers, stampedes, and weather. Grant's attention to accurate detail makes the book worthwhile historical reading.

260 Grant, Bruce. **SIX GUN : A STORY OF THE TEXAS RANGERS**. Illustrated by Jacob Landau. Cleveland. World Pub. Co. 1955. 223 p.   **(J)**

In this sequel to **Warpath**, the story of Brick and Sul Burnet as Indian captives, Brick joins the Texas Rangers. Major Jones, the Adjutant General, assigns him to track and capture Sam Bass, a legendary train robber. Brick has an adventurous pursuit of the outlaw, but the Rangers get their man in Round Rock in 1878.

261 Grant, Bruce. **WARPATH : A TALE OF THE PLAINS INDIANS**. Illustrated by Jacob Landau. Cleveland. World Pub. Co. 1954. 220 p.   **(I J)**

Indian captive Brick Burnet escapes from Comanches to warn buffalo hunters of an impending attack on Adobe Walls in 1874. Medicine man Isatai, Quanah Parker, Bat Masterson, and Billy Dixon appear in the story, which is sympathetic to Indian culture and white men's ways.

262 Grant, Matthew G. **CORONADO : EXPLORER OF THE SOUTHWEST.** Illustrated by Harold Henriksen. Mankato, Minn. Creative Education; distributed by Childrens Press, Chicago. 1974. 26 p. (Gallery of Great Americans Series) **(P)**

An illustrated history of Coronado's search for the Seven Cities of Cibola and Quivira in 1540-41, which led him into the Staked Plains, is presented in easy- to-read format.

263 Grant, Matthew G. **DAVY CROCKETT, FRONTIER ADVENTURER.** Illustrated by Jack Norman. Mankato, Minn. Creative Education; distributed by Childrens Press, Chicago. 1973. 29 p. (Gallery of Great Americans Series) **(P)**

This easy-to-read biography of Crockett--pioneer, politician, hero of the Alamo in 1836--begins at age eight and features the highlights of his life and his heroic death. Alternate full-color and black-and-white drawings illustrate the simple text.

264 Grant, Matthew G. **SAM HOUSTON OF TEXAS.** Illustrated by Harold Henriksen. Mankato, Minn. Creative Education; distributed by Childrens Press, Chicago. 1974. 29 p. (Gallery of Great Americans Series. War Heroes of America) **(P)**

This easy-to-read biography highlights Houston's important role in the Texas Revolution and in political affairs in the days of the Republic and early statehood. Alternate full-color and black-and-white drawings illustrate the simple text.

265 Gray, Joan. **THE BALL BOYS ON THE BAY.** Philadelphia. Dorrance. 1971. 51 p. **(I)**

Corbin and Warren, two young boys, travel across East Texas from Shreveport to Ingleside for a family reunion. Texas weather and wildlife are in evidence as the happy group explores Corpus Christi Bay, Goose Island State Park, and Rockport and enjoys crabbing and trout fishing.

266 Greer, James Kimmins. **EARLY IN THE SADDLE**. Dallas. Dealey & Lowe. 1936. 269 p.   **(I J)**

A biographical narrative of a boy who was born in a log cabin in Corsicana, whose father was a sheriff and former Texas Ranger, and who grew up on the Texas frontier. After the family moved to Meridian in 1856, he hunted wild animals and Indians, rode on trail drives, and married his childhood sweetheart. This is an abridged edition of **Bois d'Arc to Barb'd Wire**.

267 Griffin, John Howard. **A TIME TO BE HUMAN**. New York. Macmillan. 1977. 102 p.   **(I J)**

The author of **Black Like Me** critically appraises racial prejudice in this country, including his experience as a black man in the South in 1959. He explores the effects of behavior patterns learned as a boy growing up in Texas on his thinking as an adult.

268 Griffith, Mary Matlock. **WESTWARD THE COURSE OF EMPIRE : THE HISTORY OF TEXAS FROM EXPLORATION TO ANNEXATION IN A SEQUENCE OF ONE ACT PLAYS.**. Austin. Steck. 1924. 219 p.   **(I J)**

Eighteen one-act plays about events in Texas history from the French period to the Republic are introduced in the foreword by Eugene C. Barker.

269 Grimmer, Glenda Gardiner. **THE ABCs OF TEXAS WILDFLOWERS**. Illustrated by Mary Jo Laughlin. Burnet, Tex. Eakin. 1982. 70 p.   **(P I)**

This introduction to wildflowers includes twenty-six flowers common to Texas, with a full-page illustration of each and a facing-page narrative of characteristics and locale; a glossary of botanical terms; and brief descriptions of the sixteen flower families represented. Scientific names are used for the letters x and z, with common names used for the other letters. This useful book would be improved by coloring the detailed black- and-white illustrations.

270 Grisham, Noel. **CROSSROADS AT SAN FELIPE**. Illustrated by Tim Grisham. Burnet, Tex. Eakin. 1980. 73 p. (Stories for Young Americans)   **(J)**

The author set out to write a concise volume about San Felipe, with the explanation that the history of the town, 1823-1836, is the history of Stephen F. Austin. The text recounts the establishment of the town and its burning in the Runaway Scrape, but goes far afield in discussing the broader events leading to the Texas Revolution and conflicts with the Indians. The maps are useful, but the faded photographs and black-and-white drawings leave room for improvement. A list of The Old Three Hundred is also included.

271 Hahn, James and Hahn, Lynn. **ZAHARIAS! : THE SPORTS CAREER OF MILDRED ZAHARIAS**. Mankato, Minn. Crestwood. 1981. 47 p. (Sports Legends)   **(P I)**

"Babe" Didrikson Zaharias, from a large family in Port Arthur, excelled in basketball, baseball, track and field, bowling, and golf. She was named "Greatest Woman Athlete of the Half-Century" by the Associated Press in 1949. The brief biography is heavily illustrated with black-and-white photographs.

272 Haines, Paul G. **GROWING UP IN THE HILL COUNTRY**. Burnet, Tex. Nortex. 1976. 135 p.   **(J)**

Episodic reminiscences of his Hill Country youth by Haines, who was born in Blanco in 1892, was graduated from Texas A&M University, and served as a county extension agent. Boyhood pranks, local eccentrics, and community customs are recalled in colorful language with a strong Christian overtone. Line drawings and old photographs illustrate the vignettes.

273 Haislet, John. **FAMOUS TREES OF TEXAS**. College Station. Texas Forest Service. 1970. 193 p.   **(I J)**

The expressed purpose of this book is to memorialize those trees which have been a witness to some of the exciting periods and events in Texas's frontier history. A full-page color photograph of each tree is accompanied by a vignette about its location and historical significance. A map of Texas on the endpapers shows the location of the ninety-six trees. The volume was distributed free of charge to Texas schools.

274 Hall-Quest, Olga Wilbourne. **SHRINE OF LIBERTY, THE ALAMO**. New York. Dutton. 1948. 120 p.   **(I J)**

The story of the Alamo, from the beginning of the missions to the siege and battle of 1836, with a chapter about the present-day site. The historical study is authoritative and unbiased, neither condescending nor overly patriotic, and is presented in a clear, readable style.

275 Hamilton, Dorothy. **BUSBOYS AT BIG BEND**. Illustrated by Betty Baker Fraley. Scottdale, Pa. Herald Press. 1974. 100 p.   **(I J)**

Ben Martinez, poor Mexican American, and Wesley Cameron, nephew of the lodge manager, work as busboys at Chisos Mountain Lodge, explore Big Bend National Park together, and become good friends by the end of the summer.

276 Hancock, Sibyl. **BILL PICKETT : FIRST BLACK RODEO STAR**. Illustrated by Lorinda Bryan Cauley. New York. Harcourt, Brace, Jovanovich. 1977. 61 p. (A Let Me Read Book)   **(P I)**

Pickett, born in 1860 on a ranch near Taylor, worked on ranches and in rodeos worldwide. This easy-to-read biography portrays the adventurous life of the famous black cowboy.

277 Hancock, Sibyl. **THE BLAZING HILLS**. Illustrated by Richard Cuffari. New York. Putnam. 1975. 47 p. (A See and Read Book)   **(P I)**

On Easter Eve 1846 German settlers in Fredericksburg made a peace treaty with Comanche and Apache tribes. Signal fires on the hills, lit by suspicious Indians, were interpreted to the settlers' children as the Easter bunny dyeing eggs. The easy-to-read format explains the Easter fires tradition that is practiced even now.

278 Hancock, Sibyl. **OLD BLUE**. Illustrated by Erick Ingraham. New York. Putnam. 1980. 46 p. (A See and Read Book)   **(P)**

From Palo Duro Canyon to Dodge City, Davy, a young boy on his first trail drive, watches Old Blue, a tame longhorn with a brass bell around his neck, lead cattle through a stampede and bad weather, and sleeps around the campfire with the cowboys. This is 1878 history in easy-to-read form.

279 Hancock, Sibyl. **SPINDLETOP**. Illustrated by Virginia Scott Gholson. Burnet, Tex. Eakin. 1980. 26 p. (Stories for Young Americans)   **(P)**

January 10, 1901, was the day Jimmy's father struck oil, the day the well on Spindletop hill near Beaumont "blew in." The suspense of drilling, the excitement of striking oil, and the dangers of explosions and fires are portrayed in simple text with black-and- white line drawings. Eakin published a revised illustrated edition in 1984.

280 Hancock, Sibyl and Venable, Fay. **TEXAS : YESTERDAY AND TODAY**. Burnet, Tex. Eakin. 1982. 48 p. (Stories for Young Americans)   **(P I)**

A simple, large-type introduction to Texas history, heavily illustrated with photographs, containing basic facts of history, geography, weather, industry, and information about eleven cities.

281 Hanna, Betty Elliott. **LANTERN IN THE VALLEY**. Burnet, Tex. Eakin. 1981. 49 p. (Stories for Young Americans)   **(J)**

Christina Torstensen Swenson was a stalwart pioneer woman from Norway who arrived in Texas in 1877 with her Swedish husband, Peter, and settled in Stephens County. Her inspirational story includes standing firm as a sheep rancher in cattle country; meeting Clara Barton, founder of the Red Cross, as a victim of drought; and surviving the arduous work of a pioneer farm wife and mother.

282 Hardesty, Vida Ann. **THE TURN-OF-THE-CENTURY PARTY**. Illustrated by Steven Kahl. Austin. Stevenson. 1977. 32 p. (National History Series: USA)   **(P I)**

Life on a West Texas ranch at the turn of the century included moving to town in the winter so the children could attend school. On New Year's Eve of 1899 the pioneer families had a special century party, with dancing, eating, and the exploding of two anvils as a real "bang-up" ending. Black-and-white drawings illustrate the story.

283 Harris, Leon A. **THE NIGHT BEFORE CHRISTMAS, IN TEXAS, THAT IS**. Illustrated by Meg Wohlberg. New York. Crown. 1968. 1 v. (unpaged)   **(P)**

In this Texas parody of Clement Moore's famous poem, Santa, dressed in a ten-gallon Stetson and Levis, arrives in a buckboard to fill the cowboy boots the children have left out. Colorful full-page drawings illustrate the story.

284 Harris, Lorle. **BIOGRAPHY OF A WHOOPING CRANE.** Illustrated by Kazue Mizumura. New York. Putnam. 1977. 63 p.   **(P I)**

A year in the life of a whooping crane, from birth at Wood Buffalo National Park in northern Canada through growth and winter migration to Aransas National Wildlife Refuge on the Texas Gulf Coast, is the framework for presentation of scientific information about the life cycle and behavior patterns of an endangered species. A map of migration and numerous detailed black-and-white drawings enhance the simple, lucid text.

285 Haskins, James. **BARBARA JORDAN : SPEAKING OUT.** New York. Dial. 1977. 215 p.   **(J)**

This biography of a contemporary pioneer illustrates Barbara Jordan's tremendous strength of character, steadfastness of purpose, intelligence, and eloquence. Her Houston childhood, scholastic honors, and involvement in local politics developed her facility for hard work and dedication, which were necessary as she achieved prominence as the first black woman in the Texas Senate, the first black woman from a Southern state in the U.S. House of Representatives, and the only black woman on the House Judiciary Committee during the impeachment proceedings against Richard Nixon. Black-and-white photographs and reference aids add to the book's value.

286 Hawthorne, Dorothy. **A WISH FOR LUTIE.** Illustrated by Kathleen Voute. New York. Longmans, Green. 1955. 117 p.   **(I)**

Pioneer children Lutie Rollins and her brother Will help their parents homestead while living in a dugout on the prairie near Tascosa. Lutie plants petunias, collects buffalo bones for money, cooks dinner for Panhandle outlaw Jake Ringo when her parents are away, hauls water from a nearby ranch, and begin to feel at home on the High Plains.

287 Haynes, Nelma. **PANTHER LICK CREEK.** Illustrated by William Moyers. Nashville. Abingdon. 1970. 157 p.   **(I J)**

Homesteading in Peters' Colony near the Trinity River where Dallas now stands, Chet Merrifield's family experiences the 1840s frontier dangers of wild animals and Indians. After a series of frontier adventures, Chet and his friend Tolly Tigus succeed in gaining their hearts' desire: wild mustangs to ride.

288 Hays, Wilma Pitchford. **EASTER FIRES**. Illustrated by Peter Burchard. New York. Coward-McCann. 1960. 62 p.   **(I)**

Silver Arrow, a Tonkawa Indian, saves his sweetheart from human sacrifice to the Rain God by telling the tribe the Easter story he learned when he guided the Spanish missionaries. This variant version of the Fredericksburg Easter fires is a dignified retelling of the Easter story which also respects the Indian philosophy and lifestyle. The drought of withering heat and the joy of Easter are evoked in three-color yellow, black, and white drawings.

289 Haywood, Carolyn. **EDDIE AND GARDENIA**. New York. Morrow. 1951. 191 p. (Morrow Junior Books)   **(I)**

Eddie's goat Gardenia is sent to a Texas ranch when she eats a hole in the top of Mr. Wilson's convertible. Eddie accompanies Gardenia to visit his relatives and wins his spurs by participating in ranch activities. The setting for this humorous, wholesome story is in the early 1950s.

290 Henry, Will. **THE TEXAS RANGERS**. Illustrated by Charles Banks Wilson. New York. Random House. 1957. 181 p. (Landmark Books, 72)   **(I)**

This history is based on official Ranger records. Beginning in 1835 and continuing through the excitement of battles with Indians, border bandits, and outlaws, the famous law force established a legendary reputation and honorable traditions. The lively text includes anecdotes of heroic and humorous events, such as the rescue of a three-year-old boy from Comanches, the capture of John Wesley Hardin and Sam Bass, and the settlement of the Fence Cutters' War. Line drawings at the chapter headings illustrate the text.

291 Heyliger, William. **WILDCAT**. Illustrated by Gordon Grant. New York. Appleton. 1937. 286 p.   **(I J)**

An adventure story about a seismograph engineer who "poor-boys" wildcats in the Texas Gulf Coast oil field. Stock characters include the lease-buster, the wise old driller, the large company executive, and the eccentric landowner. Details of industry practice and life in the 1930s are woven into the story.

292 Hiller, Illo. **YOUNG NATURALIST : FROM TEXAS PARKS AND WILDLIFE MAGAZINE**. College Station. Texas A&M University.

1983. 160 p. (Louise Lindsey Merrick Texas Environment Series, No. 6) (I J)

Scientific and practical information about animals, plants, earth science, and the scientific method are combined in a pleasant, conversational style in thirty-nine articles which originally appeared in the **Texas Parks and Wildlife Magazine**. Vivid, detailed full-color photographs, drawings, charts, crossword puzzles, and an index enhance this book about the Texas environment.

293 Hirschfeld, Burt. **AFTER THE ALAMO : THE STORY OF THE MEXICAN WAR**. Illustrated by Barry Martin. New York. Messner. 1966. 191 p. (I J)

This lively, well-written history of the war between the United States and Mexico, 1845 to 1848, analyzes the social and political factors which influenced each side. The colonization of Texas and the subsequent revolution were a significant part of the background of the war which, in turn, had a vital impact on the state's future. The book has excellent maps and reference aids.

294 Hoff, Carol. **CHRIS**. Chicago. Follett. 1960. 157 p. (I)

Chris, son of an oilfield driller in South Texas, has difficulty adjusting to his father's frequent moves. The lonely boy is befriended by his new sixth grade teacher, who makes life more pleasant in a traditional, predictable manner. Details of the countryside and the lifestyle of oil workers give local color to the story.

295 Hoff, Carol. **HEAD TO THE WEST**. Illustrated by William Moyers. Chicago. Follett. 1957. 159 p. (I)

The von Dohn family immigrates from Germany to Texas in 1840. The pioneers learn about their new surroundings, but struggle with the unaccustomed farm life. Mr. von Dohn, educated as a lawyer, moves the family to Galveston and a more familiar lifestyle.

296 Hoff, Carol. **JOHNNY TEXAS:**. Illustrated by Bob Meyers. Chicago. Wilcox & Follett. 1950. 149 p. (I)

This modern classic children's novel, set in the Texas revolutionary period, relates the experiences of ten-year-old Johann Friedricks, who migrated with his German family to Texas in 1836. While his father is away fighting for independence, "Johnny Texas" and his mother and sister join the Runaway Scrape. The pleasures and hardships of pioneer life are seen through the boy's experiences. The author, a descendant of pioneers, won the 1950 Wilcox-Follett Award and the 1950 Texas Institute of Letters Award for the book, which has been reprinted several times.

297 Hoff, Carol. **JOHNNY TEXAS ON THE SAN ANTONIO ROAD**. Chicago. Wilcox & Follett. 1953. 191 p. **(I)**

In this sequel to **Johnny Texas**, which takes place in the late 1830s, Johnny sets out in place of his injured father with a load of cornmeal to deliver across the Mexican border in return for gold to pay the note on the family's mill. His adventures on the 600-mile journey include a raid by wild pigs, a wild turkey hunt, attacks by an Indian and a thief, and encounters with many sympathetic adults who help the boy. Pioneer stories of the author's grandparents add authentic flavor to the boy's adventures. A slightly revised edition was published by Hendrick-Long in 1984.

298 Hoff, Carol. **WILDERNESS PIONEER : STEPHEN F. AUSTIN OF TEXAS**. Illustrated by Robert Todd. Chicago. Follett. 1955. 192 p. **(I J)**

This outstanding juvenile biography of Austin by a well-known Texas author is based on Eugene C. Barker's definitive work, **The Father of Texas**, and source material from the Austin papers. The incredible hardships and dangers Austin survived in order to establish his colony and the selfless devotion he sustained to maintain it are portrayed sensitively and in depth. This is a well-written, comprehensive portrait which is intelligible to the younger reader.

299 Hofland, Barbara Wreaks Hoole. **LITTLE MANUEL : THE CAPTIVE BOY**. New York. Garland Pub. 1978. 63 p. (The Garland Library of Narratives of North American Indian Captivities, V.44) **(I J)**

This reprint of a miniature children's book first published by B.F. Edmands, Boston, as **Edmand's Lilliputian Quarto**, is a fanciful account of customs and daily life in colonial Texas. Little Manuel, the nine-year-old son of a Spanish gentleman, is captured by the Comanches in a raid and lives among them for three years until he escapes. This is a charming melodrama with pious religious sentiments.

300 Holbrook, Stewart Hall. **DAVY CROCKETT.** Illustrated by Ernest Richardson. New York. Random House. 1955. 179 p. (Landmark Books, 57)   **(I J)**

This well-written biography of Crockett covers the period from his youth through his death at the Alamo. The folk hero's legendary exploits, including his fight for freedom in Texas, are retold. An appendix lists memorials to Crockett in Tennessee and Texas.

301 Hollander, Paul. **SAM HOUSTON.** Illustrated by Salem Tamer. New York. Putnam. 1968. 61 p. (A See and Read Beginning to Read Biography)   **(P)**

Many two-color sketches illustrate this easy-to-read biography of a Texas hero which highlights his military and political achievements.

302 Holt, Roy D. **CHILDREN INDIAN CAPTIVES.** Illustrated by S.J. Stout. Burnet, Tex. Eakin. 1980. 92 p. (Stories for Young Americans)   **(I)**

An episodic story of captives of the Comanches and Kiowas on the Texas frontier. The marauding Indians spared the lives of older children and teenagers and forced them to adopt Indian ways. A range of experiences from horrendous to humorous is told of these young captives who sometimes were bartered or escaped back to the world of their heritage.

303 Hooper, Byrd. **BEEF FOR BEAUREGARD.** Illustrated by Charles Geer. New York. Putnam. 1959. 218 p.   **(I J)**

Sixteen-year-old Breck Garland leads a cattle drive from Texas to Mobile to sell longhorns to the Confederate troops. Breck matures as he witnesses the reality of war and experiences the burden of decision making inherent in leadership.

304 Horn, Madeline Darrough. **DANNIE : A TALE OF THE GALVESTON HURRICANE OF 1900.** San Antonio. Naylor. 1952. 118 p.   **(I J)**

The violent 1900 hurricane is seen through the eyes of Dannie Major, a fourteen-year-old girl from Oklahoma who is a visitor in Galveston. Dannie is helped by adults and is of help to younger children in an incredible struggle for survival.

305 Howard, William Neal. **ARTHUR'S AUSTIN ABC : ARTURO EN AUSTIN: UN ABECEDARIO.** Illustrated by Ben Sargent. Austin. Winter Wheat House. 1980. 48 p. **(P)**

Authur the armadillo lands at Bergstrom AFB, swims in Barton Springs, and explores the history and landmarks of the state capital. The lively text is illustrated by Pulitzer Prize winning cartoonist Ben Sargent. The latest printing is in patriotic red, white and blue.

306 Hubbard, Margaret Ann. **SERAPHINA TODD.** Illustrated by Manning de V. Lee. New York. Macmillan. 1941. 308 p. **(I J)**

In 1777 thirteen-year-old Seraphina's family leaves New Orleans to establish trade in San Antonio. The pioneers meet hostile Indians and Spaniards before they settle in Villa San Fernando, from which the city of San Antonio grew. Accurate historical details paint the background for the fictitious adventures of Seraphina and her friend Barney, who warn the village of an Apache attack, thus saving it from destruction.

307 Huebel, Russ. **THE BIG BAD WOLF IN TEXAS.** Illustrated by Tony Espinosa. Kingsville,Tex. Cayo Del Grullo Press. 1983. 1 v. (unpaged) **(I J)**

This parody of **The Three Little Pigs** features a wolf who eats ham on rye and pumpkin pie and visits the sunbelt, where he downs Lone Star and tamales on the beach. Full-page black-and-white drawings illustrate the story, which is good for a a light moment or for older children to practice identifying cliches.

308 Hunter, Warren. **TEXAS MISSIONS AND LANDMARKS.** Illustrated by the author. San Antonio. Institute of Texan Cultures. 1978. 57 p. **(J)**

Hunter's copper-plate etchings, originally used as Christmas cards by the Southwest Research Institute, are the outstanding feature of the book. Jack Harmon wrote brief, readable sketches of the history, architecture, and current status of the San Antonio missions, the Spanish Governors' Palace, and the missions La Bahia del Espiritu Santo, Ysleta, Nuestra Senora de la Concepion del Socorro, and San Elizario.

309 Hutto, Nelson. **BREAKAWAY BACK.** New York. Harper & Row. 1963. 213 p. **(I J)**

Scotty Clayburn's move to a large West Texas town is suspected to be an effort to play at a larger school, because he is an outstanding football player. Scotty, a nice boy, has actually moved to study vocational education courses not available in his small town. When another player sustains an injury, Scotty is accused of planning it.

310 Hutto, Nelson. **VICTORY VOLLEY.** New York. Harper & Row. 1967. 249 p.   **(I J)**

Sports rivalry is played out between a natural tennis player, high school senior Doug Cameron, who needs a college scholarship, and Maury Alford, who has played for years at his parents' exclusive tennis club. Conciliation of two different social groups at Central High School is brought about by an important match. The novel reflects the author's background as a teacher and tennis coach at a Dallas high school.

311 Iglehart, Fanny Chambers Gooch. **THE BOY CAPTIVE OF THE TEXAS MIER EXPEDITION.** Illustrated by Charles Peter Bock. San Antonio. J. R. Wood Printing Co. 1909. 331 p.   **(J)**

A fascinating biography of John C.C. Hill of La Grange, who as a thirteen-year-old joined his father and brother on the Mier Expedition. When captured by the Mexicans, he shattered his rifle rather than give it up. He thereby came under the protection of General Ampudia and was reared as a Mexican gentleman and trusted friend of both Texans and Mexicans. Hill told his story to the author with the request, "Please tell this story to the children of Texas with my love."

312 Institute of Texan Cultures. **THE AFRO-AMERICAN TEXANS.** San Antonio. The Institute. 1975. 32 p. (The Texians and the Texans)   **(I J)**

A brief history of Afro-Americans in Texas, including cultural contributions and biographies of important individuals, illustrated with drawings and photographs.

313 Institute of Texan Cultures. **THE ANGLO-AMERICAN TEXANS.** San Antonio. The Institute. 1975. 32 p. (The Texians and the Texans)   **(I J)**

A brief history of Anglo-Americans in Texas, including cultural contributions and biographies of important individuals, illustrated with drawings and photographs.

Institute-Institute

314 Institute of Texan Cultures. **THE BELGIAN TEXANS.** San Antonio. The Institute. 1975. 32 p. (The Texians and the Texans) **(I J)**

A brief history of Belgian Americans in Texas, including cultural contributions and biographies of important individuals, illustrated with drawings and photographs.

315 Institute of Texan Cultures. **THE CHINESE TEXANS.** San Antonio. The Institute. 1978. 23 p. (The Texians and the Texans) **(I J)**

A brief history of Chinese Americans in Texas, including cultural contributions and biographies of important individuals, illustrated with drawings and photographs.

316 Institute of Texan Cultures. **THE CZECH TEXANS.** San Antonio. The Institute. 1972. 32 p. (The Texians and the Texans) **(I J)**

A brief history of Czech Americans in Texas, including cultural contributions and biographies of important individuals, illustrated with drawings and photographs.

317 Institute of Texan Cultures. **THE FRENCH TEXANS.** San Antonio. The Institute. 1973. 32 p. (The Texians and the Texans) **(I J)**

A brief history of French Americans in Texas, including cultural contributions and biographies of important individuals, illustrated with drawings and photographs.

318 Institute of Texan Cultures. **THE GERMAN TEXANS.** San Antonio. The Institute. 1970. 32 p. (The Texians and the Texans) **(I J)**

A brief history of German Americans in Texas, including cultural contributions and biographies of important individuals, illustrated with drawings and photographs.

319 Institute of Texan Cultures. **THE GREEK TEXANS.** San Antonio. The Institute. 1974. 32 p. (The Texians and the Texans) **(I J)**

A brief history of Greek Americans in Texas, including cultural contributions and biographies of important individuals, illustrated with drawings and photographs.

320 Institute of Texan Cultures. **THE INDIAN TEXANS**. San Antonio. The Institute. 1970. 25 p. (The Texians and the Texans)   **(I J)**

A brief history of Indians in Texas, including cultural contributions and biographies of important individuals, illustrated with drawings and photographs.

321 Institute of Texan Cultures. **THE ITALIAN TEXANS**. San Antonio. The Institute. 1973. 32 p. (The Texians and the Texans)   **(I J)**

A brief history of Italian Americans in Texas, including cultural contributions and biographies of important individuals, illustrated with drawings and photographs.

322 Institute of Texan Cultures. **THE JEWISH TEXANS**. San Antonio. The Institute. 1974. 32 p. (The Texians and the Texans)   **(I J)**

A brief history of Jewish Texans, including cultural contributions and biographies of important individuals, illustrated with drawings and photographs.

323 Institute of Texan Cultures. **THE MEXICAN TEXANS**. San Antonio. The Institute. 1975. 32 p. (The Texians and the Texans) **(I J)**

A brief history of Mexican Americans in Texas, including cultural contributions and biographies of important individuals, illustrated with drawings and photographs. The Spanish language version is **Los Tejanos Mexicanos**.

324 Institute of Texan Cultures. **THE NORWEGIAN TEXANS**. San Antonio. The Institute. 1970. 32 p. (The Texians and the Texans) **(I J)**

A brief history of Norwegian Americans in Texas, including cultural contributions and biographies of important individuals, illustrated with drawings and photographs.

325 Institute of Texan Cultures. **THE POLISH TEXANS**. San Antonio. The Institute. 1972. 32 p. (The Texians and the Texans) **(I J)**

A brief history of Polish Americans in Texas, including cultural contributions and biographies of important individuals, illustrated with drawings and photographs.

326 Institute of Texan Cultures. **THE SPANISH TEXANS**. San Antonio. The Institute. 1972. 32 p. (The Texians and the Texans) **(I J)**

A brief history of Spanish Americans in Texas, including cultural contributions and biographies of important individuals, illustrated with drawings and photographs.

327 Institute of Texan Cultures. **THE SWISS TEXANS**. San Antonio. The Institute. 1977. 26 p. (The Texians and the Texans) **(I J)**

A brief history of Swiss Americans in Texas, including biographies of important individuals, illustrated with drawings and photographs.

328 Institute of Texan Cultures. **THE SYRIAN AND LEBANESE TEXANS**. San Antonio. The Institute. 1974. 32 p. (The Texians and the Texans) **(I J)**

A brief history of Syrian and Lebanese Americans in Texas, including cultural contributions and biographies of important individuals, illustrated with drawings and photographs.

329 Institute of Texan Cultures. **LOS TEJANOS MEXICANOS**. San Antonio. The Institute. 1971. 32 p. (The Texians and the Texans) **(I J)**

A brief history of Mexican Americans in Texas, including cultural contributions and biographies of important individuals, illustrated with drawings and photographs. The English language version is **The Mexican Texans**.

330 Institute of Texan Cultures. **TEXAS AND THE AMERICAN REVOLUTION**. San Antonio. The Institute. 1975. 72 p. **(J)**

Although this heavily illustrated book was designed to be a companion to the Institute of Texan Cultures' traveling exhibit of the same name, it also stands on its own. The history of the American Revolution is contrasted with contemporary events in Spanish Texas. The influence of the philosophy and the pioneering, freedom-loving spirit of the Anglos who migrated west and the Mexicans who won independence from Spain is shown in events leading to the Texas Revolution. A list of veterans and descendants and in-depth biographical sketches put the revolutionary ferment on a personal basis.

331 Jackson, Louise A. **GRANDPA HAD A WINDMILL, GRANDMA HAD A CHURN.** Illustrated by George Ancona. New York. Parents Magazine Press. 1977. 32 p.   **(P I)**

The author's childhood memories of life on her grandparents' farm in Central Texas in the 1940s are expressed in a churn song and illustrated with black-and-white photographs. Significant objects used by each grandparent for work or play give clues about farm activities. The grandfather is associated with the windmill, whetstone, corn crib, goldfish, chopping block, gold watch, and fiddle. The grandmother is associated with her silver thimble, churn, cellar, guineas, quilting frame, friendship ring, and piano.

332 Jackson, Robert B. **SUPERMEX : THE LEE TREVINO STORY.** New York. Walck. 1973. 72 p.   **(I)**

This biography of Dallas native Trevino highlights his successful struggle from humble Mexican American background to internationally recognized golf professional. The easy-to-read text is illustrated with photographs.

333 Jackson, Sarah and Patterson, Mary Ann. **A CHILD'S HISTORY OF TEXAS COLORING BOOK.** Illustrated by the authors. Quanah, Tex. Nortex. 1974. 78 p. (Historical Coloring Books of Texas)   **(P I)**

Important historical events are presented in easy- to-read text, illustrated with simple line drawings, in this basic introduction to Texas history. It is appropriate for elementary grade children who need a brief, straightforward history.

334 Jacobs, Caroline Elliott Hoogs and Read, Edyth Ellerbeck. **BLUE BONNET'S RANCH PARTY**. Illustrated by John Goss. Boston. L.C. Page. 1912. 305 p. **(I J)**

Elizabeth Ashe, better known as Blue Bonnet, takes five of her Boston school friends to her Texas ranch for the summer. With the assistance of her uncle, the wealthy orphan organizes entertainments of riding, swimming, and camping, and celebrates her sixteenth birthday with a Mexican fiesta. A strong sense of duty and class pervades this novel from the publisher of **The Little Colonel Books**.

335 Jacobs, Linda. **BARBARA JORDAN : KEEPING FAITH**. St. Paul. EMC Corp. 1978. 39 p. (Headliners II) **(I)**

This easy-to-read biography of an exceptional black woman shows her dedication to high principles of honesty, loyalty, and justice. Jordan's struggles to win election to the Texas Senate and the U.S. House of Representatives are outlined. Her achievements are illustrated with photographs.

336 Jacobs, Linda. **JOHN DENVER : A NATURAL HIGH**. St. Paul. EMC Corp. 1975. 40 p. (Men Behind the Bright Lights) **(I)**

John Deutschendorf's growth from a shy Air Force officer's son to a superstar singer is told in this simple biography. A graduate of Arlington Heights High School, Fort Worth, he left Texas with his guitar to seek fame. The text is illustrated with numerous photographs.

337 Jakes, John W. **THE TEXANS RIDE NORTH : THE STORY OF THE CATTLE TRAILS**. Illustrated by Arthur Edrop. Philadelphia. Winston. 1952. 184 p. (Winston Adventure Books) **(I J)**

The lifestyle and hardships of Texas cowboys on a trail drive from Dallas to Missouri in 1866, following the fall of the Confederacy, are central to the story. Fourteen-year-old Tom Logan is a hero in the fictional episodes as the group moves up the Sedalia Trail with a herd of cattle to sell for good legal Yankee money, battling weather, Indians, and Jayhawkers along the way.

338 James, Bessie Rowland. **SIX FEET SIX; THE HEROIC STORY OF SAM HOUSTON**. Illustrated by Lowell Balcom. Indianapolis. Bobbs-Merrill. 1931. 251 p. **(I J)**

This biography of Sam Houston was adapted from **The Raven**, an adult book by Marquis James. The readable text is illustrated with Balcom's dramatic woodcuts. Chapter XI, "Who Shall Rule Texas?" clearly explains the political situation at the time of the Texas Revolution by means of a discussion between President Andrew Jackson and Houston. A glimpse of Houston as a person is shown as the successes and failures of his life are explored.

339 Jefferies, Madeleine Milner. **KATEY**. Illustrated by the author. New York. Hastings House. 1961. 32 p.   **(P)**

Young Katey lives with her parents on their late 19th-century Texas ranch, where they are joined by Katey's pretty young aunt from Paris, who brings fashionable dresses and a ruffly parasol. Mr. Higgins, the neighbor on the next ranch, courts and marries the aunt, causing excitement and delight in the family. The author's appealing pastel drawings illustrate the charming story.

340 Jensen, Ann Oden. **THE TIME OF ROSIE**. Austin. Steck-Vaughn. 1967. 172 p.   **(I)**

Rosie, a pet pig born in 1912 on the Oden family ranch twenty miles from El Paso, is trained to be a lady by ten-year-old Anita Oden. Instead, Rosie sits in a visiting Congressman's white Stetson, crawls into bed with a visiting minister, and gets drunk in Juarez. In one episode the family witnesses Pancho Villa's raid on Juarez in November 1913.

341 Johansen, Margaret Alison. **HAWK OF HAWK CLAN**. Illustrated by William O'Brian. New York. Longmans, Green. 1941. 280 p.
(I J)

This is a story of two Indian boys from enemy Caddo tribes who become blood brothers and are able to end the hatred between the tribes. Details about the differing lifestyles of the Hasinai of the plains and the Nacogdoches of the forest before the arrival of the white settlers form the background of the many adventures the boys share.

342 Johnson, August Wisdom. **TELL US ABOUT TEXAS**. Illustrated by Lynn Walcott Benton. Dallas. Tardy Pub. Co. 1935. 115 p.
(I J)

Short stories about the colonial and revolutionary periods of Texas history, folklore, and natural history are told by grandfather to his inquisitive grandchildren. The first edition, written in 1935 for the Centennial, was revised in 1947.

343 Johnson, James Ralph. **CAMELS WEST**. New York. McKay. 1964. 154 p.   **(I J)**

When the U.S. Army decided to use camels as beasts of burden on the survey of a wagon road from Fort Defiance to the Colorado River, Hi Jolly, a young camel driver, was contacted in Smyrna in 1855 to purchase camels and care for them on the long ocean voyage to Indianola, Texas. The 1857 expedition westward and Hi Jolly's remarkable adaptation to his adopted country, while overcoming an over-grown bully mule skinner, Comanche and Apache Indians, and conflicts between mule teamsters and camel drivers at Camp Verde near San Antonio, make this a fascinating narrative.

344 Johnson, Olive McClintic and Chute, Mary. **LITTLE TEJAS : CHILD OF THE TWILIGHT**. Illustrated by B.J. Lore and T.G. Hamilton. Fort Worth. Economy Co. 1937. 256 p.   **(I)**

Daily life and customs of Central Texas Indians are portrayed in the experiences of the son of the chief. Brief, episodic chapters show the changes brought by the white man in this charming 1930s-style book.

345 Johnson, Ramond. **THE RIO GRANDE**. Morristown, N.J. Silver Burdette. 1981. 69 p. (Rivers of the World)   **(J)**

The historical and economic significance of the Rio Grande from its source to its mouth is clearly explained and illustrated with color photographs, maps, and drawings.

346 Johnson, Siddie Joe. **CAT HOTEL**. Illustrated by Janice Holland. New York. Longmans, Green. 1955. 132 p.   **(I)**

Ted Mahon stays with Mrs. Dietrich for a year while his parents work in South America. Sympathetic adults help Ted have a good year. He improves his grades, learns to get along with his peers, and accepts responsibility in helping Mrs. Dietrich run a cat-boarding business. Several cats with distinctive personalities are an important part of the story, which is set in Dallas in the 1950s.

347 Johnson, Siddie Joe. **CATHY**. Illustrated by Mary Lee Baker. New York. Longmans, Green. 1945. 146 p.   **(P I)**

Ten-year-old Cathy's mother works at the aircraft plant in Corpus Christi while her father fights as an Air Corps pilot in World War II. Cathy picks tomato worms and babysits to help out. Then she escapes her loneliness by entering the world of Sarah, Gilbert, and Linda, three children growing up on a farm during World War I, whose long-forgotten diaries and letters Cathy has found in the attic. She finally meets the three and is reunited with her father in a happy ending.

348 Johnson, Siddie Joe. **DEBBY**. Illustrated by Ninon MacKnight. New York. Longmans, Green. 1940. 213 p.   **(I)**

The Sanders' small, white farmhouse, set in a grove of crooked old mesquite trees near Corpus Christi, appeals to ten-year-old Debby, who lives in a trailer nearby. Debby fishes, picks cotton, picnics on Padre Island, visits the McGloin home in San Patricio, and becomes acquainted with Mrs. Sanders, who gives her a beautiful antique china doll named Deborah. This is a lovely family story with strong regional flavor.

349 Johnson, Siddie Joe. **JOE AND ANDY WANT A BOAT**. Illustrated by Lucille Jeffries and Barbara Maples. Austin. Steck. 1951. 38 p.   **(P)**

A picture story with large, colorful drawings about Joe and Andy, eight- and nine-year-old brothers, who find an old rowboat during a visit to their grandmother's farm on the Texas coast. The boys give a good oarlock to Uncle Harry, who in return takes them floundering on his boat. The simple, easy-to-read text tells a happy, carefree story.

350 Johnson, Siddie Joe. **A MONTH OF CHRISTMASES**. Illustrated by Henrietta Jones Moon. New York. Longmans, Green. 1952. 132 p.   **(P I)**

Milla and John visit their Aunt Katrin and Uncle Karl for the month of December in Fredericksburg, where they learn family traditions brought from Germany. Smudge, a black-and-white cat with a face like a little clown, introduces an element of fantasy by taking the children back in time to pioneer days.

351 Johnson, Siddie Joe. **NEW TOWN IN TEXAS**. Illustrated by Margaret Ayer. New York. Longmans, Green. 1942. 301 p.   **(I J)**

When the large Thompson family arrives by covered wagon in North Texas in the 1870s, curious, exuberant young Abigail is disappointed not to have been part of the exciting revolutionary period but is determined, nevertheless, to be cunning and strong. As she encounters cowboys, Indians, and early settlers and witnesses the arrival of the first train in Denison, she comes to the realization that history is ongoing and that she has a part in it.

352 Johnson, Siddie Joe. **RABBIT FIRES**. Illustrated by Emilie Toepperwein. Boerne, Tex. Highland Press. 1951. 32 p. **(P I)**

This charming story, about the Easter fires and the Easter rabbit's boiling kettles of flower-dye to color eggs, told by a Fredricksburg grandmother to her grandchildren, combines Texas history and German customs. The children prepare a nest for the rabbit of Hill Country spring wildflowers, the colors of which are repeated in the pastel pages of the beautifully constructed book.

353 Johnson, Siddie Joe. **SUSAN'S YEAR**. Illustrated by Anne Merriman Peck. New York. Longmans, Green. 1948. 168 p. **(I J)**

At the beginning of her eleventh year, Susan Brent moves with her professor aunt from a small college town to Dalbert, a fictionalized Dallas. Susan's adventures include a trip to the State Fair, a library story hour, city shopping, finding historic letters about General Sam Houston, and looking for a dog of her own. The reader gains a sense of place and of the 1940s in Dallas.

354 Johnson, Siddie Joe. **TEXAS, THE LAND OF THE TEJAS**. Illustrated by Fanita Lanier. New York. Random House. 1943. 55 p. **(P I J)**

The lively text of this especially attractive picture history of Texas from the time of Spanish exploration to World War II is illustrated with colorful drawings which sweep across the pages and large, decorative headings. The endpapers map shows the homes of Indian tribes and villages, missions, and presidios of the colonial era. The book was reprinted in 1950 and is worthy of another reprinting.

355 Johnson, William Weber. **THE BIRTH OF TEXAS**. Illustrated by Herb Mott. Boston. Houghton Mifflin. 1960. 183 p. (North Star Books) **(I J)**

A dramatic presentation of little-known historical details of the events preceding the Battle of the Alamo and the founding of the Republic.

356 Johnson, William Weber. **SAM HOUSTON, THE TALLEST TEXAN**. Illustrated by William Reusswig. New York. Random House. 1953. 185 p. (Landmark Books, 32) **(I J)**

The Landmark Books biography of the soldier statesman who became President of Texas emphasizes events in which Houston displayed his outstanding ability for leadership.

357 Johnston, Annie Fellows. **MARY WARE IN TEXAS**. Illustrated by Frank T. Merrill. Boston. L.C. Page. 1910. 385 p. (The Little Colonel Series) **(I)**

Mary Ware brings her invalid brother to Texas in search of health.

358 Johnston, Leah Carter. **SAN ANTONIO, ST. ANTHONY'S TOWN**. Illustrated by Eduardo Cardenas and Allen Richards. San Antonio. Librarians' Council. 1947. 146 p. **(I J)**

This is an intimate and detailed portrait of San Antonio based on material compiled by local public library staff members to answer school children's questions. Drawings and photographs illustrate the factual material about the city's Indian, Spanish, and Revolutionary heritage, local government, institutions, buildings, activities, holy days, and holidays. Retellings of legends about the first Christmas tree at the Alamo, the bluebonnet, and the bells of Mission San Jose are included.

359 Jones, Weyman B. **EDGE OF TWO WORLDS**. Illustrated by J.C. Kocsis. New York. Dial. 1968. 143 p. **(J)**

In 1842 Sequoyah, the seventy-year-old Cherokee chief, travels across Texas in search of a lost band of Cherokees which is purportedly living in Mexico. On the way he meets fifteen-year-old Calvin Harper, the only survivor of a Comanche raid, who had been traveling to Harvard. Seqouyah's journey is historical, the character of Calvin fictional. As they assist each other in order to survive, the boy becomes a man who can make his own decisions and who learns to respect the remarkable Indian, inventor of the Cherokee alphabet, leader, and craftsman. The beautifully constructed, moving story is illustrated with bold, rhythmic drawings.

360 Katz, William Loren. **BLACK PEOPLE WHO MADE THE OLD WEST.** New York. Crowell. 1977. 181 p.   (I J)

A juvenile version of the author's **The Black West: A Documentary and Pictorial History**, which gives biographical sketches of thirty-five who explored and settled the Old West. Early settlers in Texas include William Goings; Greenbury Logan; Pompey Factor, a Seminole scout for the U.S. Army and a Congressional Medal of Honor winner; members of the Ninth and Tenth U.S. Cavalry; and Sutton E. Griggs, Baptist pastor and author. A bibliography and index add to its value.

361 Kelly, Eric Philbrook. **ON THE STAKED PLAIN : EL LLANO ESTACADO.** Illustrated by Harve Stein. New York. Macmillan. 1940. 250 p.   (I J)

In 1938 Flo Harbison discovers an unsolved mystery in the files of her father's and grandfather's law office in Amarillo. The 1850 deaths of three and a buried treasure of California gold intertwine the lives of three families. Details of the boomtown days of Tascosa and an author's note about the Llano Estacado (Staked Plain) are of historical interest.

362 Kerman, Gertrude Lerner. **CABEZA DE VACA, DEFENDER OF THE INDIANS.** Illustrated by Ray Abel. New York. Harvey House. 1974. 142 p.   (I)

The carefully written text of this biographical adventure story is based on the explorer's published journals. Cabeza de Vaca's experiences in Texas and his growing understanding of Indian culture are presented in a sympathetic manner.

363 Kerr, Rita. **THE GIRL OF THE ALAMO : SUSANNA DICKENSON.** Austin. Eakin. 1984. 64 p. (Stories for Young Americans)   (I)

The Battle of the Alamo, told from the perspective of the only Anglo-American woman to survive those thirteen important days of the Texas Revolution, is the focal point of Susanna Dickenson's biography. Her report of the battle and the message she carried from Santa Anna to Houston influenced the course of the war.

364 King, C. Richard. **A BIRTHDAY IN TEXAS.** Illustrated by Mark Donaldson. Austin. Shoal Creek Publishers. 1980. 60 p.   (I)

Catherine Anderson celebrates her tenth birthday on the family's Brazos River plantation and matures quickly in the events of the Texas Revolution. While the historical details of the settlers' lives are accurate, the characters do not come alive in this story.

365 King, Larry L. **THAT TERRIBLE NIGHT SANTA GOT LOST IN THE WOODS.** Illustrated by Patrick Oliphant. Austin. Encino Press. 1981. 29 p.   **(I J)**

A personal recollection of a family Christmas in Eastland County, Texas, in 1933 when the author's "rag-tag poor, dirt farmer" father went out in a blizzard to get presents for his four-year-old son. The Texas Institute of Letters award winning author and illustrator Patrick Oliphant have created a heart-warming story.

366 Kjelgaard, James Arthur. **HI JOLLY.** Illustrated by Kendall Rossi. Dodd, Mead. 1959. 183 p.   **(J)**

The exotic story of Hadji Ali, or Hi Jolly, a Syrian camel driver who arrived in Indianola, Texas, with his camel as part of the 1850s Army Camel Corps experiment, is based on historical research. The lively story includes detailed characterizations of Hi Jolly and the military personnel he encounters, an explanation of the role the Camel Corps was intended to play in westward expansion, and reasons for failure of the experiment.

367 Knapp, George Leonard. **LONE STAR OF COURAGE.** New York. Dodd, Mead. 1931. 240 p.   **(J)**

Timid sixteen-year-old Perry Duval Farnham sets out for Texas in 1835 in the company of Doc Benson, traveling medicine salesman. The significant events of the Texas Revolution are the background for Perry's adventures and his increasing bravery. This is a boys' adventure story with plentiful historical detail, including the music for "Deguello."

368 Kubiak, Daniel James. **TEN TALL TEXANS.** San Antonio. Naylor. 1967. 132 p.   **(I J)**

This collective biography contains sketches of the lives of ten Revolutionary heroes: Sam Houston, Lorenzo de Zavala, Stephen F. Austin, Jose Antonio Navarro, Ben Milam, Andrea Candelaria, David Crockett, James Bowie, William B. Travis, and Juan N. Seguin. The personal experiences of each person are documented with quotations from primary sources, a sketch, and a brief chronology. A bibliography and index are included.

369 Kupper, Mike. **DRIVEN TO WIN : A.J. FOYT**. Milwaukee. Raintree. 1975. 47 p.   **(I)**

Automobile racer Foyt, winner of the Indianapolis 500 and the United States Auto Club championships, is introduced in a brief biography.

370 Kurland, Gerald. **LYNDON BAINES JOHNSON : PRESIDENT CAUGHT IN AN ORDEAL OF POWER**. Charlotteville, N.Y. SamHar Press. 1972. 32 p. (Outstanding Personalities, No. 25) **(J)**

A biography of Johnson that emphasizes his vice-presidential and presidential years, the social programs he championed, and the consequences of the Vietnam War. The book has a bibliography but no illustrations.

371 Kyger, John Charles Fremont, comp. **TEXAS GEMS**. Dennison, Tex. Murray's Steam Printing House. 1885. 160 p.   **(I J)**

A patriotic tone and optimism about the future of the state are reflected in this collection of poetry, extracts of speeches, declamations, and readings, selected, according to the compiler, "from the richest and best-loved literary pieces of the Lone Star State." An explanatory or biographical sketch precedes each selection. Kyger, a teacher of elocution and oratory, dedicated the book to the young men of Texas.

372 Ladd, Ileta Kerr. **SEEING TEXAS : A CHILDREN'S TRAVELOG OF TEXAS**. Dallas. Mathis, Van Nort. 1943. 186 p.   **(I J)**

Ten-year-old Bill travels throughout Texas as he takes trips with his parents and relatives in the early 1940s. Each of the twenty brief chapters in this geographical reader is descriptive of a different Texas place. The book has a pleasant, didactic text illustrated with black-and-white photographs. The endpapers contain a map of the state parks.

373 Latham, Jean Lee.**RETREAT TO GLORY : THE STORY OF SAM HOUSTON**. New York. Harper & Row. 1965. 274 p.   **(I J)**

This fictionalized biography of Houston spans his boyhood and life with the Cherokees, his soldiering under Andrew Jackson, and his political career in Tennessee and Texas, with emphasis on his role in the formation of the Republic and the transition to statehood. Imaginary dialogue adds to the vivid portrayal of his extraordinary life. His unique leadership qualities, the unpopular positions he espoused on principle, and the personal cost of his achievements to himself and his family are portrayed in lively style by the Newbery Award winning author.

374 Latham, Jean Lee. **SAM HOUSTON, HERO OF TEXAS.** Champaign, Ill. Garrard. 1965. 80 p. (A Discovery Book) **(P I)**

An easy-to-read biography of Sam Houston, friend of the Cherokees and President Andrew Jackson, Commander-in-Chief of the Texas army that fought for independence from Mexico and won the Battle of San Jacinto. He later became President of the Republic of Texas, U.S. Senator, and Governor. This is a simplified version of the author's **Retreat to Glory**.

375 Latham, John H. **LONESOME LONGHORN.** Philadelphia. Westminster. 1951. 220 p. **(I J)**

Eight-year-old Purdy Cobb raised Sancho as a pet, feeding him hot tamales and other Mexican food, until Sancho was taken north in a cattle drive. Sancho walked all winter, two thousand miles from Wyoming, to return to Purdy. This is an adaptation of a Texas folk tale recorded by J. Frank Dobie and also used as the basis of Bosworth's **Sancho of the Long, Long Horns**. Lathams's version is rich in detail of character development and place.

376 Lawson, Don. **THE UNITED STATES IN THE MEXICAN WAR.** Illustrated by Robert F. McCullough. New York. Abelard-Schuman. 1976. 145 p. (The Young People's History of America's Wars Series) **(I J)**

Military campaigns and political battles of the Mexican War are placed in the appropriate historical context from the dispute over Texas's southern boundary in 1836 to the end of the war in 1848. The well-written text presents a balanced view of the war, including details of the soldiers' hardships. Outstanding reference aids include drawings and paintings of the period, a timeline, a bibliography, and an index.

377 Lazarus, Keo Felker. **RATTLESNAKE RUN.** Illustrated by Ken Nisson. Chicago. Follett. 1968. 192 p. **(I J)**

Thirteen-year-old Adam Vance tends a mail station in the Texas brush country while his father and uncle meet at noon to eat dinner and exchange mail bags. Adam has to maintain the camp, cook for the men, kill game, and confront escaped convicts and rattlesnakes in his frontier life.

378 Lazarus, Keo Felker. **TADPOLE TAYLOR.** Illustrated by Don Collins. Austin. Steck-Vaughn. 1970. 132 p. **(P I)**

Nine-year-old Thaddeus "Tadpole" Taylor travels with his parents when they take the archives of the Republic of Texas to Austin in the fall of 1839. Tad's adventures include being captured by the Comanches and rescued by the Tonkawas, moving the archives as far as Brushy Creek when the capital is moved to Washington-on-the Brazos, and an incident with the French Ambassador Count Saligny and a pig.

379 Leach, Christopher. **MEETING MISS HANNAH.** New York. Warne. 1980. 135 p. **(J)**

Fourteen-year-old Louise Challoner's world expands when she meets the mysterious stranger who moves to Sinclair in Critch County, Texas. The small-town girl attempts to identify the stranger in town and instead becomes involved in Miss Hannah's life. A Texas setting portrayed by an Englishman provides the background for a strange mystery.

380 Le Grand. **AUGUSTUS RIDES THE BORDER.** Indianapolis. Bobbs-Merrill. 1947. 134 p. **(P I)**

Augustus and his family tour Texas, selling plaster statues for cash and having "noodlehead" adventures until they lose their car in an arroyo and become goatherders in Sonora. There Augustus and Manuel corner "Old Poison," the mountain lion who has been killing goats. This is an entertaining story of a happy-go-lucky family, full of silliness, sure to bring on giggles.

381 Le Grand. **WHY COWBOYS SING, IN TEXAS.** New York. Abingdon-Cokesbury. 1950. 40 p. **(P I)**

When Slim Jim Bean opened his mouth and sang, the cattle all stampeded, according to this humorous tall tale. Then one day Slim Jim rode through thorny brush country without his chaps, shouting in pain "Yippee yi, yippee yay!" Surprisingly, the cattle loved the sound, and the other cowboys began to imitate it. Plentiful, colorful drawings illustrate the rib-tickling text.

382 Lehr, Delores. **TURNABOUT SUMMER.** Garden City, N.Y. Doubleday. 1965. 192 p. **(I J)**

A summer in the early 1960s at her widowed mother's family home on the Gulf Coast at fictional Seaport on Madre Island challenges sixteen-year-old Ellen Bennett's sheltered lifestyle. After leaving her popular, handsome boyfriend in San Antonio, weathering a hurricane, and bearing the stress of her mother's heart attack, Ellen experiences a change of attitude, develops her own values, and matures. Descriptions of the quiet pleasures of small-town coastal life and double romances add interest to this story for girls.

383 Lenski, Lois. **COWBOY SMALL**. Illustrated by the author. London, New York. Oxford. 1949. 48 p. **(P)**

Cowboy activities, clothes, and equipment are described in simple narrative and conversational text and charming, childlike three-color drawings. According to Mildred P. Harrington's annotation, the idea for this classic picture book began with Lenski's visit to a Texas Hill Country ranch.

384 Lenski, Lois. **TEXAS TOMBOY**. Illustrated by the author. Philadelphia. Lippincott. 1950. 180 p. **(I J)**

Charlotte Clarissa Carter grew up on the Triangle Ranch west of San Angelo, longing for her own horse and helping her father do the chores, while her older sister helped their mother with the housework. "Charlie Boy" matures as she accepts responsibility for her family and her own actions. The author's foreword, written at Eldorado in 1948, discusses the tomboy girls who loved animals and outdoor life and places the story in a transition period prior to 1920 and the introduction of ranch machinery. One of a series of regional stories by Lenski, this is a realistic description of the struggles necessary to survive the hardships of a cattle ranch, enhanced by the author's charming drawings.

385 Le Sueur, Meridel. **CHANTICLEER OF WILDERNESS ROAD : A STORY OF DAVY CROCKETT**. Illustrated by Aldren A. Watson. New York. Knopf. 1951. 160 p. **(I J)**

Crockett's biography is told in colorful frontier language as a family tale learned from an Irish grandmother. The familiar figures of the Crockett legend--Thimblerig, the Bee Hunter, the Pirate, and the Indian--appear, along with folk song lyrics and long segments of dialogue within the text. The wild goose which flies against the wind is used as a symbol of Crockett's life. The fourth part of the book, "Remember the Alamo," brings Crockett to Texas in this rich literary introduction to the folk hero.

386 Liffring, Joan. **JIM AND ALAN ON A COTTON FARM**. Chicago. Follett. 1959. 64 p. (The Farm Life Series)   **(P)**

This picture book illustrated with photographs tells the story of cotton from planting to processing. In the 1950s Jim lives on a farm on the Great High Plains of West Texas, where he plants five acres of cotton as a 4-H project. He learns how to battle drought and insects to grow his crop.

387 Lippincott, Joseph Wharton. **OLD BILL : THE WHOOPING CRANE**. Philadelphia. Lippincott. 1958. 176 p.   **(I J)**

A detailed description of the endangered species, including the whooping crane's courtship, nesting, migration, and predators, centered around Old Bill, a tough survivor who wintered in the Aransas National Wildlife Refuge with the other twenty-three known cranes. A callous hunter and several sympathetic game wardens enliven this inspirational story. Black-and-white photographs illustrate the text.

388 Livingston, Myra Cohn. **NO WAY OF KNOWING : DALLAS POEMS**. New York. Atheneum. 1980. 45 p. (A Margaret K. McElderry Book)   **(J)**

Poetic vignettes depicting lifestyles, livelihoods, religion, and everyday activities of young and old, at work and at play, flavored with the cadences of black speech. The characters are universal; no last names are given. Little mention is made of specific place, although Livingston wrote these poems based on experiences she had while living in Dallas.

389 Lockwood, Myna. **BECKONING STAR : A STORY OF OLD TEXAS**. New York. Dutton. 1943. 242 p.   **(I J)**

The Paine family's move from New Orleans to join the Austin colony in 1821-22 is told from the perspective of thirteen-year-old Margot Paine. The family leaves the frivolous life of the city for a dangerous trip across the prairie to San Antonio, meeting renegades and Indians along the way. The long and sometimes historically inaccurate story introduces historical persons, such as Stephen F. Austin, Jane Long, the Bee Hunter, and Governor Martinez. Lockwood's other books about the Paines before they move to Texas are **Delecta Ann** and **Free River**.

390 Lockwood, Myna. **UP WITH YOUR BANNER**. New York. Dutton. 1945. 256 p.   **(J)**

Incidents based on historical events of the Texas Revolution; the battles of the Alamo, Goliad, and San Jacinto; the Runaway Scrape; and the burning of San Felipe de Austin are adapted by the author as the background for the Paine family's adventures from 1834 to 1836. The affluent family's history from 1821, when they leave New Orleans to join the Austin colony, is recorded in an earlier novel, **Beckoning Star**.

391 LOOK AT ME! EXPERIENCES OF CHILDREN OF DALLAS.
Illustrated by Bob McCown. Dallas. Dallas Public Library. 1973. 61 p.   **(P I)**

This collection of black-and-white photographs and brief comments by Dallas children about themselves, their families, friendships, schools, neighborhoods, and adventures was created as part of a literacy program focusing on the development of communication skills. The purpose of this product of the Dallas Public Library's Project "Look at Me!" is summarized in the statement, "Once you've made a book of your own, you're not afraid of books any more."

392 Lowrey, Janette Sebring. **ANNUNCIATA AND THE SHEPHERDS.**
Illustrated by Willard Clark. New York. Gentry Press. 1938. 40 p.
(I J)

Annunciata, a little girl who lives with her grandmother in San Antonio, witnesses the neighborhood pastorela in this charming Christmas story. As presented in South Texas, "Los Pastores," the 16th-century miracle play about the birth of Jesus, is a combination of Spanish and Indian traditions. Lovely wood engravings convey the folklore quality of the story.

393 Lowrey, Janette Sebring. **THE LAVENDER CAT.** Illustrated by Rafaello Busoni. New York. Harper. 1944. 180 p.   **(I)**

This beautifully written story in the style of a folk tale is set in the Hill Country of Central Texas at an indeterminate time in the past. Jemmy, a young orphan boy, is befriended by Shawn, a charming Irish wanderer who rescues Jemmy from a brutish, insensitive family of charcoal burners. A playful kitten and an elusive leprechaun are part of the magic of the story.

394 Lowrey, Janette Sebring. **LOVE, BID ME WELCOME.** New York. Harper & Row. 1964. 249 p.   **(I J)**

In this sequel to **Margaret**, Margaret McLeod is seventeen years old in

1912, the year she faces the death of a favorite aunt. The leisurely pace of the story allows for rich details of small-town East Texas life and the introspective thoughts of a teenage girl in love.

395 Lowrey, Janette Sebring. **MARGARET.** New York. Harper. 1950. 277 p. **(J)**

In 1909, fourteen-year-old Margaret McLeod is suddenly invited to move from her simple country foster home to Ashford, a small East Texas town, by her great-aunt and great-uncle, descendants of the pioneer settlers. The contrast of manners brought about by the change in social station and the intricate social relationships are explored in depth. A satisfying sense of place is given in the description of the natural beauty of the unfolding seasons. The sensitive story of a teen-age girl learning about her past as she matures is continued in **Love, Bid Me Welcome**.

396 Lowrey, Janette Sebring. **RINGS ON HER FINGERS.** Illustrated by Janice Holland. New York. Harper. 1941. 192 p. **(I)**

Sisters Claire, Carey, and Katherine Ann plan to purchase Johnne Parks's Shetland pony, Flossie, with their three gold rings. The summer of 1901 in a small town on the Sabine River in the southeast corner of Texas comes alive as the little girls search for their lost rings, disrupting their comfortable, middle-class lives. Detailed character development and many literary allusions contribute to the richness of the story.

397 Lowrey, Janette Sebring. **THE SILVER DOLLAR.** Illustrated by Barbara Latham. New York. Harper. 1940. 48 p. **(P)**

Sixteen full-page color lithographs and many black-and-white drawings illustrate the tale of Bill, a small boy, exploring a ranch on the banks of the Nueces River. He shows his silver dollar to all of the kind people on the ranch, participates in a roundup, and is rewarded for his bravery with a new cowboy outfit of red bandana, Stetson hat, brush jacket, leather chaps, spurs, and cowboy boots. This is a beautiful picture book written on a child's level.

398 Luttrell, Ida. **NOT LIKE THAT, ARMADILLO.** Illustrated by Janet Stevens. New York. Harcourt, Brace, Jovanovich. 1982. 62 p. (A Let Me Read Book)   **(P)**

The adventures of Armadillo, Rabbit, and Turtle, friends who wear cowboy gear, include running a lemonade stand, reading a book about exercise, and making a wish on a penny. The three chapters, written for the early reader, are heavily illustrated with amusing black-and-white drawings.

399 Lyman, Nanci A. **PECOS BILL.** Illustrated by Bert Dodson. Mahwah, N.J. Troll Associates. 1980. 48 p. (Folk Tales of America) **(P I)**

This easy-to-read story of the legendary supercowboy tells of the major events in Pecos Bill's life.

400 Lynch, Dudley M. **THE PRESIDENT FROM TEXAS : LYNDON BAINES JOHNSON.** New York. Crowell. 1975. 169 p. **(J)**

The political and private lives of Lyndon Johnson are portrayed in this biography of the thirty-sixth president.

401 Maddox, Bill and Beeson, Harold. **RAGS AND PATCHES.** Chicago. Follett. 1978. 192 p. **(I J)**

Thirteen-year-old Danny Ragsdale (Rags) and his dog Patches leave their home on the Texas bayou to search around Port Arthur for Danny's widower Dad. Cock fighting, fiddle playing, shrimping, a hurricane and Cajun festivities and characters give a regional flavor to their picturesque adventures.

402 Magee, Agnes Davis. **WHEN THE PINES GREW TALL.** Illustrated by Bruce Good. San Antonio. Naylor. 1968. 73 p. **(I)**

Based on the experiences of the author's great-great-grandmother Elizabeth Davis, whose pioneer family moved to Beulah Springs in 1837 from Georgia, this is a simple story of pioneer life in the piney woods of East Texas. Ten-year-old Jim befriends a sick, abandoned Indian boy, White Feather. The growing friendship of the boys leads to cross-cultural understanding. The adventure climaxes when the young friends go to Natchitoches for supplies and are attacked by river pirates on the way home.

403 Maher, Ramona. **THE GLORY HORSE : A STORY OF THE BATTLE OF SAN JACINTO AND TEXAS IN 1836.** Illustrated by Stephen Gammell. New York. Coward, McCann & Geoghegan. 1974. 61 p. **(I)**

April 21, 1836, at the Battle of San Jacinto, Texas won independence from Mexico. Seen through the eyes of twelve-year-old Jimmy Brown, the activity surrounding the fight for independence comes alive. Sam Houston, Deaf Smith, and General Santa Anna appear while Jimmy loses and reclaims his beloved Old Whip, a tall black race horse. A vivid portrayal of an important point in Texas history.

404 Maher, Ramona. **MYSTERY OF THE STOLEN FISH POND.** New York. Dodd, Mead. 1969. 210 p. **(J)**

When Cassie Sherman spends the summer at the Chapultepec Castle, a new luxury San Antonio hotel modeled on the famous Mexico City site, she and her friend investigate several incidents which interrupt the completion of the hotel. They discover rare panoramas associated with Empress Carlotta which had been painted on canvas by an author of dime novels. The use of historical evidence as the basis of the mystery provides an unusual twist of plot.

405 Maher, Ramona. **THEIR SHINING HOUR.** New York. Day. 1960. 192 p. (The Daughters of Valor Series) **(I J)**

The story of Susanna Dickenson, the eighteen-year-old wife of Almaron Dickenson from Gonzales, focuses on the thirteen-day siege and battle of the Alamo, in which her husband dies, and on her role in conveying Santa Anna's message to Houston. A feminine perspective is well documented in the author's note and list of sources.

406 Makerney, Edna Smith. **CISSY'S TEXAS PRIDE.** Illustrated by Margaret Leibold. Nashville. Abingdon. 1975. 80 p. **(P I J)**

When the main crop on the Russells' West Texas farm is ruined by a hard freeze, Cissy tries to help her family raise money to pay off a bank note. She hopes to prevent the sale of her beautiful mare, Texas Pride, in a series of fund-raising ventures.

407 Martinello, Marian L. and Sance, Melvin M. **A PERSONAL HISTORY : THE AFRO-AMERICAN TEXANS.** San Antonio. Institute of Texan Cultures. 1982. 97 p. (Stories for Young Readers) **(I J)**

A fine introduction to black history for children, which captures interest with its interview, question-and-answer format and numerous drawings and paintings. Brief sketches of black heroes and common people who have influenced Texas history, from Esteban, Kiamata, Scott Joplin, Dorris Miller, and Barbara Jordan to military figures, cowboys, and sportsmen, are included. A list of questions for children to use in writing their own family history is an added tool found in this excellent work.

408 Martinello, Marian L. and Field, William T. **WHO ARE THE CHINESE TEXANS?** San Antonio. Institute of Texan Cultures. 1979. 80 p. (Stories for Young Readers)   **(I J)**

A chronological, question-and-answer format history of the Chinese in Texas and their contributions to the state from the first railroad workers in 1870 to 1979, beautifully illustrated with drawings and photographs.

409 Martinello, Marian L. and Nesmith, Samuel P. **WITH DOMINGO LEAL IN SAN ANTONIO, 1734.** San Antonio. Institute of Texan Cultures. 1979. 78 p. (Stories for Young Readers)   **(I J)**

An exciting day in the life of ten-year-old Domingo, whose family migrated from the Canary Islands to San Antonio in 1731. Domingo goes from his family chores to the mission, visits a blacksmith and soldiers at the barracks, and sees hostile Indians. Daily customs and Spanish phrases are introduced in the story.

410 Mason, Herbert Molloy. **THE TEXAS RANGERS.** New York. Meredith Press. 1967. 171 p.   **(J)**

The official Texas Ranger files were used as the primary source for this lively, readable history of the Rangers covering the period from their beginning during the Texas Revolution to the 1960s. Numerous black-and-white photographs and paintings of early and modern Rangers illustrate the text. An index is included.

411 Mason, Miriam Evangeline. **THE MAJOR AND HIS CAMELS.** Illustrated by Zhenya Gay. New York. Macmillan. 1953. 130 p. **(P)**

This fictional account of three camels--Finefellow, Chili, and their offspring Tibboo Funnyface--adjusting to life in Texas is based on historical fact. In the 1850s the U.S. Army acquired camels from the Middle East to use as pack animals in building a road from Texas to California. The simple text, illustrated with black-and-white sketches, tells a good-natured animal story without overwhelming historical detail.

412 Mauzey, Merritt. **COTTON-FARM BOY**. Illustrated by the author. New York. Abelard-Schuman. 1953. 79 p.   **(I J)**

The folklore and customs of the cotton growers in West Texas who replaced the sheep and cattle ranchers on the prairies is told in two parts, "The Frontier" and "The Fields." The raising of cotton from planting to product is seen through the eyes of Billy, a thinly disguised representation of Mauzey, who was born on a cotton farm at Clifton, Texas, in 1898. The back-breaking work of tending the crop and the fun of neigborhood gatherings are shown in outstanding lithographs.

413 Mauzey, Merritt. **OILFIELD BOY**. Illustrated by the author. New York. Abelard-Schuman. 1957. 80 p.   **(I J)**

The development of the oil industry, seen through the life of Albert Clay, is told in simple explanatory text and fine lithographs. The natural environment, human characters, and industrial process form a background for Albert's success through hard work, faith, and purpose.

414 Mauzey, Merritt. **TEXAS RANCH BOY**. Illustrated by the author. New York. Abelard-Schuman. 1955. 77 p.   **(I J)**

The pictorial story of a ranch boy, Gene Ballard, who lived in West Texas on a typical ranch during the early part of the 20th century. As in his other books, Mauzey illustrates the natural environment, everyday life, and folklore of the period in excellent lithographs.

415 May, Julian. **THE DALLAS COWBOYS**. Mankato, Minn. Creative Education; distributed by Childrens Press, Chicago. 1974. 45 p.   **(I)**

This brief history of the Cowboys from 1960 to 1973 highlights their Super Bowl VI win over the Miami Dolphins. Coach Landry and star players are featured in black-and-white action photographs.

416 May, Julian. **LEE TREVINO : THE GOLF EXPLOSION**. Mankato, Minn. Crestwood. 1974. 48 p. (Sports Close-up Books)   **(I)**

Lee Trevino was born in Dallas where the Glen Lakes Country Club is now located. His rise from humble Mexican American beginnings to world-famous golf professional is told in simple text illustrated with photographs.

417 May, Julian. **QUANAH, LEADER OF THE COMANCHE.** Illustrated by Phero Thomas. Mankato, Minn. Creative Educational Society. 1973. 39 p. (Personal Close-up Books) **(P I)**

A brief, clearly written biography of the last warrior chief of the Comanches. It begins with the capture of Cynthia Ann Parker, Quanah's mother, then describes his youth and his achievements in helping the Indians to adapt to their new life in the white culture. Black-and-white sketches illustrate his exciting, varied life.

418 McCague, James. **WHEN COWBOYS RODE THE CHISHOLM TRAIL.** Illustrated by George Loh. Champaign, Ill. Garrard. 1969. 95 p. (How They Lived Series) **(I J)**

Bill Blocker, a typical cowboy, rides six hundred miles with the Backward Seven herd on an 1870 trail drive from Texas to Abilene, Kansas, the railhead promoted by Joseph McCoy. Starting on the Pedernales River, the drive follows the Old Chisholm Trail, now U.S. Highway 81. The excitement and dangers of the trail are portrayed in the clearly written text and illustrated with drawings, paintings by Remington and Russell, and old photographs. The factual information within the text is accessible through the index and is supplemented by a glossary.

419 McCaleb, Walter Flavius. **THE ALAMO.** San Antonio. Naylor. 1956. 80 p. **(I J)**

In this history of the Alamo from its construction as a Spanish mission, through the period of the Texas Revolution, to its rescue from demolition by Clara Driscoll, the building is depicted as "the holiest relic of a desperate war for independence" and a monument to the Franciscans and Texans. The author uses sources from the Spanish Archives in San Antonio, Yoakum's history, and excerpts from letters and documents within the framework of a conversation between grandson and grandfather.

420 McCaleb, Walter Flavius. **BIGFOOT WALLACE.** San Antonio. Naylor. 1956. 121 p. **(I J)**

This biography, written for boys "with red blood in their veins" and told from the perspective of the biographee, recounts Wallace's extraordinary frontier experiences as a Texas Ranger, Indian captive, soldier in the Mier Expedition, rancher, and mail coach driver. When Wallace spent two months in the summer of 1893 at the McCaleb family home, he related his life adventures to the young McCaleb, who wrote the biography from notes he had taken of Wallace's conversations.

421 McCaleb, Walter Flavius. **THE MIER EXPEDITION.** San Antonio. Naylor. 1959. 122 p. **(I J)**

This is a chronicle of the 304 men who crossed the Rio Grande in December 1842 to continue the Texas fight for freedom. The men were captured, subjected to the drawing of black or white beans for life or death, incarcerated in Perote Prison, and finally returned to Texas. Writing from notes dictated by Big Foot Wallace in his old age, the author condemns Houston for nonintervention in freeing the Texas patriots. Two-color drawings illustrate the chapter headings.

422 McCaleb, Walter Flavius. **SAM HOUSTON.** San Antonio. Naylor. 1958. 128 p. **(I J)**

This biography of Houston focuses on his role in Texas history and includes character flaws, noting both his genius and his eccentricities. As in other of his works, McCaleb uses conversations between a grandfather and his grandson as a storytelling device. A revised and enlarged edition was published in 1967 with illustrations at the chapter headings.

423 McCaleb, Walter Flavius. **THE SANTA FE EXPEDITION.** San Antonio. Naylor. 1964. 86 p. **(I J)**

This heroic account of the Santa Fe Expedition, begun in 1841 by President Mirabeau Lamar to secure for Texas the territory of New Mexico, includes excerpts from the histories of Kendall and Falconer. The hardships on the trail, defeat at San Miguel, and mistreatment on the way to Mexico City of the party of merchants and volunteers is told from the perspective of great sympathy for the expedition's purpose. Black-and-white and color drawings illustrate the history, which is presented as a conversation between a grandfather and his grandson.

424 McCaleb, Walter Flavius. **STEPHEN F. AUSTIN.** San Antonio. Naylor. 1957. 90 p. **(I J)**

This is an objective biography of the Father of Texas which focuses on his great achievements in the colonization of the state. The author acknowledges Eugene C. Barker's writings as his primary source. The use of conversations between a grandfather and his grandson in the telling of Austin's life story gives the book a didactic tone.

425 McCaleb, Walter Flavius. **WILLIAM BARRET TRAVIS.** San Antonio. Naylor. 1957. 96 p. **(I J)**

After a brief sketch of Travis's early life, this biography focuses on his activities in Texas and contains excerpts from letters and documents within the text. The device of beginning and ending each chapter with a conversation between a grandfather and his grandson gives the book a didactic tone.

426 McCall, Edith S. **COWBOYS AND CATTLE DRIVES.** Illustrated by Carol Rogers. Chicago. Childrens Press. 1964. 126 p. (Frontiers of America) **(P I)**

This easy-to-read, clearly written collective biography is primarily about the cowboy and ranching experiences of Charlie Goodnight and James Cook in frontier Texas. Brief sketches about Tom Smith, an early marshall, and Will Rogers complete the volume. Bold black-and-white drawings in keeping with the cowboy subjects illustrate the text.

427 McCall, Edith S. **STALWART MEN OF EARLY TEXAS.** Illustrated by Lou Aronson. Chicago. Childrens Press. 1970. 127 p. (Frontiers of America) **(I)**

Dramatic episodes and personalities in Texas history from 1528 to 1836 are presented in lively, fictionalized accounts of Cabeza de Vaca, La Salle, the Austins, Houston, Bowie, Crockett, and the heroes of the Alamo. The readable text is illustrated with numerous black-and-white sketches.

428 McClendon, Marie Millicent Dancy. **MYSTERY CAMP.** Illustrated by P.L. Martin. Boston. L.C. Page. 1926. 308 p. **(I J)**

Speck Evans and his friends Snappy Dean and Blooey Browne camp in an abandoned cabin on a small island near Seabrook. Their carefree 1920s summer fun is interrupted when they discover buried treasure for which the villainous Eyeless Moke is searching. The opening chapter was first published as a short story in **St. Nicholas Magazine**.

429 McClendon, Marie Millicent Dancy. **SECRETS INSIDE.** Illustrated by Dean Freeman. Boston. L.C. Page. 1928. 315 p. **(I J)**

A little orphan girl travels by train from North Carolina to Houston, where she is lost while looking for a new home. The old silver locket she wears is the link that leads to her wealthy father and her inheritance of an oil well. This sentimental girls' story provides action, mystery, and a happy ending based on the Texas dream.

430 McCoy, Joseph J. **THE HUNT FOR THE WHOOPING CRANE : A NATURAL HISTORY DETECTIVE STORY**. Illustrated by Rey Abruzzi. New York. Lothrop, Lee & Shepard. 1966. 223 p.   **(I J)**

A scientific adventure story, this book describes the detective work of the National Audubon Society, the U.S. Fish and Wildlife Service, and the Canadian Wildlife Service in an eleven-year search to locate the nesting grounds of the whooping cranes and to protect the cranes along their migration routes and in their winter home at the Aransas National Wildlife Refuge. Photographs and maps illustrate the reports of scientific observations of the endangered species.

431 McDaniel, Ruel. **DEEP WATER BOY**. Illustrated by Parker Edwards. San Carlos, Calif. Golden Gate Junior Books. 1964. 138 p.   **(I)**

The work of Port Isabel shrimpers forms a background as Captain Clegg's North Star, shrimp trawler, rescues a young stowaway from the Gulf waters after he escapes from a pirate cruiser carrying illegal aliens from Mexico to Florida.

432 McGiffin, Lee. **THE FIFER OF SAN JACINTO**. Illustrated by Frank Nicholas. New York. Lothrop, Lee & Shepard. 1956. 191 p.   **(I)**

Fifteen-year-old Page Carter and his widowed mother arrive in Serena, Texas, in April 1835. Marker Wilson, the local blacksmith, befriends the Carters, helping them build a cabin and set up a school and teaching Page pioneer skills. When war comes, Page is ready to volunteer to fight at San Jacinto.

433 McGiffin, Lee. **THE HORSE HUNTERS**. New York. Dutton. 1963. 156 p.   **(I J)**

In 1862 Jeff Hunter and his adopted brother Sam Britt leave camp on the Frio River with a herd of mustangs they plan to sell to the Confederates in New Orleans. After the herd is stolen, the two mustangers join the Army to track down the horse thieves. Surviving the hardships of war and daring adventures in capturing the horse thieves, the brothers return to Texas to build their dream ranch.

434 McGiffin, Lee. **THE MUSTANGERS**. New York. Dutton. 1965. 160 p.   **(J)**

Andy Taylor, fifteen-year-old office boy in a New York publishing company, reads dime novels and dreams about life in the West. In 1873 he sets out for San Antonio in hope of meeting his wandering father. Befriended instead by Matt, a seasoned cowboy, Andy learns to ride, rope, and love the real Texas. While fighting Indians at Adobe Walls, Andy makes a surprising discovery which leads to a more mature stage of life.

435 McGiffin, Lee. **RIDE FOR TEXAS**. New York. Dutton. 1960. 160 p. **(I J)**

Instead of returning home to Texas, Confederate soldier Doby Taylor follows General Jo Shelby into Mexico to join the army of Emperor Maximilian rather than surrender after Appomattox. After Doby suffers hardship and disillusion about life in Mexico, he courageously sets out for the far-off Rio Grande and his homeland. He realizes his desire of settling on a farm on the Angelina River.

436 McGiffin, Lee. **TEN TALL TEXANS : TALES OF THE TEXAS RANGERS**. Illustrated by John Alan Maxwell. New York. Lothrop, Lee & Shepard. 1956. 220 p. **(I J)**

In this collective biography, sketches of the exciting, brave deeds of ten early Rangers and brief histories of their later lives include Noah Smithwick, Big Foot Wallace, Jack Hays, Sam Walker, John B. Armstrong, Jim Gillett, Lee Hall, John R. Hughes, Bill McDonald, and M.T. Gonzaullas. An introductory chapter gives a brief history of the Ranger tradition and a description of the qualifications and duties of contemporary Rangers. Black-and-white drawings illustrate the narrative of legendary exploits.

437 McGiffin, Norton. **THE DOMINO HORSE**. New York. McKay. 1958. 182 p. **(I)**

Jim Carson, a young rancher from forty miles northeast of Corpus Christi, falls in love at first sight with Nopalero, an unusual spotted Appaloosa. After Jim is given Nopalero, Alberto Garza, a border outlaw who covets the horse, causes trouble for the family. This adventure story describes life of the brush country ranchers in the 1870s.

438 McGiffin, Norton. **SAM HENDERSON, TEXAS RANGER**. New York. McKay. 1959. 198 p. **(I J)**

Leaving the homestead on the Guadalupe River where he had been taken in after his father died at the Alamo, Sam Henderson, fifteen-year-old orphan, joins the Texas Rangers with the assistance of Don Jose Navarro of San Antonio. Sam experiences the life of an 1840s Ranger, fighting Comanches and a former Ranger turned outlaw, in an exciting story of a boy growing up on the frontier.

439 McGreane, Meagan. **ON STAGE: JOHN DENVER**. Mankato, Minn. Creative Eductional Society. 1976. 47 p. (The Entertainers) **(I)**

The story of John Deutschendorf's life after his graduation from Arlington Heights High School in Fort Worth explores Denver's musical career as an expression of his joy of life and his lifestyle in a secluded Colorado mountain retreat.

440 McIntyre, John Thomas. **IN TEXAS WITH DAVY CROCKETT**. Illustrated by John A. Huybers. Philadelphia. Penn Pub. Co. 1914. 208 p. (The Buckskin Books) **(I)**

In this Wild West adventure story, two boys on their way to Texas in 1836 encounter a scheme to rob a young woman of an unexpected inheritance. Davy Crockett befriends the boys and aids them in outsmarting the unscrupulous swindlers. While searching across Texas for the young woman, the boys are involved in events of the Texas Revolution. The final chapter is a brief biographical sketch of Crockett.

441 McKone, Jim. **LONE STAR FULLBACK**. New York. Vanguard. 1966. 189 p. **(I J)**

A Rio Grande Valley town learns to appreciate the determination and skill of Sangre de Cristo High School's first black football player. The message of equality is embodied in the attitudes of the coach and the newspaper's sports editor. Most of the people in the football-crazy town travel to West Texas to watch the team play in the state play-off, where they meet another form of prejudice. The novel explores racism in Texas in the 1960s within the framework of schoolboy sports.

442 McNeil, Everett. **IN TEXAS WITH DAVY CROCKETT : A STORY OF THE TEXAS WAR FOR INDEPENDENCE**. New York. Dutton. 1908. 398 p. **(I J)**

Two boys meet Davy Crockett near their home in the canebrakes and witness the events of the Texas Revolution in this lengthy adventure story.

The didactic text describes daily customs of the pioneers as well as the hostility and series of confrontations between Mexicans and Texans. The book went through four printings in the ten years 1908-1918.

443 McSpadden, Joseph Walker. **TEXAS : A ROMANTIC STORY FOR YOUNG PEOPLE.** Illustrated by Howard L. Hastings. New York. J.H. Sears. 1927. 124 p. (Romantic Stories of the States) **(I J)**

In a series of stories told by ranch owner Uncle Jack to a group of students visiting his ranch for a roundup, episodes of Texas history from Cabeza de Vaca to the Mexican War are unfolded in conversational style. One of a patriotic series of books about states, the book contains a chronology, 1513-1920, a map of forts, missions, and battlegrounds on the endpapers, and black-and-white drawings.

444 Meadowcroft, Enid LaMonte. **TEXAS STAR.** Illustrated by Lloyd Coe. New York. Crowell. 1950. 148 p. **(I J)**

Texas Star, a black horse with a white star on his forehead, is a dream come true for pioneer boy Andy Blake. On the journey to his family's new home near Austin, Andy meets a Texas Ranger who teaches him tracking and survival skills. Family adventures include an encounter with Waco Indians and participation in the 1846 statehood ceremony.

445 Michels, Barbara and White, Bettye, eds. **APPLES ON A STICK : THE FOLKLORE OF BLACK CHILDREN.** Illustrated by Jerry Pinkney. New York. Coward, McCann & Geoghegan. 1983. 53 p. **(P I)**

Active, joyful black-and-white drawings illustrate this collection of black children's rhymes gathered at a Houston school. Fifty-one brief verses are included, both universal, such as "Teddy Bear, Teddy Bear," and "One Two Buckle My Shoe," and unusual.

446 Miller, Helen Markley. **BABE DIDRIKSON ZAHARIAS.** Illustrated by Richard Mlodock. Chicago. Encyclopaedia Britannica. 1961. 191 p. (Britannica Bookshelf. Great Lives Series) **(I J)**

This biography of the outstanding woman athlete from Beaumont includes extensive background about her warm, loving family and her determination to perfect her skill at each sport she attempts in her extraordinary career. Her struggles to overcome cancer after operations in Texas give a sympathetic view of her as a symbol of courage and hope to the nation.

447 Mills, Betty J. **AMANDA GOES WEST : A JOURNAL OF FASHION HISTORY THROUGH PAPER DOLLS.** Illustrated by Lynette C. Ross. Lubbock. Texas Tech Press. 1983. l v. (unpaged) (The Amanda Series, Book I)   **(P I J)**

An accurate fashion history in paper doll format, with color illustrations of clothing and artifacts of the period 1838-42. Brief journal entries describing the life of Amanda, a fictional girl, and her family tell the story of a long journey to Texas by wagon, life in a frontier home far from neighbors and with limited supplies, a frontier Christmas, and Amanda's romance and engagement, based on factual accounts. This delightful book is the first of three in the Amanda Series.

448 Mills, Betty J. **AMANDA'S NEW LIFE: A JOURNAL OF FASHION HISTORY THROUGH FASHION DOLLS.** Illustrated by Lynette C. Ross. Lubbock. Texas Tech Press. 1 v. (unpaged) (The Amanda Series, Book II)   **(P I J)**

Amanda prepares her trousseau, marries a Texas Ranger, and has a family amid the danger and hardships of the Texas frontier. Journal entries tell of the daily activities and political events of the period 1843 to 1862. Full-color paper dolls display period costumes and artifacts.

449 Moffitt, Virginia May. **THE JAYHAWKER.** Illustrated by Robert Candy. Boston. L.C. Page. 1949. 275 p.   **(J)**

This adventure story about Confederate cotton freighters, a heroic adolescent who was formerly an Indian captive, and a dashing Jayhawker, leader of a band of outlaws, is set in South Texas in 1862. The foreword by Frank E. Vandiver contains explanatory notes of the period. The harsh realities of life on both sides of the Rio Grande during the Civil War are portrayed in Brett Pruitt's struggle to survive.

450 Moffitt, Virginia May. **POLLYANNA OF MAGIC VALLEY.** Boston. L.C. Page. 1949. 292 p.   **(I J)**

The Pendletons rent an old house in the Rio Grande Valley, where they solve a family mystery of a missing daughter and grandson while keeping alive the heritage of a joyful heart by playing the "Glad Game" of finding something to be glad about. The harvest of the fertile "Magic Valley" is celebrated with a style show parade in which costumes are created with leaves and petals of fruits and vegetables. The action-filled story of the series book is told in a decidedly didactic tone.

451 Moffitt, Virginia May. **TEXAS--THE GOLDEN LAND.** Illustrated by Robert Candy. Dallas. Banks Upshaw. 1950. 232 p.   **(P I J)**

This supplementary reader for grade three contains stories about animals and birds of Texas as they have been encountered by Indian, pioneer, and contemporary children. The emphasis is on the concept that all living things are our neighbors and should be treated in a respectful manner. The book is heavily illustrated with color plates, black-and-white photographs, and colored borders with drawings of birds and animals.

452 Mohn, Peter B. **THE GHOST SQUADRON : CONFEDERATE AIR FORCE.** Chicago. Childrens Press. 1981. 47 p. (Performers in Uniform)   **(I)**

Airplanes used by the United States and its allies in World War II are painstakingly preserved as living history by the Confederate Air Force at Rebel Field, Harlingen. This book provides a brief history of the CAF and is illustrated with many fine color photographs.

453 Molnar, Joe. **GRACIELA : A MEXICAN AMERICAN CHILD TELLS HER STORY.** New York. Watts. 1972. 48 p.   **(I)**

The biography of a Mexican American girl from a Texas border town, told in textual transcription of taped conversations and informal black-and-white photographs, shows a large, warm, close-knit family, summer trips to Michigan to earn money, prejudice experienced, and efforts to better their lot by study and hard work.

454 Montgomery, Rutherford G. **THORNBUSH JUNGLE.** Illustrated by Lorence Bjorklund. Cleveland. World Pub. Co. 1966. 159 p.   **(I J)**

Jody Carson lives with his Uncle Oats Andrews on Frio Creek in the Brush Country south of San Antonio. While Uncle Oats carves wooden curios to sell and teaches Juan Clovis, a neighbor boy, the craft, Jody learns about the local wildlife, adopting two orphaned ocelots and an old cow pony. The story of rural life close to nature, but with disputes about water and cattle, offers a carefully drawn picture of the plant and animal life of the desert country. Bjorklund's sketches enhance the sense of place.

455 Montgomery, Vivian. **MR. JELLYBEAN.** Illustrated by Jan Waide. Austin. Shoal Creek Publishers. 1980. 16 p.   **(P)**

This picture story of a neighboring rancher who stops at a small kindergarten to visit with the children, look at their drawings, and give them jellybeans is based on President Johnson's visits to the Stonewall, Texas, Head Start program. The identity of Mr. Jellybean is not revealed until the end of the simple text.

456 Mooney, Booth. **SAM HOUSTON**. Illustrated by George Roth. Chicago. Follett. 1966. 144 p. (Library of American Heroes) **(I J)**

This clearly written biography of Houston describes his life and career from boyhood until death. A feature of the book is an eleven-page section entitled "Highlights in the Life of Sam Houston," which contains color drawings and brief text about his achievements. The second half of the book is concerned with his life in Texas.

457 Moore, Jim. **THE SAN ANTONIO SPURS**. Mankato, Minn. Creative Education. 1984. 48 p. (The NBA Today) **(I)**

This easy-to-read history of the popular San Antonio basketball team is one of a series about the NBA teams. Black-and-white sports action photographs illustrate the text.

458 Morechamp, Arthur. **LIVE BOYS : OR, CHARLEY AND NASHO IN TEXAS**. Boston. Lothrop and Lee. 1878. 308 p. (Choice Books of Adventure) **(I J)**

Charley Zanco, a Texan, and Nasho, a Mexican, are fourteen-year-old farm boys from Turtle Creek in Kerr County. The boys have great adventures in this very early fictional account of a cattle drive. Good manners, ingenuity, and hard work are exemplified in a didactic tone. The lengthy story includes details of wildlife and places familiar to the region. Besides their farm and trail work, the boys visit the Centennial Exhibition in Philadelphia, where they work to earn their keep and make new acquaintances.

459 Morse, Charles and Morse, Ann. **LEE TREVINO**. Illustrated by Harold Henriksen. Mankato, Minn. Amecus Street; distributed by Childrens Press, Chicago. 1974. 31 p. (Superstars) **(P I)**

Bright-colored drawings illustrate this simple biography of the championship golfer who grew up in Dallas near the present location of the Glen Lakes Country Club and later lived in El Paso, where he worked as the golf pro at the Horizon City Country Club. This inspirational rags-to-riches story demonstrates the generous spirit of an extraordinary Mexican American.

460 Moss, Helen. **LIFE IN A LOG CABIN ON THE TEXAS FRONTIER**. Illustrated by Virginia Scott Gholson. Austin. Eakin. 1982. 76 p. (Stories for Young Americans) **(I)**

The details of everyday life of Texas pioneer families of the 1850s, from building a cabin to keeping it clean, are included. Children's chores, woman's work, clothing, food, and fun are described, as is the conflict between Anglo and Indian lifestyles. Cynthia Ann Parker's story is briefly recounted in the last chapter. This simple, realistic presentation brings alive the lifestyle of the early settlers.

461 Mullins, Vera Cooper. **RONNIE AND THE TEXAS CAMEL**. Chicago. Moody. 1976. 191 p. **(I J)**

In 1856 the Army Camel Corps is stationed at Camp Verde, Texas, where twelve-year-old Ronnie Clark and his sister Sarah live with their grandparents while their Texas Ranger father is away. Ronnie meets Suliman, the camel driver, and learns to care for Nuisance, an orphaned camel. Ronnie and Nuisance perform heroic deeds together in this novel with a strong Christian message.

462 Munroe, Kirk. **WITH CROCKETT AND BOWIE : OR, FIGHTING FOR THE LONE-STAR FLAG.**. Illustrated by V. Perard. New York. Scribner. 1897. 347 p. (White Conqueror Series) **(J)**

Rex Hardin's wealthy father settles on a land grant between Gonzales and San Antonio in 1831, where Rex captures a beautiful wild horse, Tawny. Young, adventurous Rex participates in the struggle for Texas independence and is rescued from a series of close calls by his intelligent horse. The author used Yoakum's **History of Texas** and John C. Duval's memoirs as the basis for the lengthy historical background in which the protagonist encounters all of the Revolutionary heroes and witnesses all of the major events.

463 Murphy, Keith. **BATTLE OF THE ALAMO**. Illustrated by Trevor Parkin. Milwaukee. Raintree Publishers. 1979. 31 p. **(P I)**

Crockett's role in the historic battle for Texas independence is told in this concise account, which is illustrated with large color and black-and-white drawings and a diagram of the Alamo. A brief biographical sketch explains Crockett's reasons for coming to Texas. This book is appropriate for older readers who need a simple text.

464 Murphy, Robert William. **WILD GEESE CALLING.** Illustrated by John Kaufmann. New York. Dutton. 1966. 96 p.   **(I)**

The banding of wild geese at the Aransas National Wildlife Refuge in order to learn about their migration patterns begins this story, which explains the work of the Refuge and the habits of the geese. In a sentimental story within the factual account, Dan Tolliver, a lonely farm boy starved for romance, cares for a wounded gander illegally shot down near his home. The boy's curiosity is kindled by the majestic goose, and he learns to respect its yearning for freedom.

465 Newlon, Clarke. **L.B.J. : THE MAN FROM JOHNSON CITY.** New York. Dodd, Mead. 1964. 213 p.   **(J)**

This biography of the thirty-sixth president was written during Lyndon B. Johnson's life with his approval. Beginning with Johnson's sudden ascension to the presidency after the assassination of John F. Kennedy, the book continues with a brief outline of his youth and a fuller description of his career and achievements, emphasizing the powerful later years. Anecdotes from friends and colleagues enliven the narrative. Reference aids include a history of the Johnson pioneers, a genealogical chart, a section of photographs, and an index. The book was revised in 1966, 1970, and 1976 to include information about recent events.

466 Newman, Shirlee Petkin. **THE STORY OF LYNDON B. JOHNSON.** Philadelphia. Westminster. 1967. 95 p.   **(P I)**

This simple biography of Johnson encompasses the time from his boyhood to his presidency, highlighting his personality rather than his politics.

467 Nixon, Joan Lowery. **THE BUTTERFLY TREE.** Illustrated by James McIlrath. Huntington, Ind. Our Sunday Visitor. 1979. 29 p. **(P)**

As her frail great-grandmother nears death, Jennifer offers her a special gift in this full-color picture book set in Central Texas. The migration of the monarch butterflies becomes a symbol of the life cycle, a moment of beauty before moving on to another place.

468 Nixon, Joan Lowery. **A DEADLY GAME OF MAGIC.** New York. Harcourt, Brace, Jovanovich. 1983. 148 p. **(J)**

While returning to their small North Texas town from a speech and drama tournament, four teenagers spend a stormy night in a strange, big house after their car breaks down. A mysterious magician manipulates the four with his illusions to gain his deadly aims in a terrifying battle of wits. The winner of the Edgar Allan Poe Award for best juvenile mystery has written another contemporary thriller.

469 Nixon, Joan Lowery. **IF YOU SAY SO, CLAUDE.** Illustrated by Lorinda Bryan Cauley. New York. F. Warne. 1980. 48 p. **(P)**

Shirley and Claude, an amusing pioneer couple, travel across Texas in their covered wagon looking for a place to settle down. Cauley's colorful illustrations depict the settlers' adventures.

470 Nixon, Joan Lowery. **THE KIDNAPPING OF CHRISTINA LATTIMORE.** New York. Harcourt, Brace, Jovanovich. 1979. 179 p. **(I J)**

Contemporary Houston is the setting for this exciting mystery about the kidnapping of a young prep school woman. Christina, accused of scheming to extort money from her wealthy, domineering grandmother, finds the inner strength to exonerate herself and set her own life course. This novel won the Edgar Allan Poe Award for the best juvenile mystery of the year.

471 Nixon, Joan Lowery. **MYSTERY OF HURRICANE CASTLE.** Illustrated by Velma Ilsley. New York. Criterion. 1964. 144 p. **(P I)**

Thirteen-year-old Kathy, her sister, and her little brother visit friends on the Texas coast. When the three are left behind in a hurricane, they meet Seaweed Annie. This modern mystery is exciting and suspenseful, if somewhat implausible.

472 Nixon, Joan Lowery. **THE SEANCE.** New York. Harcourt, Brace, Jovanovich. 1980. 142 p. **(J)**

Sara Martin disappears during a secret high school girls' seance in a small East Texas town near the Big Thicket. Her foster sister Lauren grows increasingly terrified as the murders of Sara and Rachel, a friend, are discovered. A strong sense of place is felt in this Edgar Allan Poe Award winning mystery.

473 Nixon, Joan Lowery. **THE SPECTER.** New York. Delacorte. 1982. 184 p. **(I J)**

Dina Harrington, a seventeen-year-old orphan with Hodgkin's disease, becomes involved with her roommate, nine-year-old Julie, in a San Antonio hospital. The mystery of Julie's identity and violent past unfolds in a carefully developed plot by this award winning author. Descriptions of the San Antonio River Walk and zoo, of the countryside around Fredericksburg, and of the large, loving Cardenas family, which becomes the girls' foster family, add local color to this exciting story.

474 Nolan, Jeannette Covert. **LA SALLE AND THE GRAND ENTERPRISE.** New York. Messner. 1951. 178 p. **(I J)**

This comprehensive biography of the great French explorer focuses on his three journeys in North America. Through persistent effort La Salle obtained King Louis XIV's permission and funding to undertake his third journey, whose intended destination was the mouth of the Mississippi River. In 1685 the expedition landed instead at Matagorda Bay in Texas, where La Salle met his death in 1687. The history of the unsuccessful colony at Fort St. Louis and the aftermath of La Salle's death are recounted in the final part of the book. Reference aids include maps of La Salle's routes, a bibliography and an index.

475 Nolan, Jeannette Covert. **O. HENRY : THE STORY OF WILLIAM SYDNEY PORTER.** Illustrated by Hamilton Greene. New York. Messner. 1943. 263 p. **(I J)**

A substantial portion of this biography of the well-known author concerns his life in Texas, where he first came to a sheep ranch near Cotulla as sickly young man and later lived as a dashing bachelor in Austin. He fell in love, was married, worked in the Land Office and then fled Texas when accused of embezzlement. Reference aids include a bibliography and index.

476 O'Brien, Esse Forrester. **THE FIRST BULLDOGGER.** San Antonio. Naylor. 1961. 58 p. **(J)**

This biography of Bill Pickett, the Taylor native who became a world-famous cowboy, includes his early training in ranch skills, his special ability in caring for animals, his long-time association with the 101 Ranch and the 101 Wild West Show, and some of his successes as a rodeo star in this country and abroad. One photograph of Pickett and several black-and-white drawings illustrate the text.

477 Olds, Helen Diehl. **LYNDON BAINES JOHNSON.** Illustrated by Paul Frame. New York. Putnam. 1965. 64 p. (A See and Read Beginning to Read Biography) **(P)**

This easy-to-read biography encompasses Johnson's life from his rural boyhood to his election for a full term as U.S. President. Each page contains a few lines of text and drawings of Johnson's activities.

478 Olgin, Joseph. **SAM HOUSTON, FRIEND OF THE INDIANS.** Illustrated by Andre Le Blanc. Boston. Houghton Mifflin. 1958. 192 p. (Piper Books) **(I)**

This biography of Houston gives a somewhat fictional version of his childhood, as facts are tempered by incidents invented by the author. His unusual relationship with the Cherokee Indians and long-time friendship with Andrew Jackson are shown as influences on his actions as a Texas patriot, President of the Republic, State Governor, and U.S. Senator. The simple text is illustrated with two-color drawings.

479 Olsen, James T. **A.J. FOYT : "FANCY PANTS" AT THE WHEEL.** Illustrated by John Keely. Mankato, Minn. Creative Education. 1973. 29 p. (Creative's Superstars) **(P I)**

This easy-to-read biography of the automobile racing superstar begins with an incident when, at age eleven and without his parents' permission, Foyt raced around the family yard, ruining both yard and car and foreshadowing his lifelong desire to race. More than an account of his numerous racing achievements and championships, this text includes information about his personality, lifestyle, injuries, and enormous determination to win. Alternating black-and-white drawings illustrate the text.

480 Otis, James. **PHILIP OF TEXAS : A STORY OF SHEEP RAISING IN TEXAS.** New York. American Book Co. 1913. 155 p. (James Otis's Pioneer Series) **(I)**

The events of a pioneer family's move to the west fork of the Trinity River in 1843 are unfolded in brief chapters narrated by Philip, the young son. The family and five slaves travel overland, herding their cattle and sheep, meeting Kickapoo Indians and Mexican gunrunners. The pleasant, didactic text centers on the struggles of establishing a new home but also discusses the political events of the period. Black-and-white drawings illustrate the text, which is one of a series of pioneer stories for children.

481 Owens, William A. **LOOK TO THE RIVER.** New York. Atheneum. 1963. 185 p.   **(I J)**

Orphaned and homeless, young Jed binds himself to work on Basil and Cannie's farm, where he is treated kindly. Old Peddler John's tales of exotic travel kindle Jed's wanderlust, and he accepts a cheap pocket watch as a token that he will work for John. Accused of stealing the watch, Jed attempts to prove his innocence by searching for the peddler. He is detained by the cruel boss of a chain gang and meets a black boy being treated cruelly for stealing food. Set in Texas south of the Red River in 1910, this moving story contains philosophical themes about life. Reprinted by McGraw-Hill, 1970.

482 Paradis, Adrian A. **GAIL BORDEN, A RESOURCEFUL BOY.** Illustrated by Nate Goldstein. Indianapolis. Bobbs-Merrill. 1964. 200 p. (Childhood of Famous Americans)   **(P I)**

This easy-to-read biography of the inventor of the condensed milk process includes Borden's role in the Texas Revolution as a patriot and newpaper publisher, his friendship with Sam Houston, and his work as a surveyor of the site of Houston and as a customs official in Galveston. Reference aids include a brief chronology, 1801-1874, and study questions.

483 Parsons, Chuck. **THE CAPTURE OF JOHN WESLEY HARDIN.** College Station. Creative Pub. Co. 1978. 121 p. (The Young West Series)   **(I J)**

Credit for Hardin's capture on the train in Pensacola is given to William Henry Hutchinson, sheriff of Escambia County, Florida, instead of to Texas Ranger Jack Armstrong. The account of Hardin's crimes in Texas, his family relations and friends, and the changing climate of law enforcement in Texas as the frontier disappeared reads as an exciting detective story. The carefully researched account includes period letters, newspaper articles, maps, drawings, photographs, and extensive chapter notes.

484 Paschal, Nancy. **CLOVER CREEK.** Illustrated by Alice Carsey. New York. Nelson. 1964. 272 p.   **(J)**

Sixteen-year-old Lucy Ann Lee, oldest child in a large family, finds a job as a botanical assistant at Martin's Nursery on Clover Creek and uses her knowledge of Texas wildflowers to help the business. Paschal's first career girl romance for teenagers reflects the values of the 1940s. The setting, by the author's admission, is Texas.

485 Paschal, Nancy. **EMERALDS ON HER HANDS**. New York. Farrar, Straus & Giroux. 1965. 211 p.   **(J)**

High school graduate Arlin Brooks finds a high-paying job at Kimberley's jewelry store, where she catches the eye of handsome young Kevin Kimberley. In this improbable romance the intelligent, beautiful girl learns all about gems, catches a jewel thief, assists her cousin in attending college, and becomes engaged to the wealthy jeweler. The setting for the novel is a fictional Texas city similar to Dallas.

486 Paschal, Nancy. **HILLVIEW HOUSE**. Philadelphia. Westminster. 1963. 206 p.   **(J)**

Sensible, self-possessed Cary Bennett is employed for the summer as a literary secretary to help wealthy Mrs. Wendell complete a biography of her Texas pioneer grandmother. Also spending the summer at the Wendell estate, Hillview House, are Mrs. Wendell's nephew, Dixon King, and his sister from New York. Double romances and difficulties in completing the fascinating biography give interest to the novel, which is set in suburban Dallas.

487 Paschal, Nancy. **MAGNOLIA HEIGHTS**. Illustrated by Ruth King. New York. Nelson. 1947. 272 p.   **(J)**

Fifteen-year-old orphan Mary Jo Mills finds a job as receptionist to veterinarian Dr. Grant Milton to help Mrs. Loving, her poor grandmother, maintain their home. Mary Jo's eagerness to learn more about animals and to work hard at the clinic earn her a permanent job and home in spite of conflicts with a substitute veterinarian and a major fire. The fictional setting of Mrs. Loving's house surrounded by magnolia trees in the Magnolia Heights section of town is in the Dallas area.

488 Paschal, Nancy. **MAKE WAY FOR LAUREN**. Philadelphia. Westminster. 1963. 229 p.   **(J)**

When Lauren Lacy's widowed father is transferred from their small North Texas town to Chicago, Lauren spends the summer in the family home with their kindly housekeeper Edna, a young interior decorator, and her dog Boots. Lauren faces a difficult adjustment when her father returns with a stepmother and stepsister who take over the house. Her adjustment to being part of a stepfamily with two teenage daughters and a new baby is aided by her friendship with Kal Meadows and her interest in becoming an interior decorator.

489 Paschal, Nancy. **NAME THE DAY**. Philadelphia. Westminster. 1959. 204 p.   **(J)**

Nineteen-year-old Sandra Dodson is pampered by her wealthy parents. Her main objective in life is to have fun until the night her boy friend smashes his guardian's car fender. When she is challenged to earn the money to pay for the damage herself, a new world based on the satisfaction of work opens to her. Becoming an assistant to a large manufacturing company editor, Sandra meets many employees, including handsome, ambitious Craig Calvert, with whom she falls in love. Set in suburban 1950s Texas, this career girl romance places emphasis on traditional values.

490 Paschal, Nancy. **PORTRAIT BY SHERYL**. Philadelphia. Westminster. 1958. 205 p.   **(J)**

When Sheryl Lane arrives in suburban North Texas to take over the photographic studio inherited from her grandfather, she faces trouble from the unethical owner of a rival studio. Befriended by building contractor Kim Roberts, Sheryl learns business and political skills and gains a husband in the process. This is another of Paschal's pleasant romantic career girl novels.

491 Paschal, Nancy. **PROMISE OF JUNE**. New York. Nelson. 1955. 189 p.   **(J)**

Debra Deering faces a sudden change of plans when her boy friend moves to Venezuela, giving her his dog to care for, and her older sister marries and gives up her job which was to provide financial support for art school. The young woman earns money by modeling animal figurines at home and falls in love with her supportive young sculpture teacher. This career girl romance is set in a 1950s Texas city.

492 Paschal, Nancy. **SONG OF THE HEART**. Philadelphia. Westminster. 1961. 218 p.   **(J)**

Talented twenty-one-year-old college senior Lonna Henderson is the adopted daughter of a wealthy Texas family. Lonna discovers that in order to develop the potential of her beautiful voice, inherited from her grandmother, a famous turn-of-the-century singer, she needs strict discipline. Her handsome boy friend Stanley Lowell encourages Lonna in spite of his mother's displeasure. This is another of Paschal's romantic novels of a young woman making career choices.

493 Paschal, Nancy. **SPRING IN THE AIR.** Illustrated by Susan Knight. New York. Viking. 1953. 192 p.   **(J)**

Sudie Emerson returns to her 1950s small Texas city with a new degree in landscape architecture and a strong desire to work. Complications arise when Grandfather Emerson wants her to marry, as her younger sister Glenda plans to do, and attractive young Californian Warren Eads takes all the landscape business in town. Sudie takes a job with Eads and is soon designing beautiful gardens and winning Warren's heart. The author attributes the Texas settings in her books to her Texas pioneer great-grandfather.

494 Paschal, Nancy. **SYLVAN CITY.** Illustrated by Dorothy Bayley Moore. New York. Viking. 1950. 254 p.   **(J)**

East Texas farm girl Callie Taylor is sent to a private girls' school with money made from newly discovered oil. Callie adjusts to living with her affluent, sophisticated relatives in Sylvan City and to studying at Miss Brown's school. Appreciating her grandmother's plans for her to receive an education, she continues in school after reverses in family finances. Paschal's novel reflects traditional values and has a thread of romantic interest.

495 Peacock, Howard H. **THE BIG THICKET OF TEXAS : AMERICA'S ECOLOGICAL WONDER.** Boston. Little, Brown. 1984. 89 p.   **(I J)**

The ecology and history of the Big Thicket in southeast Texas from prehistoric times to 1974, when the Big Thicket National Preserve was created, are told in a factual, fascinating text with photographs. Meat-eating plants, Indians, pioneers, bear hunters, lumbermen, oil field roughnecks, and environmentalists all appear in this delightful book. The work also includes a recipe for hush puppies to cook on a camping trip. Maps, an index, and a bibliography aid in the easy use of the book.

496 Peare, Catherine Owens. **THE LOST LAKES : A STORY OF THE TEXAS RANGERS.** Illustrated by Lorence F. Bjorklund. Philadelphia. Winston. 1953. 176 p.   **(I J)**

This is a fast-paced story about fourteen-year-old Chett Roberts's adventures with the Texas Rangers. Set in the 1880s in the Panhandle, the carefully authenticated action involves a scouting party looking for the Lost Lakes, which the Rangers believed were helping the Comanches maintain devastating raids on settlers.

497 Peck, Leigh. **DON COYOTE.** Illustrated by Virginia Lee Burton. Boston. Houghton Mifflin. 1942. 78 p.   **(I J)**

Sixteen brief tales in this collection are about the coyote, the animal the Indians and Mexicans of the Rio Grande region considered the wisest of all. Variants of well-known stories include a Cinderella tale and a hare and tortoise tale with a humorous twist. Virginia Lee Burton's lively, colorful drawings sweep across the pages, complementing the text.

498 Peck, Leigh. **PECOS BILL AND LIGHTNING.** Illustrated by Kurt Wiese. Boston. Houghton Mifflin. 1940. 68 p.   **(I J)**

This collection of twelve tales presents the high adventure of the cowboy folk hero's life. His youth with the coyotes on the Pecos, cowboy feats, capture of the pacing white mustang, and meeting with Paul Bunyan and Slue-Foot Sue are told in a lively, lucid style. Kurt Wiese's colorful, informal drawings mirror the good-natured quality of the text.

499 Peck, Leigh. **THEY WERE MADE OF RAWHIDE.** Illustrated by Aldren Watson. Boston. Houghton Mifflin. 1954. 181 p.   **(I J)**

In the 1880s Jed rides his horse from Galveston to Rutland, Vermont, to be with his father. Suffering from amnesia after a shipwreck on a horse-buying trip to South America, father is hospitalized. Jed's adventures as he crosses the country on his mustang and those of his sister Tibby, who remains at home, provide an exciting story.

500 Perry, George Sessions. **THE STORY OF TEXAS.** Illustrated by John N. Barron. Garden City, N.Y. Garden City Books. 1956. 56 p.   **(I)**

This heavily illustrated, oversize book presents a brief, readable narrative of Texas history from the Spanish explorers to the 1950s, concentrating on the period of the Revolution and the Republic and the importance of Stephen F. Austin and Sam Houston. The endpapers are decorated with a historical map of the state.

501 Phegley, Mallie. **THE FATHER OF TEXAS, STEPHEN F. AUSTIN.** San Antonio. Naylor. 1960. 123 p.   **(I J)**

This fictional biography begins in 1821 as Austin leads a wagon train of settlers to San Felipe. A sketch of his younger life is given, but the major portion of the book concentrates on Austin's work in Texas, the difficulties he encounters, and his personal and patriotic perspective. Some conversations of colonists are written in heavy dialect. An index is included.

502 Phillips, Betty Lou. **EARL CAMPBELL : HOUSTON OILER SUPERSTAR.** New York McKay. 1979. 122 p. **(I J)**

An inspirational biography of the "Tyler Rose," college and professional football star and Heisman Trophy winner, which uses frequent dialogue in presenting a positive portrait of Campbell. His humor, hard work, and closeness of family are shown along with his impressive achievements as a sports hero. Black-and- white photographs, an index, and a list of Campbell's twenty-seven post-season awards through 1979 are included. This book has more substance than the average sports biography.

503 Place, Marian Templeton. **AMERICAN CATTLE TRAILS.** Illustrated by Gil Walker. New York. Holt. 1967. 148 p. **(I J)**

This informative account reports the history and lore of cattle trails from Coronado's explorations to the establishment of the railroads. While the seldom mentioned Colonial and Wilderness Trails of the East and the trails to California and Oregon are discussed, the central focus is Texas, where the vast, sparely populated spaces yielded huge herds which often brought fortunes when driven to population centers. The danger and hardship experienced, the personalities of the trail blazers and cowboys, and the economic advantages of each trail are presented with unusual depth of coverage. The detailed map, bibliography, index, and brown drawings enhance the value of the book.

504 Place, Marian Templeton. **COMANCHES AND OTHER INDIANS OF TEXAS.** New York. Harcourt, Brace. 1970. 131 p. **(I J)**

The history and daily life of the early tribes--the Karankawas, Coahuiltecans, Jumanos, Atakapans, Caddoes, Wichitas, and Tonkawas-- are explored, from 12,000-year-old "Midland Minnie" to the subjugation of the Indians in 1901. The second part of the book contains detailed explanations of beliefs and practices of the Comanches, the dominant "Lords of the Plains." Authentic illustrations accompany the text.

505 Polk, Stella Gipson. **THE TEXAS HILL COUNTRY : A CHILD'S HISTORY.** Burnet, Tex. Eakin. 1980. 60 p. (Stories for Young Americans) **(P I)**

The Hill Country's history, pioneers, plants, and animals are described by a resident of a ranch west of Mason. The author is the sister of the late Fred Gipson.

506 Potter, Fannie Cora Bellows. **TEXAS IN HISTORY--STORY--LEGEND**. Dallas. Southwest Press. 1933. 220 p.   (I J)

This supplementary reader in Texas history for fifth to seventh graders has brief selections of prose and poetry about the entire span of the state's history. Attitudes of the 1930s are reflected in the stories depicting Indian raids, the role of the blacks, the inevitability of the survival of the the fittest, and the United Daughters of the Confederacy. Several pieces are signed by Olive McClintic Johnson.

507 Pritchett, Jewell G. **TAGALONG WITH CODY**. Abilene, Tex. J.G. Pritchett. 1980. 100 p.   (I J)

Intrigued by his study of Indian fighter Ranald Slidell Mackenzie, small-town boy Cody Johnson decides to spend two weeks of the summer of 1959 backpacking through central West Texas to sites of Captain Mackenzie's skirmishes. Cody's experiences include acquiring a stray dog, being captured by a World War I deserter in a Comanchero hideout, and returning home more mature and self-assured. A map of Cody's hike, black-and-white photographs of several sites, and a glossary aid the reader's understanding of the story.

508 Puttcamp, Rita. **BORROWED BOOTS**. Illustrated by Clifford N. Geary. New York. Viking. 1956. 186 p.   (I J)

Small fifteen-year-old Sam Houston Randal yearns to meet the expectations of Captain Pete, his large, loud-mouthed father. Sam is torn between love for his Mexican War veteran father, who plans to take the beautiful Cortina hacienda by force, and his desire for fair play and admiration for the gracious Don Juan Cortina, who desires to remain on the land given his family in a 1669 land grant. Within the cultural conflict of 1859 Brownsville, the boy learns to walk in the shoes of the men he admires and matures as he gains insights into their strengths and weaknesses.

509 Puttcamp, Rita. **TEXAS TREASURE**. Illustrated by Kurt Werth. New York. Lothrop, Lee, and Shepard. 1959. 155 p.   (I)

Twelve-year-old Jim Bradford joins his father's scholarly archaeological expedition in the Big Bend along the Rio Grande. While staying on his uncle's Loopy Y Ranch, Jim meets Pedro Barillo, a boy his age, who tells him of an old buried treasure on the land given to Don Pedro Barillo in 1667 by Queen Regent Maria Ana for Charles II of Spain and guarded by a ghost who is supposed to sing when a member of the Barillo family approaches. The summer becomes an exciting adventure as the boys search for the buried treasure.

510 Radlauer, Ed and Radlauer, Ruth. **COWBOY MANIA**. Chicago. Childrens Press. 1981. 32 p. (Radlauer Mania Book) **(P)**

An easy-to-read, controlled-vocabulary description of rodeo activities of cowgirls and cowboys. The text is illustrated with color photographs on each page.

511 Ranson, Nancy Richey. **TEXAS WILD FLOWER LEGENDS**. Dallas. Kaleidograph. 1933. 119 p. **(I J)**

Forty-four popular Texas wildflowers, arranged alphabetically by name, are presented in material first used as a series in **The Dallas Journal**. Botanical facts, folklore and legend, an original poem, and a poor quality black-and-white photograph describe each flower. The coverage is uneven, with some flowers receiving a more detailed description than others.

512 Ray, Frederic. **THE STORY OF THE ALAMO : AN ILLUSTRATED HISTORY OF THE SIEGE AND FALL OF THE ALAMO**. n.p. 1955. 32 p. **(I)**

This is a brief history of the site and of the heroic battle called a monument to the spirit of Texan liberty. The factual text is illustrated with large black-and-white drawings which give the book a comic book appearance. The centerfold map contains an overview of the Alamo as it appeared during the siege.

513 Ray, Ophelia. **DAUGHTER OF TEJAS**. Greenwich, Conn. New York Graphic Society. 1965. 120 p. **(I)**

Tiwana, twelve-year-old granddaughter of a Tejas chief, learns useful skills at Mission San Jose, where she spends the winter of 1725-26. On returning home she instructs the women of her tribe in the new skills before being taken captive by an Apache. Reunited with her mother, also an Apache captive, Tiwana courageously manages their escape, returning to stand tall in the village of her own people. The customs of the Tejas, the Apaches, and the Spanish missions at San Antonio are skillfully woven into an intriguing story.

514 Ray, Ophelia. **YOUNG HIDALGO : CARLOS DE MENDOZA OF SAN ANTONIO**. New York. Weybright & Talley. 1968. 117 p. **(I)**

Sixteen families leave Tenerife, Canary Islands, in March 1730 on a two-year journey to Texas, where they settle in San Antonio on land grants from the King of Spain. This unique episode in the settlement of Texas unfolds from two perspectives, as excerpts from the journal of young Carlos are interspersed with a lively narrative of the grueling land and sea journey and the establishment of new homes. A map of the journey illustrates the masterfully written story.

515 Read, Esther Bonilla. **JUANITO**. Corpus Christi. Cerca del Mar Pub. House. 1980. 31 p. **(P)**

During his first term at school, Juanito learns to respect the property of others. The easy-to-read Spanish text was written by a bilingual kindergarten teacher. Brightly colored drawings alternate with the didactic text.

516 Regli, Adolph Casper. **FIDDLING COWBOY**. Illustrated by Nat Edson. Philadelphia. McKay. 1949. 230 p. **(I J)**

Ross Gordon, a sixteen-year-old from Illinois, looks for a job as a cowboy in 1874 Texas. Blackie Spencer, the foreman at the Double Bee Ranch near Fort Griffin, hires Ross because of his fiddling and riding skills. With new friend Jeff Boyd, the ranch owner's son, Ross faces Indians, rustlers, and all the dangers of a trail drive to Dodge City. In this predictable western, the boy hero's honesty, hard work, and talent win him a place of respect.

517 Regli, Adolph Casper. **PARTNERS IN THE SADDLE**. New York. Watts. 1950. 248 p. **(I J)**

Fourteen-year-old Kemp Gifford's younger cousin, Peter, spends 1877 on the Crown W Ranch in the Texas Panhandle. The boys ride the line, fight Apache cattle thieves, are captured by Comanches, and escape to warn buffalo hunters of an Indian attack. The high spirited adventures of this western are predictable; the Indians are stereotypes who speak in broken English.

518 Reid, Mayne. **THE BOY HUNTERS : OR, ADVENTURES IN SEARCH OF A WHITE BUFFALLO**. Boston. Ticknor & Fields. 1852. 364 p. **(J)**

Colonel Landi, a wealthy former French soldier, raises his three sons to be self-sufficient and share his interest in nature found near their Louisiana home. When Landi receives a request from Prince Bonaparte to send a white buffalo skin for exhibition at a European museum, Basil, Lucien, and Francois set out to hunt the great prairie for it. The boys live off the land and have a series of encounters with all manner of wildlife, whose Latin names and lengthy descriptions are included. This boys' adventure by Captain Reid, a prolific English author, was published in several English and American editions.

519 Rice, James. **COWBOY ALPHABET FOR GROWNUPS AND YOUNG'UNS TOO**. Illustrated by the author. Austin. Shoal Creek Publishers. 1977. 48 p. **(P)**

Words pertaining to the habitat and vocabulary of the cowboy are used to introduce letters of the alphabet; for example, armadillo, arrowhead, and arroyo introduce the letter "a." Simple upper and lower case letters and colorful, humorous drawings illustrate the cowboy dialectal terms relating to animals, equipment, work, leisure activity, and other aspects of ranch life. The book is appropriate for older students who can read.

520 Rice, James. **GASTON DRILLS AN OFFSHORE OIL WELL**. Illustrated by the author. Gretna, La. Pelican Pub. Co. 1982. 46 p. **(P I)**

Gaston, the Cajun alligator, leaves the Louisiana bayou to drill for oil in the Gulf of Mexico and become the richest alligator in the world. More technical terminology is used in the text than in previous Gaston adventure books, and a glossary of terms is included. Rice's appealing drawings and text create a cheerful, lively introduction to the offshore oil business.

521 Rice, James. **GASTON GOES TO TEXAS**. Illustrated by the author. Gretna, La. Pelican Pub. Co. 1978. 32 p. **(P)**

Blown by a storm from the Louisiana bayou to a West Texas ranch, Gaston, the Cajun alligator, learns the skills of a cowhand, riding and roping with the best. Large color drawings illustrate the light-verse text.

522 Rice, James. **GASTON LAYS AN OFFSHORE PIPELINE**. Illustrated by the author. Gretna, La. Pelican Pub. Co. 1979. 32 p. **(P)**

Gaston, the Cajun alligator, leaves the bayou to lay a pipeline in the Gulf of Mexico. The story is told in light verse and is colorfully illustrated with double-page drawings.

523 Rice, James. **PRAIRIE CHRISTMAS**. Illustrated by the author. Gretna, La. Pelican Pub. Co. 1977. 48 p.   **(P)**

When a Christmas Eve "norther" slows down Santa in the Panhandle, two freezing cowboys help him hitch longhorns to his wagon and be on his way. The large, colorful drawings and light verse capture the Texas Christmas spirit. Reprinted in 1983.

524 Richards, Norman. **THE STORY OF THE ALAMO**. Illustrated by Tom Dunnington. Chicago. Childrens Press. 1970. 30 p. (Cornerstones of Freedom)   **(P I)**

The causes and history of the Texas Revolution, the siege of the Alamo, and the victory at San Jacinto are briefly narrated and heroes are sketched. Brown-and-black drawings illustrate the clearly written text.

525 Richey, Dorothy Hilliard. **ROAD TO SAN JACINTO**. San Antonio. Naylor. 1961. 102 p.   **(I)**

Teenage cousins Ken and Bill arrive with their pioneer parents in Texas in December 1835. The boys have a series of improbable adventures with Comanches and Mexicans and fight at San Jacinto before returning home to help rebuild their burned homes. Black-and-white drawings at the chapter headings illustrate the story.

526 Rickard, John Allison. **FAMOUS TEXANS**. Dallas. Banks Upshaw. 1955. 367 p.   **(I J)**

Biographical sketches of important figures in Texas history from Stephen F. Austin to John Nance Garner include political leaders, Texas Rangers, artists, Indian chiefs, and city founders, some of which are not found in other juvenile biography. Revised editions with minor changes were published in 1962 and 1980 under the title **Brief Biographies of Brave Texans**. The book contains facts and questions after each chapter, a glossary, a bibliography, and black-and-white photographs of poor quality.

527 Rickard, John Allison. **THE OLD AZTEC STORY TELLER**. Illustrated by William Brady. New York. B. Ackerman. 1944. 59 p.   **(I J)**

Don Patricio, an old shepherd, delights the children around the ranch who flock to him. They listen to his stories about honest and wily boys, a romantic princess, and supernatural beings. The nine brief stories in this collection are filled with details familiar to the Mexican child, such as burros, machetes, figs, and tortillas, and are illustrated with bold three-color drawings. Some stories in the collection first appeared in **Jack and Jill** and **Junior Life**. A new edition was published by Barnes in 1961.

528 Roberts, Naurice. **BARBARA JORDAN, THE GREAT LADY FROM TEXAS**. Chicago. Childrens Press. 1984. 31 p.   **(P I)**

This easy-to-read biography of an extraordinary black woman emphasizes her political and educational achievements. Numerous black-and-white photographs illustrate the large-type text.

529 Rogers, Mary Beth and Smith, Sherry A. and Scott, Janelle D. **WE CAN FLY : STORIES OF KATHERINE STINSON AND OTHER GUTSY WOMEN**. Illustrated by Charles Shaw. Austin. E.C. Temple: Texas Foundation for Women's Resources. 1983. 184 p.   **(I J)**

Exuberant individual sketches of twelve women who have made unusual contributions in the arts, politics, business, and the professions, and group sketches of WAFS pilots and NASA space women exemplify the theme of women having the ability to do whatever they choose. The lively, inspirational sketches are illustrated with photographs and line drawings. Reference aids include sources and a capsule biography of each subject.

530 Rosenfield, John. **TEXAS HISTORY MOVIES**. Illustrated by Jack I. Patton. Dallas. Southwest Press. 1928. 217 p.   **(I J)**

This history of Texas, which uses brief, fast-moving text in combination with cartoons in comic strip format, replete with dialogue in balloons, to tell the story, encompasses primarily the period from the early Indians through the Battle of San Jacinto. Its purpose is to entertain and stimulate interest in Texas history, not to present history fully and accurately. The work has also been published in an abridged paperback, which was distributed to Texas schools by the Magnolia Petroleum Company, and in a revised edition, with different author and illustrator, by Graphic Ideas.

531 Rostiser, Leila Brechenser. **MASCOT PERUNA**. San Antonio. Naylor. 1951. 67 p.   **(P I)**

This fictional biography of the Southern Methodist University mascot, a black midget Shetland pony, describes the pony's intensive training and excitement of being in the spotlight. Peruna was named for a medicine made in Texas and taken to gain pep. The partisan story, printed in bright blue text with bright red drawings, ends with an S.M.U. football victory.

532 Rothaus, James. **THE HOUSTON OILERS**. Mankato, Minn. Creative Education. 1981. 48 p. (The NFL Today)   (I)

A history of the Houston Oilers from their beginnings in 1960 through the 1979 season, with easy text illustrated by numerous black-and-white sports action photographs. Fans will enjoy reading about star players and coaches and studying the statistics.

533 Rourke, Constance Mayfield. **DAVY CROCKETT**. Illustrated by James MacDonald. New York. Harcourt, Brace. 1934. 276 p.   (J)

Crockett's reasons for coming to Texas, the Battle of the Alamo, and the rich folklore legacy he left are a major portion of this biography for older children. The narrative contains historical references and cites sources and evidence substantiating incidents. The author includes scholarly notes about the Crockett almanacs and the development of the legends from origins in other cultures. This biography, richer than some of the later juvenile biographies of Crockett, was republished in 1956 by Junior Deluxe Editions.

534 Roy, Lillian Elizabeth. **FIVE LITTLE STARRS ON A RANCH**. New York. Burt. 1913. 193 p. (Five Little Starrs Series)   (P I)

The five Starr children and their parents from New Jersey accept Grandpa Starr's invitation to spend the summer on his ranch near Laredo. Traveling up the Rio Grande in "The Five Starrs" boat and by private train to the ranch, the children begin an adventurous summer. A cougar, a runaway train engine, an Indian raid, and cattle thieves provide plenty of action in this easy-to-read series book.

535 Ruby, Lois. **WHAT DO YOU DO IN QUICKSAND?**. New York. Viking. 1979. 199 p.   (J)

Set in contemporary Houston, this problem novel explores teenage pregnancy, stepparents, child abuse, and mental breakdown in a story with an abrupt, improbable conclusion.

536 Rushmore, Helen. **BIGFOOT WALLACE AND THE HICKORY NUT BATTLE**. Illustrated by George Wilde. Champaign, Ill. Garrard. 1970. 45 p.   **(P I)**

When all the horses in Bug Hollow are stolen, Bigfoot Wallace proves that his feet are smaller than the huge moccasin tracks of the thief. Then he sets off on Chili Bean, his favorite horse, to fight the Comanches, the real thieves. He uses his knowledge of the Indians' superstitious nature to outwit them by stuffing his clothes with hickory nuts and pretending to be the spirit of Limping Grizzly, a powerful medicine man, thereby scaring away the Indians, who leave the stolen horses behind. The humorous tall tale is illustrated with four-color cartoon drawings.

537 Rushmore, Helen. **SANCHO, THE HOMESICK STEER**. Illustrated by Jack Hearne. Champaign, Ill. Garrard. 1972. 62 p.   **(P I)**

Sancho, a motherless calf on the Kerr ranch on San Miguel Creek south of San Antonio, becomes Rosita Kerr's pet, eating her tamales. Taken on a trail drive to Wyoming when he is three years old, the big black-and-white longhorn is homesick all the way, according to Charlie, a cowboy who befriends him. Months later, after retracing the 2,000 mile walk, Sancho returns to the Kerrs. This delightful retelling of a Texas folk tale is more accessible to young readers than Bosworth's longer novel on the same theme.

538 Russell, Donald. **COWBOY ON THE TRAIL**. Illustrated by May Ranft. Westchester, Ill. Benefic Press. 1970. 95 p. (Cowboys of Many Races)   **(P I)**

Cowboy Adam Bradford, a former slave, rides the Chisholm Trail from Texas to Kansas and shows how to develop trust between people of different backgorunds. This 400-word, controlled-vocabulary story portrays the activities of the trail drive, but the excitement, struggle, and flavor of the Old West are missing. Three-color drawings illustrate the six chapters.

539 Sabin, Edwin Legrand. **WITH SAM HOUSTON IN TEXAS: A BOY VOLUNTEER IN THE TEXAS STRUGGLES FOR INDEPENDENCE**. Philadelphia. Lippincott. 1916. 320 p.   **(J)**

Ernest Merrill, a boy on his way to Texas in 1832, meets Sam Houston near Fort Gibson. The character of Houston is explored in considerably more depth than in later juvenile novels. The dark side of his personality is portrayed, as is his rise to leadership in the new nation. Ernest's participation in events, the conversations he overhears, and explanations of the political situation given him by adults are woven into the didactic text, which also includes letters and documents. The story concludes with Houston's inauguration as President of the Republic. The volume includes extensive chronologies of Texas history.

540 Sasek, Miroslav. **THIS IS TEXAS**. New York. Macmillan. 1967. 60 p. **(P)**

Texas geography and history are presented in stylized illustrations in this large picture book. The trait of exaggeration is exhibited in descriptive comments about physical features and important buildings. Sasek's lively style is maintained in another "This Is" book.

541 Saunders, Susan. **FISH FRY**. Illustrated by S.D. Schindler. New York. Viking. 1982. 1 v. (unpaged) **(P)**

Edith, a bright young girl, lives at Chandler in the piney woods of East Texas in 1912. She enjoys the simple pleasures of waving at the train engineer, looking up at the clouds, and socializing at the town fish fry by the river. She is teased by Eugene Greene, the mischievous boy next door, who gets a good spanking for pushing Edith into the river. Text and full-color drawings contain a wealth of detail in this nostalgic picture of turn-of-the-century life.

542 Savitt, Sam. **A DAY AT THE LBJ RANCH**. New York. Random House. 1965. 54 p. **(I P)**

Dennis Hallman, Boy Scout, and Jackie Dixon, Girl Scout, visit President Johnson in this contrived view of the LBJ Ranch on the Pedernales River. Barbecues, calf roping, and other ranch customs are illustrated in a graphic manner.

543 Sayers, Frances Clarke. **BLUEBONNETS FOR LUCINDA**. Illustrated by Helen Sewell. New York. Viking. 1934. 32 p. **(P)**

Lucinda's kind German neighbors on Oleander Island (Galveston) give her a lovely silver music box with a picture on top of a girl gooseherd playing a flute. When Herr and Frau Geranium move to a little farm on the mainland, they invite Lucinda to visit. There she sees a field of bluebonnets for the first time and bewitches the geese with the music box. Sayers's masterful storytelling creates a gentle, charming world, which is reproduced in Sewell's full color folk-style illustrations.

544 Sayers, Frances Clarke. **SALLY TAIT**. Illustrated by Eileen Evans. New York. Viking. 1948. 126 p. **(I J)**

This charming story of nine-year-old Sally Tait's life on Oleander Island in 1912-13 describes in delightful detail her home and school; the pleasures of shopping in town; the social debut of Aunt Cornelia, who comes home from New York for an eight-month visit; and sharing in a loving family. The author's gifts as a storyteller shine in this tale of historic Galveston. Her portrayal of the intensity of the universal pleasures and pains of childhood should appeal to many children.

545 Sayers, Frances Clarke. **TAG-ALONG-TOOLOO**. Illustrated by Helen Sewell. New York. Viking. 1941. 87 p. **(P I)**

Five-year-old Talluluh earns the nickname Tag-along-Tooloo by trying to keep up with her older sister. This an enchanting picture of a little girl's adventures on Oleander Island (Galveston) in a bygone era. She celebrates Christmas, dresses up for the Mardi Gras parade, goes crabbing on the beach, and visits the circus. Tooloo is protected from her misadventures by the cook, kindly Aunt Melaynay, who speaks in dialect. Pastel full-page drawing illustrate the gentle, happy text.

546 Scarborough, Willard Frances. **STORIES FROM THE HISTORY OF TEXAS**. Illustrated by H. Wedemeyer. Dallas. Turner Co. 1929. 138 p. **(I)**

This supplementary reader, written "to kindle human interest in history," meets its objectives within the seven chapters about state history from the period of the Spanish explorers through the war for independence. The readable text, illustrated with maps and black-and-white sketches, provides insights into the human qualities of the historical figures. Reference aids are a word list, bibliography, and pronunciation guide.

547 Schoor, Gene. **BABE DIDRIKSON : THE WORLD'S GREATEST WOMAN ATHLETE**. Garden City, N.Y. Doubleday. 1978. 185 p. **(I J)**

This biography presents a warm, human portrait of the outstanding woman athlete from Beaumont. Dialogue and insights from teachers, sportswriters, and friends enliven the text, which includes background about the social and political climate of the times as well as the record of an exceptional career in sports and a courageous battle against cancer. Sections of black-and-white photographs illustrate the text. An appendix of sports records and an index are included.

548 Schulz, Ellen Dorothy. **TEXAS WILD FLOWERS : A POPULAR ACCOUNT OF THE COMMON WILD FLOWERS OF TEXAS.** Chicago. Laidlaw. 1928. 505 p. **(I J)**

This comprehensive guide to wildflowers, dedicated to the children and flower-loving public of Texas, includes the following information for each flower: scientific name; common name(s); field identification; habitat; and general information about economic value, usefulness, unique characteristics, and folklore or traditions. Black-and-white photographs and color plates illustrate a few of the plants. The user must make a botanical indentification to use the keys to families and know a flower's popular name to locate information through the index.

549 Seaman, Augusta Huiell. **BLUE BONNET BEND.** Illustrated by C.M. Relyea. New York. Century. 1925. 253 p. **(I J)**

Accepting the invitation of Uncle Ezra, sixteen-year-old Katherine and her mother visit Fernandra Ranch near San Antonio in this mystery with a picturesque Texas setting and the intrigue of lost treasure. Katherine's reading of Texas history and interest in the local sites connected with the Revolution enable her and her cousins to discover a valuable old mine which had been lost since its former owner died at the Battle of the Alamo.

550 Sebestyen, Ouida. **FAR FROM HOME.** Boston. Little, Brown. 1980. 187 P. **(J)**

After his mother's death, thirteen-year-old Salty Yeager takes over her job as a servant in a small- town East Texas boardinghouse to support his elderly grandmother and himself. The harsh economic realities of the Depression are interwoven with a complex familial relationship as the boy discovers his past and, in the process, matures.

551 Sebestyen, Ouida. **WORDS BY HEART.** Boston. Little, Brown. 1979. 162 p. **(J)**

Hoping for a better life, a black family moves to Bethel Springs, Texas, in 1910. Teenage Lena, the strong protagonist, learns about racial prejudice after she wins a scripture verse contest. Family love, Christian virtue, violence, and death are themes in this powerful story about a young woman maturing.

552 Sellars, David Kelly. **TEXAS TALES.** Dallas. Noble and Noble. 1955. 274 p. **(J)**

This anthology consists of short stories by well-known authors, songs, and a play, selected from publications of the Texas Folklore Society and other sources, about Texas pioneers, cowboys, lawmen, heroes, and ghosts, from the time of early settlers to the discovery of oil. Prepared for use in seventh grade programs integrating social studies and literature, the book, which is dedicated to J. Frank Dobie, presents the flavor and traditions of the state in a manner suitable for pleasure reading as well as class assignments.

553 Seymour, Flora Warren. **LA SALLE : EXPLORER OF OUR MIDLAND EMPIRE**. Illustrated by Edward Caswell. New York. Appleton. 1939. 236 p. , **(I J)**

A long account of La Salle's last voyage and the establishment of Fort St. Louis of the South near Matagorda Bay in 1685 concludes this biography of a visionary explorer. The hardships and failure of this early French settlement in Texas and the treachery surrounding La Salle's murder are detailed in the text, which is illustrated with black-and-white sketches.

554 Seymour, Flora Warren. **SAM HOUSTON, PATRIOT**. New York. Century. 1930. 232 p. **(I J)**

This is a straightforward biography of Houston's life from his boyhood to his death. The text is full of history, has little dialogue, and is an adequate, if not exciting, presentation by an experienced biographer. The endpapers contain a map of the United States during the period of the Texas Republic with important Houston sites indicated.

555 Shannon, George. **THE PINEY WOODS PEDDLER**. Illustrated by Nancy Tafuri. New York. Greenwillow. 1981. 32 p. **(P)**

Told in the folksong tradition, a jaunty peddler sets out in a rural setting to find a shiny silver dollar for his "dear darling daughter." He makes a series of trades with a barefoot woman, a muleman, a boy with a fine hunting dog, a man with a big wood stick, a long rattlesnake, and a railroad man. The lively, humorous page borders complement the text. The only thing missing is the music of the song.

556 Shapiro, Irwin. **GRETCHEN AND THE WHITE STEED**. Illustrated by Herman Vestal. Champaign, Ill. Garrard. 1972. 63 p. **(P)**

Gretchen, a young pioneer, is lost on the prairie when the old gray mare she is riding wanders away from her wagon train on the way to Texas.

There she meets the legendary White Steed, who shows her where to drink and sleep and leads her back to her worried family. This improbable story in easy-to-read form does not give the source of the legend on which it is based.

557 Shapiro, Irwin. **YANKEE THUNDER : THE LEGENDARY LIFE OF DAVY CROCKETT.** Illustrated by James Daugherty. New York. Messner. 1944. 205 p.   **(J)**

The multiple identities of Crockett--his historical, political, and mythical personae--are revealed in lively retellings of the tales about the hero. Slickerty Sam, the arch villain, a character not usually found in children's versions of Crockett folklore, provides a foil for the hero's exploits. The tall tale exaggeration and good humor make this an exceptional source for storytelling and reading aloud. Daugherty's bold, vital drawings capture the spirit of the character and the text.

558 Sharp, Adda Mai Cummings. **GEE WHILLIKINS.** Illustrated by Elizabeth Rice. Austin. Steck. 1950. 61 p.   **(P)**

Bryce and his wild palomino colt, Gee Whillikins, live and play on a Texas ranch in this illustrated cowboy story.

559 Shefelman, Janice Jordan. **A PARADISE CALLED TEXAS.** Austin. Eakin. 1983. 126 p. (Stories for Young Americans)   **(I)**

In 1845 ten-year-old Mina Jordan and her family leave home in Germany for a new life in Fredericksburg. As a pioneer girl she experiences many hardships and faces hostile Indians before happiness comes to her in her new home. This carefully written novel is based on family stories of the author's ancestors.

560 Shepherd, Elizabeth. **THE DISCOVERIES OF ESTEBAN THE BLACK.** New York. Dodd, Mead. 1970. 122 p.   **(I J)**

The adventures of a 16th-century black who traveled across the Southwest with Cabeza de Vaca are chronicled in this story. Esteban was a member of the small band of survivors from Narvaez's ill-fated Florida expedition which searched for the Seven Cities of Gold, escaped from hostile Indians, and traveled to Mexico City.

561 Sheppard, William Henry Crispin. **THE RAMBLER CLUB ON**

THE TEXAS BORDER. Illustrated by the author. Philadelphia. Penn. 1915. 320 p. **(I J)**

The Rambler Club, composed of five young men from Wisconsin, visit the Texas border country, where they meet some Texas Rangers, become involved in the Mexican struggle between the Constitutionalists and Federalists, help a friend while he decides on a career, and catch some cattle rustlers. One of a series of adventure stories about the Rambler Club boys, the book advocates the healthy outdoor life and the work ethic.

562 Sherwood, Elmer. **TED MARSH AND THE ENEMY.** Illustrated by Neil O'Keeffe. Racine, Wisc. Whitman Pub. Co. 191-. 125 p. **(I J)**

Ted Marsh and his friend Red Mack capture a German spy in Columbus, New Mexico, and return to El Paso, where they hunt down troublemakers on both sides of the border in 1917. One of the Ted Marsh series of adventure stories, whose predictable plot of stereotypes and heroics draws on the political situation of the period for colorful characters such as Pancho Villa and General "Fighting Fred" Funston.

563 Shuffler, Ralph Henderson. **MANY TEXANS : A GATHERING OF CULTURES.** Illustrated by Barbara Whitehead. Dallas. Hendrick-Long. 1970. 222 p. **(I J)**

This anthology consists of forty-six readings, mainly biographical sketches of Texans from the first settlers to more recent residents, but with some selections about ethnic customs, historical events, and places, which first appeared in the **Houston Chronicle**. The supplementary reader was designed to improve reading skills with aids of marginal headings and study questions. Attractive, bold, detailed woodcuts decorate the text.

564 Silcott, Philip B. **COWBOYS.** Illustrated by Martin Rogers. Washington, D.C. National Geographic Society. 1975. 32 p. (Books for Young Explorers Series) **(P)**

Contemporary cowboy life on a large Texas ranch is depicted in picture-book format with simple text and full-color photographs. Rancher Mac Morrow and his family are shown caring for cattle and horses and doing chores such as windmill repair and fence mending.

565 Silliman, Leland. **GOLDEN CLOUD IN TEXAS.** Illustrated by Pers Crowell. Philadelphia. Winston. 1953. 243 p. **(J)**

Golden Cloud, a palomino horse, is brought from Oklahoma to Texas to compete in a contest. The kidnapping of the horse adds suspense to the story of ranch life.

566 Silverthorne, Elizabeth. **THE GHOST OF PADRE ISLAND**. Illustrated by Dennis Anderson. Nashville. Abingdon. 1975. 174 p. **(I)**

A family camping on Padre Island searches for a lost Indian site and finds treasure and the identity of a ghost. Descriptions of the vacation trip are spiced by a gentle mystery.

567 Simond, Ada DeBlanc. **LET'S PRETEND : MAE DEE AND HER FAMILY AND THE FIRST WEDDING OF THE YEAR**. Illustrated by Sarochin Shannon. Austin. Stevenson. 1979. 145 p. (National History Series, USA) **(I J)**

This fifth book in the "Let's Pretend" series tells of preparations for a January wedding, including sewing a friendship quilt as a gift.

568 Simond, Ada DeBlanc. **LET'S PRETEND : MAE DEE AND HER FAMILY GO TO TOWN**. Illustrated by Sarochin Shannon. Austin. Stevenson. 1977. 63 p. (National History Series, USA) **(I J)**

In this first of the "Let's Pretend" series about a rural black family at the turn of the 20th century, the family goes to Austin for the day to shop and do errands. Illustrated with drawings and photographs, the book gives a realistic glimpse of life at that time.

569 Simond, Ada DeBlanc. **LET'S PRETEND : MAE DEE AND HER FAMILY IN THE MERRY, MERRY SEASON**. Illustrated by Sarochin Shannon. Austin. Stevenson. 1978. 131 p. (National History Series, USA) **(I J)**

This fourth book in the "Let's Pretend" series highlights family and community activities during the Thanksgiving and Christmas holidays and visits to an orphanage and to an "old folks' home."

570 Simond, Ada DeBlanc. **LET'S PRETEND : MAE DEE AND HER FAMILY JOIN THE JUNETEENTH CELEBRATION**. Illustrated by Sarochin Shannon. Austin. Stevenson. 1978. 165 p. (National History Series, USA) **(I J)**

This third book in the "Let's Pretend" series describes festivities in honor of Emancipation Day, including speeches, music, games, and a barbecue. The Knights of Pythias convention brings more summertime activities.

571 Simond, Ada DeBlanc. **LET'S PRETEND : MAE DEE AND HER FAMILY ON A WEEKEND IN MAY.** Illustrated by Sarochin Shannon. Austin. Stevenson. 1977. 95 p. (National History Series, USA)   **(I J)**

This second book in the "Let's Pretend" series finds the family doing its Saturday chores and enjoying the May Day celebration in which young Emmaressa has a major role. The father teaches the children self-respect and respect for each other.

572 Simond, Ada DeBlanc. **LET'S PRETEND : MAE DEE AND HER FAMILY TEN YEARS LATER.** Illustrated by Sarochin Shannon. Austin. Stevenson. 1980. 151 p. (National History Series, USA) **(I J)**

This sixth book in the "Let's Pretend" series, winner of a special award from the Texas Historical Commission, relates the death of Emmaressa, Charley's joining the Army during "The Great War," and the beginning of Mae Dee's teaching career in 1922 after her graduation from Prairie View A&M.

573 Slicer, Margaret O. **THE BALLOON FARM.** Illustrated by William Hunter. Nashville. Abingdon. 1968. 40 p.   **(P)**

This picture book fantasy with bright pink and orange illustrations is an account of what happens when Malone's Carnival Show is swapped for Farmer Merryfield's land in Crazy County, Texas. The Malones grow balloons and send baskets filled with candy hearts tied to bunches of balloons all over the country, causing people to be nice to each other. Texas exaggeration, sunny weather, and wide-open spaces add a light touch to the story, which first appeared in **The Instructor.**

574 Smith, Beatrice S. **THE ROAD TO GALVESTON.** Minneapolis. Lerner. 1973. 127 p.   **(J)**

After his mother dies of typhoid fever, fourteen-year-old Joe Reno leaves the small Colorado town where he grew up in search of his father, who he hates for abandoning him and his mother. Joe is robbed while traveling by train to Spurr Center, Texas, his father's last known address. As he locates clues to his father's whereabouts, Joe works and learns about his own talents. He finds his father in Galveston, just as the 1901 hurricane destroys the city, killing his father. This story of a boy's search for identity is full of adventure and humor.

575 Smyrl, Frank Herbert. **POLEY MORGAN : SON OF A TEXAS SCALAWAG.** Illustrated by Donald Van Horn. Tyler. Book Publishers of Texas. 1982. 63 p.   **(I J)**

Smyrl writes about his grandfather's youth in a carefully researched novel of rural life during Reconstruction in Smith County. Poley had to run the family farm after his father was killed in 1870.

576 **SONGS TEXAS SINGS.** Dallas. Turner Co. 1936. 31 p.   **(I J)**

Compiled by the Public School Division of the Texas Department of Publicity for Centennial Celebrations for use by Texas school children, this collection of twenty-eight cowboy, patriotic, and traditional songs represents the spirit and regional color of the state. Comments by John Lomax indicate that the most popular song in the collection is "The Eyes of Texas" and that the twelve cowboy songs best represent the state. Most of the songs are still familiar fifty years later.

577 Spears, Patricia Lynn. **ANGELINA.** Illustrated by Ann Pressly. Austin. Eakin. 1984. 142 p. (Stories for Young Americans)   **(I)**

The daughter of a Hasinai Indian Princess and a Spanish soldier, Angelina came to the Franciscan mission of San Juan Bautista in the early 1700s. The dangers and hardships of mission life, the beauty of the natural surroundings, and acts of human kindness are woven into this fictionalized story of a historical person.

578 Sprague, William Cyrus. **DAVY CROCKETT.** New York. Macmillan. 1915. 189 p.   **(J)**

This straightforward biography of a Texas hero Includes long excerpts from writings and dairies attributed to Crockett. He is portrayed as a pure patriot and martyr to freedom, singing "Up with Your Banner Freedom" at the Alamo. The book is one of a series about events in the careers of makers of the nation published prior to World War I.

579 Staffelbach, Elmer Hubert. **FOR TEXAS AND FREEDOM.** Illustrated by Hugh Wiley. Philadelphia. Macrae Smith. 1948. 271 p. **(I J)**

President Andrew Jackson entrusts Pierre Garonne, an orphaned French noble, with a secret message for Sam Houston. In spite of Mexican spies who try to waylay him, Pierre reaches Texas in time to deliver the message; spy on Santa Anna's camp; escape from El Tigre, a treacherous scout; and witness major battles of the Revolution. Political intrigue in the struggle for westward expansion and fictional villains provide more adventures than the usual ones found in novels set in the Texas Revolution.

580 Steen, Ralph Wright. **TEXAS NEWS : A MISCELLANY OF TEXAS HISTORY IN NEWSPAPER STYLE.** Austin. Steck. 1955. 187 p. **(J)**

Historical events from March 1493 to December 31, 1940, are presented in newspaper format for the purpose of enlivening the study of history and encouraging students to use newspapers as a historical reference source. International and national events give perspective to state and local happenings reported for the same period. The format might be misleading, because the pages which contain historically accurate materials are not actual reproductions of newspapers.

581 Steiner, Stanley. **THE TIGUAS : THE LOST TRIBE OF CITY INDIANS.** New York. Crowell-Collier. 1972. 90 p. **(I J)**

Tigua Indians, believed by many to be extinct, have actually maintained their tribal society in Ysleta del Sur, an El Paso suburb, since 1682. Speaking Spanish and English in addition to Tiwa, the old tongue, members of the state's oldest identifiable tribe blend into modern society; Catholic feast days and old Indian rituals are combined. This fascinating exploration of tribal history and modern status is ilustrated with black-and-white photographs.

582 Stevens, Mary Ellen and Sayles, Edwin Booth. **LITTLE CLOUD AND THE GREAT PLAINS HUNTERS, 15,000 YEARS AGO.** Illustrated by Barton Wright. Chicago. Reilly & Lee. 1962. 155 p. **(I J)**

Little Cloud, a twelve-year-old boy who yearns to be a hunter, belongs to the Camel Band of prehistoric hunters who roam the Great Plains in search of food. This fictional reconstruction brings to life the social organization and habits of an ancient people. Little Cloud's courage in finding a path into the Palo Duro Canyon and frightening off the enormous elephants leads to his acceptance among his people. The carefully illustrated story is the result of collaboration among a writer, an anthropologist, and an archaeologist.

583 Stevenson, Augusta. **SAM HOUSTON : BOY CHIEFTAIN.** Illustrated by Paul Laune. Indianapolis. Bobbs-Merrill. 1944. 199 p. (The Childhood of Famous Americans Series)   **(I)**

This simple biography of the Texas hero concentrates on the formative period between his seventh year and his teens, when he lived with the Cherokees. The final chapter outlines Houston's career and achievements. The easy text illustrated with black silhouettes, typical of the series, has been updated in a 1962 edition, in which dialect is deleted but the text remains basically unchanged.

584 Stoddard, William Osborn. **THE LOST GOLD OF THE MONTEZUMAS : A STORY OF THE ALAMO.** Illustrated by Charles H. Stephens. Philadelphia. Lippincott. 1900. 309 p.
(J)

In 1835 the Tlascalan Indians are dying out and need some way to meet the demands of the old gods for human sacrifice without reducing their own number. They devise a plan to use Texas revolutionaries as cat's-paws to kill their enemies, the Mexicans, and thereby appease the gods. Red Wolf, a young Indian, lures Jim Bowie to Mexico with the promise of hidden Aztec treasure to buy weapons for the Texas army. Bowie returns to Texas and dies at the Alamo before the treasure can be transported and put to use, and Red Wolf witnesses the battle knowing that Bowie, having viewed the secret treasure of the gods, is doomed. The adventure is a farfetched mixture of history, legend, and imagination.

585 Stong, Philip Duffield. **COWHAND GOES TO TOWN.** Illustrated by Kurt Wiese. New York. Dodd, Mead. 1939. 85 p.   **(I)**

The playful, light-hearted story of twelve-year-old Sam, beloved son of a prosperous Texas rancher, relates his adventures at a Circle V Ranch roundup and his first trip to Kansas City. Storytelling and good-natured teasing fill the humorous text, which is illustrated with Kurt Wiese's bright, informal drawings.

586 Stover, Marjorie Filley. **TRAIL BOSS IN PIGTAILS**. Illustrated by Lydia Dabcovich. New York. Atheneum. 1972. 220 p.   **(I J)**

After Emma Jane Burke's father dies, having charged her with the responsibility of providing for her mother and five younger siblings, the fifteen-year-old girl serves as trail boss for the family's eighty-two longhorns on their 1859 drive from Waco to Chicago. The shrewd, spunky girl meets danger head-on, getting the herd to Chicago, where it earns enough to provide the independent future her father wished for the family. The colorful cattle trail story, with a young woman as the unusual protagonist, is based on family history.

587 Stratton, Florence. **WHEN THE STORM GOD RIDES : TEJAS AND OTHER INDIAN LEGENDS**. Illustrated by Benniece Burrough. New York. Scribner. 1936. 243 p.   **(I)**

This absorbing collection of thirty-one simple retellings of legends of the Indians of Texas includes the legend of the bluebonnet, "Kachina Brings the Spring," and variants of "The Hare and the Tortoise" and "Pandora," as well as stories of the origin of familiar plants and animals. Bold drawings of Indian motifs, colored in bright earth tones, enhance the feeling of the text. A concluding chapter, "About the Tejas Indians," presents their history, beliefs, appearance, and daily life. A key to symbols in the drawings is included in this outstanding book.

588 Syme, Ronald. **FIRST MAN TO CROSS AMERICA : THE STORY OF CABEZA DE VACA** Illustrated by William Stobbs. New York. Morrow. 1961. 190 p.   **(I)**

This well-written, insightful biography of Alvar Nunez de Vaca, better known by his noble name, Cabeza de Vaca, includes a detailed account of his landing in Texas and the years he spent living with the Indians from the Gulf Coast to El Paso, 1528 to 1536, as recorded in his amazing diary. Cabeza de Vaca's extraordinary will to live and ability to communicate with the Indians are sympathetically portrayed.

589 Tarkington, Kate. **REX GOES TO THE RODEO**. San Antonio. Naylor. 1955. 38 p.   **(I)**

Eight-year-old Rex visits the midway and attends the rodeo at San Antonio Coliseum. He meets Cowboy Steve, who tells him about ranch life in Wyoming and the Cheyenne Frontier Days celebration, and gives him a rodeo ticket to replace the one he lost. The simple, slight story reflects the safe 1950s, when children were not afraid of strangers.

590 Taylor, Florance Walton. **FROM TEXAS TO ILLINOIS.** Minneapolis. Lerner. 1971. 32 p. (A Felipe Adventure Story) **(P I)**

Ten-year-old Felipe Fuentes and his family leave their home in the Rio Grande Valley for summer farm work in Illinois. Big Pablo, the crew leader, takes the group to a farm near a large canning company, where they have decent living quarters with their friends from home. The children attend school while the adults work. This large-type, simple text presents a sanitized version of the life of migrant workers.

591 Taylor, Florance Walton. **NAVY WINGS OF GOLD.** Illustrated by Harve Stein. Chicago. Whitman. 1944. 232 p. **(I)**

Three young men go through a year of training during World War II to be commissioned as ensigns in the U.S. Naval Reserve and earn the gold wings signifying a naval aviator. They are introduced to flying at primary training in Grand Prairie, Texas, and move to the University of the Air at Corpus Christi for advanced training. Military routine and terminology, the excitement of flying the PBY (the flying boxcar) and the Grumman fighters in preparation for war service, and the reality of the Texas weather, with its hot sun, hurricanes, and northers, are combined in this authentic boys' story.

592 Taylor, Ross McLaury. **WE WERE THERE ON THE CHISHOLM TRAIL.** Illustrated by Charles Banks Wilson. New York. Grosset & Dunlap. 1957. 176 p. (We Were There Series, 14) **(I)**

Fourteen-year-old Lance Calhoun sets out on a trail drive from his father's ranch near San Antonio to Abilene with the first herd over the Chisholm Trail in 1868. Colonel Calhoun's crew meets the dangers of weather, Indians, and outlaws with the assistance of an Army Cavalry escort through part of the Indian Territory. Young hero Lance's fast action in emergencies saves the herd and the crew on several dangerous occasions in this fast-paced novel.

593 Templeton, R. Lee. **ALAMO SOLDIER : THE STORY OF PEACEFUL MITCHELL.** Quanah, Tex. Nortex. 1976. 158 p. (Stories for Young Americans) **(J)**

Napoleon Bonaparte Mitchell, a seventeen-year-old member of the Tennessee Mounted Volunteers, sees the events leading up to the battle of the Alamo from the perspective of a young man who does not like to fight. This realistic portrayal of a soldier's life, including its seamier side, is for mature readers who enjoy a lively, historically accurate story.

594 Templeton, R. Lee. **CANNON BOY OF THE ALAMO**. Quanah, Tex. Nortex. 1975. 137 p. (Stories for Young Americas)   **(J)**

A fifteen-year-old farm boy from Gonzales, Billy King was the youngest volunteer to fight and die at the Alamo. He was assigned to work for Sergeant Ward, the cannoneer, who instructed him in the historical background of the cannon as well as its use.

595 Templeton, R. Lee. **THE DEATH OF JIMMY LITTLEWOLF : AN INDIAN BOY AT BOYS RANCH**. Burnet, Tex. Eakin. 1980. 105 p. (Stories for Young Americans)   **(J)**

An Indian boy runs away from Cal Farley's Boys Ranch near Amarillo, fearing he will die of tuberculosis. The young Comanche and three friends from the ranch are befriended by a deaf girl, whose faith in them leads to a happy ending. Descriptions of the Panhandle terrain form the background for a melodramatic story of a successful social agency.

596 Templeton, R. Lee. **LITTLE GIRL LOST**. Austin. Eakin. 1983. 82 p. (Stories for Young Americans)   **(I)**

Sissy, a frail, mentally retarded girl, disappears after a school bus accident. The rural Panhandle community searches the range for her. Buz, an orphaned, independent young buzzard, finds her. Colloquial dialect and description of the landscape add flavor to the mystery.

597 Templeton, R. Lee. **SILVER TIP : MY CRIPPLED COYOTE**. Austin. Eakin. 1983. 112 p. (Stories for Young Americans)   **(I J)**

Jaime Bell, a twelve-year-old boy grieving his father's death, befriends a three-legged coyote in 1896 Panhandle country. Their adventures in capturing a wild mare and her colt help Jaime in growing up and accepting death and life.

598 TEXAS WILDLIFE : PHOTOGRAPHS FROM TEXAS PARKS AND WILDLIFE MAGAZINE. College Station. Texas A&M University Press. 1978. 196 p. (Louise Lindsey Merrick Texas Environment Series)   **(P I J)**

Close-up color plates of wildlife in its natural habitat show the beauty found in abundance and diversity in ten ecological regions of Texas. Looking at these photographs of javelina, armadillo, chachalaca, alligator, coral snake, white-tailed deer, and many other species is almost as exciting as seeing them in the wild. A brief introduction gives the history and current status of wildlife management in Texas. Reference aids are notes containing frequency of occurence of the species, photographic credits, and an index of common and scientific names.

599 Thompson, Corrie. **MY BEACH BUDDIES OF BYGONE DAYS : A BOOK FOR CHILDREN ABOUT THE SEASHORE OF TEXAS**. Quanah, Tex. Nortex. 1974. 91 p. **(P I)**

The author's reminiscences of her turn-of-the-century childhood in Rockport, vignettes of nature study about seashore animals, and a few poems form this episodic potpourri, illustrated with drawings and poor quality black-and-white photographs of interesting old buildings and people.

600 Thomson, Peter. **LONGHORNS TO ABILENE**. Chicago. Follett. 1965. 191 p. **(J)**

After the Civil War sixteen-year-old, orphaned Jim Ryan is hired by the Tepee Spread as an all-around handyman. Frisco, the cook, teaches Jim to ride and rope, enabling him to be a wrangler on the Chisholm Trail cattle drive to Abilene, Kansas. Bullied and put under suspicion by a mean-tempered cowboy, Jim proves his loyalty and bravery by pursuing stolen horses, showing once again that hard work and a kind heart can overcome adversity.

601 Tinkle, Lon. **THE KEY TO DALLAS**. Philadelphia. Lippincott. 1965. 128 p. (Keys to the Cities Series) **(I J)**

This skillfully written presentation of information about Dallas--its past and present leaders, economy, traditions, cultural affairs, and growth--covers the period from 1842 Peters' Colony to the mid-1960s. Civic projects and an abiding fondness for what is new are shown to be traits of the dynamic city. Photographs and maps illustrate the people and places mentioned in this carefully produced work.

602 Tinkle, Lon. **THE VALIANT FEW : CRISIS AT THE ALAMO**. New York. Macmillan. 1964. 90 p. (The Macmillan Battle Books) **(I J)**

The thirteen-day siege of the Alamo is the focus of this outstanding book, which places the conflict within a historical context and introduces the major personalities on both sides. Details of political and military history, often lacking in juvenile literature, give an understanding of both sides of the battle. A five-page chronology, 1803-1836, diagrams of the battle, paintings, engravings, and maps embellish the text.

603 Toepperwein, Fritz Arnold. **CHINTO, THE CHAPARRAL COCK.** Illustrated by Emilie Toepperwein. Boerne, Tex. Highland Press. 1953. 48 p. **(P I)**

Eight-year-old Kenito Vinto lives with his parents on the Roberts Ranch in southwest Texas, where his family has lived for generations. Kenito loves the wildlife he observes in nature, caring for wounded birds and animals. For a birthday present, he gives Julia Roberts a chaparral cock, or road runner, he captured. Chinto, Julia's favorite gift, kills a giant diamondback rattlesnake in the ranch yard, becoming a hero. The charming, realistic story is decorated with folkstyle drawings of the people and animals in the text.

604 Toepperwein, Fritz Arnold. **I WANT TO BE A COWBOY.** Illustrated by Emilie Toepperwein. Boerne, Tex. Highland Press. 1947. 80 p. **(P I)**

Two Eastern children spend their summer vacation on the Circle H Ranch with their Uncle Frank, Aunt Mitty, and Cousin Henry. The two ask a steady stream of questions about the history, customs, and daily activities of cowboys and eagerly participate in life on the ranch. Realistic drawings visually represent the story, which is the answer to the dream of every child who wants to be a cowboy or cowgirl.

605 Toepperwein, Fritz Arnold. **LITTLE DEPUTY.** Illustrated by Emilie Toepperwein. Boerne, Tex. Highland Press. 1949. 62 p. **(I)**

A small frontier German village on the way to Fort Concho is the setting for seven-year-old Arnold Tepper's adventures as he helps his deputy sheriff father guard and care for prisoners in the county jail. The prisoners give the Little Deputy a toy pistol, carve a grave marker when his pet cat dies, and demand that he serve their meals when a new sheriff replaces the deputy. This charming tale of early Texas is the second volume in the Uncle Kris series.

606 Toepperwein, Fritz Arnold. **LITTLE MISS CRINOLINE**. Illustrated by Emilie Toepperwein. Boerne, Tex. Highland Press. 1951. 48 p. **(P I)**

Seven-year-old Gretchen Trost, blue-eyed and blond, is a favorite with the adults in her small village near Comal Springs. The sweet girl is nicknamed Miss Crinoline because of the crinoline her mother sews in her dresses. Four bad boys play pranks on her, getting her into trouble with her dancing teacher and the man she helps herd cattle. This is a charming, nostalgic story of the good old days in a small German community, decorated with equally charming illustrations.

607 Toepperwein, Fritz Arnold. **UNCLE KRIS AND HIS PETS**. Illustrated by Emilie Toepperwein. Boerne, Tex. Highland Press. 1949. 33 p. **(P)**

Uncle Kris is a kindly, older man who resembles Santa Claus with his white mustache and jolly face. This is a simple story about an animal lover who surrounds himself with pets: a dog, a goat, a donkey, several cats and colorful birds. Realistic, detailed woodblocks printed in a different color on each page and handset type make this a special example of fine bookmaking in Texas.

608 Toepperwein, Fritz Arnold. **UNCLE KRIS IN HIS WORKSHOP**. Illustrated by Emilie Toepperwein. Boerne, Tex. Highland Press. 1955. 32 p. **(P)**

Eighty-year-old Uncle Kris has a warm relationship with his young grandson Kenny. A talented craftsman, he uses his woodworking skills to make a small workbench for Kenny's fifth birthday and a folding rocking chair for sale. The picture story, set in a Central Texas village, demonstrates a loving relationship, an enjoyment of nature, and a pride in workmanship. Folkstyle illustrations in different colors decorate the text.

609 Treuhardt, Beverly Huie and Murdock, Marie. **SAM BASS**. Illustrated by Ralph White. Austin. Steck. 1958. 140 p. (Wings Books) **(I)**

This fictional biography of the legendary Bass, who died at age twenty-seven in Round Rock in 1878, shows his gradual change from an honest boy to a desperate outlaw. Throughout the exciting story there is a strong moral tone indicating that crime doesn't pay and that Sam goes wrong and dies because he doesn't listen "to that little voice inside him." The lively text is illustrated with realistic drawings by Ralph White.

610 Trumbull, Jane. **SHIRLEY TAKES A CHANCE.** Illustrated by Dorothy Lake Gregory. Chicago. Rand McNally. 1927. 377 p. **(I J)**

Shirley King's family moves to an old rundown farm in Midvale for father's rest and recovery from nervous collapse. The 1920s girls' story shows Shirley, a city girl, valiantly helping her family and making friends in the country. The beautiful spring flowers are described. Prevalent attitudes toward blacks are in evidence in this light novel.

611 Tveten, John L. **EXPLORING THE BAYOUS.** Illustrated by the author. New York. McKay. 1979. 88 p. **(I J)**

A clear understanding of the total environment and importance of the bayou is evident in this readable text illustrated with black-and-white photographs by a Texas author. Half of the book describes the plants and animals indigenous to the bayou region and their ecology. Other chapters of interest include a vignette of a day and night on the bayou; a sketch of Houston, the Bayou City; an outline of the economic wealth of fur, lumber, and oil taken from the bayou; and a description of Armand Bayou, the nature center near Houston.

612 Upshaw, Hazel Cooke. **THE WONDERS OF TEXAS : OR, TEXAS AT WORK.** San Antonio. Naylor. 1939. 266 p. **(J)**

Economic conditions, agriculture, and industry in Texas are presented in a textbook format of short chapters followed by questions and suggestions for study. **My State: Texas**, a revised edition, was published in 1951.

613 Van Steenwyk, Elizabeth. **RODEO.** New York. Harvey House. 1978. 78 p. (Women in Sports) **(I)**

Shelia Bussy of Hallsville and Benjie Prudom of Dallas are among the eight women in rodeo competition presented in short biographical sketches. The origin of the rodeo and standard events are described and illustrated with photographs.

614 Vinton, Iris. **PASSAGE TO TEXAS.** Illustrated by Kathleen Elgin. New York. Aladdin. 1952. 192 p. (American Heritage) **(I J)**

Hal Woodley and three friends transport cattle and other possessions by flatboat down the Mississippi from Natchez to New Orleans. From there they travel by schooner to Matagorda Bay on their way to the Mexican land grant on which they settle.

615 Vogt, Lynn McEntire. **COME COLOR DALLAS : A COLORING BOOK**. Illustrated by the author. Dallas. Dallas County Heritage Society. 1975. 24 p.   **(P)**

This picture book in coloring book format highlights Dallas history of interest to children.

616 von Rosenberg, Marjorie. **GERMAN ARTISTS OF EARLY TEXAS : HERMANN LUNGKWITZ AND RICHARD PETRI.** Austin. Eakin. 1982. 98 p. (Stories for Young Americans)   **(I)**

Richard Petri and Hermann Lungkwitz, 1850s German pioneers in Fredericksburg, were members of large, close-knit, industrious, well-educated families. Petri drew family members as they went about their daily activities and the exotic Indians and camels found in the area. Lungkwitz was the official photographer for the Texas Land Office and later painted two famous landscapes hanging in the Capitol. Charming drawings by the artists illustrate the text, which includes a bibliography.

617 Waldron, Ann. **THE HOUSE ON PENDLETON BLOCK**. Illustrated by Sonia Lisker. New York. Hastings House. 1975. 151 p.   **(I J)**

When eleven-year-old Chrissie Ranson's family moves to contemporary Dallas, her mother rents a rundown mansion from wealthy Alberta Hamilton's estate. Chrissie becomes absorbed in learning about the former mistress of the mansion, reading her letters and newspaper clippings, learning about her art collection, and discovering the valuable abstract paintings are missing. This is a plausible, breezy mystery with a bright young heroine and amusing, eccentric characters, but it lacks a sense of local color and place.

618 Waldron, Ann. **THE INTEGRATION OF MARY-LARKIN THORNHILL**. New York. Dutton. 1975. 137 p.   **(I J)**

This fictional account of Houston school desegregation revolves around the changes in a Southern girl's life as she enters an integrated junior high.

619 Waltrip, Lela and Waltrip, Rufus. **WHITE HARVEST**. Illustrated by Christine Price. New York. Longmans, Green. 1960. 118 p.   **(P I)**

Susan Mathis and her large family, poor white migrant workers, live in a tent, following the cotton crop. After industrious young Susan wins a gold piece for picking cotton and a blue ribbon for a handmade quilt, she convinces the family to travel across Texas by covered wagon to homestead in New Mexico in 1912.

620 Warren, Betsy. **INDIANS WHO LIVED IN TEXAS.** Illustrated by the author. Austin. Steck Vaughn. 1970. 48 p. **(P I)**

The daily life and customs of four Indian groups-- farmers, fishermen, plant gatherers, and hunters-- who comprised the ten major tribes in Texas are pictured in Warren's drawings and text. A useful index and glossary are included.

621 Warren, Betsy and Ingerson, Martha. **THE STORY OF TEXAS : A HISTORY PICTURE BOOK.** Illustrated by the authors. Austin. Ranch Gate. 1974. 46 p. **(P I)**

Charming line drawings illustrate the pictorial history of Texas from early Indian tribes and European explorers and settlers to modern times. Historical events, persons, and flora and fauna important to Texas are shown in this good overview suitable for any collection.

622 Warren, Robert Penn. **REMEMBER THE ALAMO.** Illustrated by William Moyers. New York. Random House. 1958. 182 p. (Landmark Books, 79) **(I)**

The battle of the Alamo is the focus of this history of the Texas Revolution written by a Pulitzer prize winning author. Background about the changing boundaries of the United States; Spanish attempts to settle northern Mexico; biographical sketches of Austin, Houston, Santa Anna, Travis, Bowie, and Crockett; and a commentary on the siege and battle are objectively presented. The text is largely narrative, with brief conversations interpreted from diaries, letters, and legends of the period. The author discusses sources of evidence and refers to technical descriptions made by retired Army Captain R.M. Potter.

623 Watson, Junius. **JOE JACOBY.** New York. McCall. 1970. 185 p. **(I J)**

Joe Jacoby, an outstanding English setter, was born in deep East Texas during the Depression in the home of Alice and Jed Crenshaw, a kind, poor young couple. Matt Brandt, a young orphan living with the Crenshaws, adored Joe and waited for his return from a rich sportsman.

624 Watson, Junius. **SHAG CHACOTA**. Quanah, Tex. Nortex. 1978. 141 p. (Stories for Young Americans)   **(I J)**

A boy-dog story about Trap, a beagle; Ben Holt, who was staying on his grandparents' East Texas farm; and Shag Chacota, an unusual, cross-cultural Indian, who befriends Ben and teaches him nature lore and woodsman's skills, bee hunting, canoe building, and survival close to nature. The story takes place in the recent past and embodies heightened multicultural awareness.

625 Webb, Walter Prescott. **THE STORY OF THE TEXAS RANGERS**. Illustrated by Nicholas Eggenhofer. New York. Grosset & Dunlap. 1957. 152 p. (Illustrated True Books)   **(J)**

This episodic history of the Texas Rangers from the time of their founding tells about colorful individuals and events, with emphasis on the glorious 19th-century battles against Indians, Mexicans, and outlaws, but with several chapters about the adventures of the 20th-century Rangers. The lifestyle of the Rangers, their work and play, are described in realistic narrative, some of which is taken from their own writings. Large black-and-white sketches enhance the text written by the renowned Texas historian. A second edition was published by Encino Press in 1971.

626 Webber, Malcolm. **JIMCO AND HARRY AT THE ROCKING H**. Illustrated by Virginia Mull. Chicago. Wilcox & Follett. 1947. 247 p.   **(I J)**

The contemporary boys' adventure story takes place on the Rocking H Ranch, where Harry visits his uncle who is boss of the ranch. Tenderfoot Harry and his friend Jimco have a rapid series of cowboy experiences climaxed by an exciting rodeo at the Plainville Cowboys' Reunion.

627 Wellman, Paul Iselin. **THE GREATEST CATTLE DRIVE**. Illustrated by Lorence Bjorklund. Boston. Houghton Mifflin. 1964. 185 p. (North Star Books, 37)   **(I J)**

In 1866 Nelson Story, with a crew of twenty-two rough, brave Texans, leads a herd of one thousand cattle from Texas to Montana over the Sedalia Trail to Fort Leavenworth, then on the Oregon Trail and the

Bozeman Trail. With incredible courage and good fortune the drive survives Jayhawkers, Indians, Army hostility, floods, a dry march, and a blizzard. This true story is more exciting than any fictional trail drive adventure. The fast-paced narrative includes extensive details of a trail drive, some of which are in footnotes, and is fully illustrated with realistic brown-and-white pencil drawings.

628 Westman, Paul. **WALTER CRONKITE : THE MOST TRUSTED MAN IN AMERICA**. Minneapolis. Dillon. 1980. 47 p. (Taking Part Books) **(P I)**

A Texan from age ten until he left the University of Texas, Cronkite is portrayed in a favorable light in this easy-to-read biography. Fifty years of American history are briefly sketched in the context of the career of the internationally esteemed news reporter.

629 Whitehead, Ruth. **THE MOTHER TREE**. Illustrated by Charles Robinson. New York. Seabury Press. 1971. 149 p.   **(I)**

In a story set in rural turn-of-the-century West Texas, eleven-year-old Tempe Foster assumes the care of her four-year-old sister Laurie after their mother's death and is frustrated by Laurie's constant questions about when her mother will be home again. The girls spend the summer on their grandparents' farm while their father and brother are working on a threshing crew. They play in a large old mesquite tree, which Laurie calls the Mother Tree. Tempe gains insight and acceptance of her mother's death during her long struggle toward maturity. The moving story gives a strong sense of place with details such as the windmill and a violent summer storm.

630 Whitehouse, Eula. **TEXAS WILDFLOWERS IN NATURAL COLORS**. Illustrated by the author. Austin. Privately published; distributed by Texas Book Store. 1936. 212 p.   **(P I J)**

This manual provides help in identifying common wildflowers with its 257 watercolor plates, notes about family characteristics, and popular descriptions which include season of appearance, color, locale, use, and origin of names. The excellent reference aids are a finding list by colors and by season of flowering, an index of common Latin names, diagrams of plant parts, and a map of plant distribution. The third edition of this useful and beautifully illustrated book was published by the Dallas County Audubon Society in 1967.

631 Whitney, David C. **THE PICTURE LIFE OF LYNDON BAINES JOHNSON.** New York. Watts. 1967. 53 p.   **(P I)**

This easy-to-read biography emphasizes Johnson's career as a prominent national political leader with strong Texas roots. Black-and-white photographs illustrate each step in his life and career.

632 Wilkerson, Jesse. **COME HOME, BILL BAILEY.** San Antonio. Naylor. 1955. 141 p.   **(I)**

Set in Cameron in 1900, this is the story of Jim Wilson, a twelve-year-old boy who wants a horse of his own. Horse Trader Hawkins, an itinerant dealer, gives Jim a bay with a black mare named Bill Bailey. When Jim goes on a trip with Horse Trader, he learn about the good and evil of human personalities. Lyric description of the rural landscape and black and white dialect in conversation provide abundant local color for the melodramatic story.

633 Wilkerson, Jesse. **COMRADES OF THE CANYONS.** San Antonio. Naylor. 1957. 54 p.   **(I)**

In 1870 Shep, an enormous shepherd dog, is stolen from a San Antonio family and taken west in a wagon train. The lone survivor of an Indian raid, Shep wanders across the desert to the Sierra Blanca country, where he saves a beautiful, young white stallion from coyotes. Shep and Big Stoney travel together in the wild until they are befriended by pioneer ranchers. The improbable story gives a sense of place of the West Texas cattle country.

634 Wilkie, Katherine Elliott. **ZACH TAYLOR, YOUNG ROUGH AND READY.** Illustrated by Syd Browne. Indianapolis. Bobbs-Merrill. 1952. 194 p. (The Childhood of Famous Americans Series)   **(I)**

In this patriotic biography of the hero of the Mexican War and the twelfth President, Taylor is portrayed in familiar series format. Taylor was commander of the U.S. troops which forced Mexico to relinquish the area between the Nueces and Rio Grande Rivers when Texas was annexed.

635 Wilkinson, Pamela Fannin. **RIDIN' THE RAINBOW : A TEXAS LEPRECHAUN TALE** Illustrated by Real Musgrave. San Antonio. Corona. 1981. 40 p.   **(P)**

Mallory O'Shea slides down the rainbow to find the pot of gold he is assigned to keep safe by the Matagorda Bay Leprechaun Assembly. Irish and Texas folklore are combined in the story, which is illustrated with greeting card style drawings and includes music and lyrics to "Ridin' the Rainbow."

636 Williams, J.R. **THE CONFEDERATE FIDDLE**. Englewood Cliffs, N.J. Prentice Hall. 1962. 192 p. **(J)**

Sixteen-year-old Vin Clayburn drives a wagonload of cotton from Missouri to Brownsville in 1863 to raise money for the Confederacy. He resents having the unglamourous job while his older brother goes to fight in the war. The novel explains the Confederate political and economic positions within the context of the family's sacrifice of treasured heirlooms for medicines for the troops. Historical figures such as Captain King and Rip Ford appear as the wagon train crosses Texas. This lively, carefully constructed story gives an unusual perspective on the period.

637 Williams, J.R. **THE HORSE TALKER**. Englewood Cliffs, N.J. Prentice Hall. 1960. 177 p. **(J)**

Adopted by the Comanches at age three after his parents die of trail fever, fifteen-year-old Lan is captured at an Army fort on the Rio Grande while stealing the colonel's favorite horse. Blanco, a Mexican mustanger, rescues Lan, takes him to search for a white stallion called the Ghost of the Plains, and assists him in recognizing his talent and finding his identity. The three cultures of the wild horse country in the 1850s provide an exciting background for the story of a boy growing up.

638 Williams, J.R. **TAME THE WILD STALLION**. Englewood Cliffs, N.J. Prentice Hall. 1957. 181 p. **(J)**

The Mitchells plan to sell the mustangs they have captured to the Army and head to California during the 1849 gold rush. Fifteen-year-old Joe falls asleep in night watch while the herd is stolen. He tries to recapture it by following it across the border. Instead he is held by Don Enrique, a large hacienda owner whose son has been killed at the battle of Chapultepec in 1847. The young Texan stays true to his own ideals while learning to appreciate Mexican culture. Winner of the 1957 Texas Institute of Letters-Cokesbury Book Store Award, this fine novel was reprinted by Sundance in 1985.

639 Williams, S.G. **A COWBOY'S NITE BEFORE CHRISTMAS.** Illustrated by Sandra Williams. Alpine, Tex. Big Bend Pub. Co. 1978. 40 p. **(P I)**

"Santy" arrives at a West Texas ranch in a buckboard pulled by eight "hosses" and Sweetwater Sue, an "ole" mule. While remaining true to the chosen ranch setting, this parody of Clement Clarke Moore's famous poem in irregular, rambling meter lacks the charm of the original. Black-and-white sketches with splashes of red illustrate the verses.

640 Willis, Kristine. **THE LONG-LEGGED, LONG-NOSED, LONG-MANED WOLF.** Illustrated by the author. Austin. Steck Vaughn. 1968. 48 p. **(P)**

This picture book fantasy set in the desert near El Paso is about a wolf who wants to be a horse so badly that he persuades the fiercest bandito in El Paso to ride him. Although they win a horse race, they are run out of town in disgrace after the wolf scratches, revealing his true identity. The humorous story is illustrated with colorful sketches which show the action of the chase and adventures of the two hapless outlaws.

641 Winders, Gertrude Hecker. **JIM BOWIE, BOY WITH A HUNTING KNIFE.** Illustrated by Harry Lees. Indianapolis. Bobbs-Merrill. 1953. 192 p. (The Childhood of Famous Americans Series) **(I)**

This fictional biography of a Texas hero spans his whole life, from his childhood in Lousiana to his death at the Alamo. He is portrayed as adventurous, jovial, and brave. The easy-to-read text, illustrated with black-and-white silhouettes, is typical of volumes in the series.

642 Wisler, G. Clifton. **BUFFALO MOON.** New York. Dutton. 1984. 105 p. **(I J)**

Set in frontier Texas in the 1850s, this is the exciting story of Willie Delamer, a fourteen-year-old boy who leaves the family ranch on the Brazos and spends six months living as a Comanche, Bright Star, proving himself and learning Indian ways. Chief Yellow Shirt guides and protects the boy in the hope that his last living son, Red Wolf, and Willie will create an atmosphere of peace in the land they all love. Wisler presents a sympathetic insight into Indian culture and a boy's struggle for maturity. **Thunder on the Tennessee** is a sequel.

643 Wisler, G. Clifton. **THUNDER ON THE TENNESSEE.** New York. Dutton. 1983. 154 p. **(I J)**

In the fall of 1861, sixteen-year-old Willie Delamer leaves the family ranch on the Brazos with his father to join the Second Texas Regiment in the battle at Shiloh, where he learns of the horror of war and the sadness of death. Told from a Texas states' rights perspective, the story has a universal, moving message. This is a sequel to **Buffalo Moon**.

644 Wisler, G. Clifton. **WINTER OF THE WOLF**. New York. Elsevier/Nelson. 1981. 124 p. **(I J)**

The winter of 1864 on a Brazos River homestead is difficult for fourteen-year-old T.J. Clinton, who is in charge after his father and older brothers leave to fight in the Civil War. With the help of Yellow Feather, a young Comanche brave he had befriended, T.J. hunts a large wolf the boys believe embodies a Comanche devil spirit. This is an inspirational story of cross-cultural understanding and courage in the face of frontier harshness.

645 Wolf, Bernard. **IN THIS PROUD LAND : THE STORY OF A MEXICAN AMERICAN FAMILY**. Philadelphia. Lippincott. 1978. 95 p. **(I J)**

The struggle of the Hernandez family of the Rio Grande Valley to overcome hardship and poverty is movingly portrayed in this photographic essay. A loving family provides support for the children's education by migrating yearly to Minnesota to do farm work.

646 Woodward, Mary Tyson. **BIRTHDAY KITTENS**. Dallas. Kaleidograph. 1949. 47 p. **(P)**

Belita, the cat, speaks in verse because she lives with two would-be Texas poetesses, whom she presents with litters of kittens on their respective birthdays. Grainy black-and-white photographs illustrate the activities of numerous kittens in the manner of a family album.

647 Woodward, Mary Tyson. **THE CHRISTMAS CARD CAT**. Illustrated by Luther Tyson. Dallas. Kaleidograph. 1948. 47 p. **(P)**

Belita, a gray and white longhaired cat, lives with Tiger, her kitten, and Black Boy in a comfortable Texas home. The very simple story of the cats' lives shows them playing in the fish pond and examining the ice on the pond after a snowstorm. Grainy black-and-white photographs illustrate the free verse text.

648 Woodward, Mary Tyson. **A DAY WITH BECKY.** Illustrated by Howard Reynolds. Dallas. Kaleidograph. 1950. 43 p. **(P)**

Two-year-old Mary Rebecca, or Becky, lives in Austin, "the fair capital city of Texas." Stylized, simple text and sepia photographs tell the story of the toddler's life as she plays in the grass with her cat, makes mud pies, and goes to bed. The book has the quality of a family album in showing the simple activities of a young child.

649 Woolford, Sam. **GULF COAST ADVENTURE.** Boerne, Tex. Highland Press. 1953. 64 p. **(I)**

Peter and Mary Ann visit Uncle Toby while their mother is in the hospital. They live in Uncle Toby's little white cottage on the Gulf Coast and help at his bait shop. They all go deep sea fishing and beachcombing, look for buried treasure, and picnic and camp on the beach. The last quarter of the book lists safety rules and contains black-and-white sketches and brief descriptions of wildlife commonly found on the Gulf Coast.

650 Wormser, Richard Edward. **THE BLACK MUSTANGER.** Illustrated by Don Bolognese. New York. Morrow. 1971. 190 p. **(I J)**

Post-Civil War Texas offers a new start for the Rikers, as thirteen-year-old Dan and his Union veteran father catch maverick cattle for the family herd. When Lafe Riker breaks his leg, Will Mesteno, an Apache-Black-Mexican known as the best mustanger in the country, sets it. Dan looks for work to support the family and convinces his parents and Will that he can hunt mustangs with Will in spite of the prejudice about a white man working for a black man. The social conflict underlies an exciting adventure of a young man growing up in a wild country.

651 Wormser, Richard Edward. **GONE TO TEXAS.** Illustrated by Don Bolognese. New York. Morrow. 1970. 222 p. **(I J)**

Desperate for a new start after the Civil War, Confederate veteran Lancey, his wife, and his thirteen-year-old son Don accept an offer to drive a wagon from Kentucky to Texas without asking about the contents. The vivid description of the slow wagon journey portrays the trials of an honest pioneer family as it is beset by renegades, thieves, trail fever, and bad weather on the way to a new life across the Red River. Lancey maintains his dignity and honor while unmasking the rogues and opportunists in the climax, which reveals the contents of the wagon.

652 Wormser, Richard Edward. **RIDE A NORTHBOUND HORSE**. Illustrated by Charles Geer. New York. Morrow. 1964. 190 p. (I J)

Orphaned, thirteen-year-old Cav Rand drives his family's oxen and wagon to Alexandria, Louisiana, where he sells them to the K-C outfit owner, Texan Cavanaugh. After unsuccessfully trying to attend school, Cav buys a horse and heads west to join the K-C on a trail drive from Brownsville to Abilene, Kansas. Tricked out of his horse by Shawnee, a peddler, Cav steals Shawnee's old horse and becomes a cook's helper for the K-C. Strong characterization of the boy and the men who help and hinder him and the adventures of the wild cattle country make this an exciting story.

653 Wright, Frances Fitzpatrick. **SAM HOUSTON, FIGHTER AND LEADER**. Illustrated by Robert Burns. Nashville. Abingdon-Cokesbury. 1953. (Makers of America)   (I)

This biography of Houston covers the period from his birth until 1861, when he steps down as Governor of Texas. Important historical events in his life, his leadership qualities, and his friendship with Andrew Jackson are emphasized, as is his preeminent role in the formation of the Republic and the entry of Texas into the United States. Fictional dialogue, large type, and black-and-white illustrations make the book accessible to younger readers.

654 Wyatt, Geraldine Tolman. **WRONGHAND**. Illustrated by Kurt Werth. New York. Longmans, Green. 1949. 206 p. (I J)

A cattle drive along the Chisholm Trail from Fort Worth to Abilene, Kansas, in 1868 led by sixteen-year-old Todd Parrish, whose father died fighting for the Confederacy, is the background of this novel. Todd, called Wronghand by the Comanches because he is left-handed, survives all of the dangers of the trail with the help of some trusty cowboys and Muster, his favorite pony. Stereotypes of cowboys, racial groups, and cattle drive occurrences are prevalent.

SUBJECT INDEX

(References are to item numbers)

Headings used in this index are based on those found in the latest edition of **Library of Congress Guide to Subject Headings**. Minor modifications have been made to reflect the specialized nature of the bibliography, such as eliminating "Texas" as a primary heading, e.g., Texas--History becomes History. Chronological history subentries follow alphabetical history subentries. Geographic headings have been used when the setting of the book is emphasized, e.g., Panhandle--Fiction. The alphabetical arrangement is word-by-word.

Adjustment, Social. **See** Social adjustment
Adobe Walls, Battle of, (1874) -- fiction, 261, 434
Adolescence -- fiction, 11, 131, 132, 200, 208, 209, 294, 382, 384, 394, 481, 550, 551, 597, 642
Adoption -- fiction, 68, 215
Adventure stories, 12, 24, 28, 44, 66, 67, 73, 107, 119, 171, 214, 258, 297, 431, 435, 440, 449, 496, 499, 516, 517, 518, 534, 549, 561, 562, 574, 584, 614, 651, 652
Afro-American folk poetry. **See** Folk poetry, Afro-American
Afro-Americans
  biography, 128, 163, 218, 276, 285, 335, 360, 407, 476, 502, 528, 650
  fiction, 92, 538, 567, 568, 569, 570, 571, 572, 650
  history, 312, 407
  poetry, 388
  social conditions, 267
    fiction, 441, 481, 551, 610
Agricultural laborers -- fiction, 233
Agricultural laborers, Migrant. **See** Migrant agricultural laborers
Agriculture, 612
Air bases, Naval -- fiction, 591
Air Force, Confederate. **See** Confederate Air Force
Air pilots, Military -- fiction, 591
Alabama Indians
  history, 229

legends, 1
Alamo
fiction,
history,
Siege (1836), 363, 463, 512, 524, 593, 602, 622
drama, 189
fiction, 23, 25, 26, 167, 168, 203, 226, 405, 584, 594
Alligators -- fiction, 520, 521, 522
Alphabet books, 22, 305, 519. **See also** use as subentry.
American bison. **See** Bison, American
Angelina (Indian girl) -- fiction, 577
Anglo-American and Indian cultures. **See** Indian and Anglo-American cultures
Anglo-American and Mexican American cultures. **See** Mexican American and Anglo-American cultures
Anglo-American and Mexican cultures. **See** Mexican and Anglo-American cultures
Anglo-Americans -- history, 313
Animals. **See also** specific animals.
 legends
Animals, Mythical -- fiction, 134
Animals, Treatment of -- fiction, 38, 39
Apache Indians
captivities -- fiction, 247
fiction, 71
history, 50
social life and customs -- fiction, 513
Appaloosa horse -- fiction, 258, 437
Aransas National Wildlife Refuge -- fiction, 464
Archaeological expeditions -- fiction, 509
Archives, State -- fiction, 378
Armadillos -- fiction, 146, 147, 183, 305, 398
Armor. **See** Arms and Armor
Arms and armor, Spanish, 190
Artists, German American, 616
Astronauts, 161
Athletes, 160, 271, 446, 547. **See also** Automobile racing drivers; Football players; Golfers; Soccer players; and names of individual athletes.
Austin, Stephen Fuller, 54, 223, 270, 298, 424, 501
Austin (City)
alphabet books, 305
fiction, 74, 75, 77, 78, 81, 85, 86, 87, 88, 90, 91, 92, 93, 94, 95, 96, 97, 98, 100, 106, 378, 567, 568, 569, 570, 571, 572, 648

Subject Index 155

Austin's Colony. **See** San Felipe de Austin
Authors -- biography, 475
Automobile racing drivers, 369, 479
Avavore Indians -- fiction, 37

Babies -- fiction, 648
Backpacking -- fiction, 507
Ballads, 34. **See also** Songs
Balloons -- fiction, 573
Barnard, Juana Cavazos -- fiction, 32
Baseball stories, 74, 75, 85, 86, 87, 88, 90, 91, 92, 93, 94, 95, 96, 97, 98
Basketball stories, 76, 102, 103
Bass, Sam -- fiction, 260, 609
Battle of Adobe Walls, (1874). **See** Adobe Walls, Battle of, (1874)
Battle of Goliad, (1836). **See** Goliad, Battle of, (1836)
Battle of San Jacinto, (1836). **See** San Jacinto, Battle of, (1836)
Battle of the Alamo, (1836). **See** Alamo--Siege, (1836)
Bayous, 611
Beale, Edward Fitzgerald -- fiction, 133
Beauregard, Pierre Gustav Toutant -- fiction, 303
Belgian Americans -- history, 314
BigBend -- fiction, 509
BigBend National Park -- fiction, 275
BigThicket National Preserve, 495
Biography, 7, 16, 19, 176, 368, 427, 526, 563. **See also** names of individuals; and use as subentry.
Biology, Seashore. **See** Seashore biology
Birds. **See also** specific types.
  legends and stories, 451
Bison, American -- fiction, 44
Black Americans. **See** Afro-Americans
Bluebonnets
  fiction,
  legends,
Boar, Wild. **See** Wild boar
Boats and boating -- fiction, 349
Books, Alphabet. **See** Alphabet books
Books, Painting. **See** Painting books
Borden, Gail, 47, 482
Bosque County -- fiction, 141
Bowie, James, 237
  fiction,

Subject Index

Boys as soldiers -- fiction, 73, 115, 116, 119, 145, 167, 168, 525, 539, 593, 594, 643
Boys' Ranch -- fiction, 595
Boys' stories, 29, 44, 51, 119, 214, 227, 238, 258, 297, 367, 432, 434, 442, 458, 481, 496, 518, 585, 592, 626, 637, 642, 644
Brewster County -- fiction, 238
British Americans. **See** Anglo-Americans
Brontosaurs, 159
Brush country -- fiction, 118, 454
Buffalo, American. **See** Bison, American
Buried treasure, 192
　fiction, 71, 138, 361, 428, 509
　legends, 192
Burton, Virginia Lee, 497
Butterflies -- fiction, 467
Buzzards -- fiction, 211, 596

Cabeza De Vaca, Alvar Nunez, 362, 560, 588
　fiction, 37, 64, 137
Caddo Indians -- social life and customs -- fiction, 341, 513
Calves -- fiction, 179
Camels -- fiction, 133, 157, 343, 366, 411, 461
Cameron County -- fiction, 632
Campbell, Earl, 128, 502
Canary Islanders in San Antonio -- fiction, 409, 514
Cannons -- fiction, 594
Career stories, 484, 485, 487, 489, 490, 491, 492, 493
Cats -- fiction, 346, 393, 646, 647
Cattle. **See** Calves; Longhorns
Cattle drives. **See** Cattle trails
Cattle trails, 150, 164, 418, 426, 503, 627. **See also** Chisholm Trail
　fiction 2, 3, 4, 51, 118, 120, 136, 236, 238, 248, 259, 278, 303, 337, 458, 537, 538, 586, 592, 600, 652, 654
Cavazos, Juana. **See** Barnard, Juana Cavazos
Center (City) -- fiction, 20
Central Texas -- fiction, 31, 331
Chachalaca, 9
Chandler (City) -- fiction, 541
Chaparral cock. **See** Road Runner (Bird)
Cherokee Indians -- fiction, 359
Chicanos. **See** Mexican Americans
Children. **See also** Babies; Orphans; School children
　Dallas
Children, Mentally handicapped. **See** Mentally handicapped children

Children, Physically handicapped. See Physically handicapped children
Chinese Americans -- history, 315, 408
Chisholm Trail, 418
 fiction, 259, 538, 592, 654
Christian ethics -- fiction, 184
Christmas
 poetry, 283, 523
 parodies,
Christmas stories, 350, 365, 392, 569
Circus stories, 18
City and town life. See also names of cities and towns.
 fiction, 20, 58, 382, 394, 541
Civil War, (1861-1865). See History -- Civil War, (1861-1865)
Civilization, 6
Clothing and dress. See Costume
Clubs -- fiction, 38, 39
College students -- social groups, 80
Collins, Michael, 161
Coloring books. See Painting books
Comal County -- fiction, 606
Comanche Indians
 biography, 30, 417
 captivities, 250, 302
 fiction, 32, 61, 69, 261, 299
 fiction, 48, 49, 216, 595, 642, 644
 legends, 185
 social life and customs, 504
 wars -- fiction, 24
Conditions, Economic. See Economic conditions
Confederate Air Force, 452
Cook, James Henry, 164, 426
Coronado, Francisco Vasquez de, 262
Corpus Christi -- fiction, 347, 348, 591
Costume, 447, 448
 history
Cotton growing -- fiction, 386, 412
Cotton trade -- Confederate States of America -- fiction, 449, 636
Country life. See Farm life; Ranch life; Rural life
Coushatta Indians
 history, 229
 legends, 1
Cowboys, 150, 254, 418, 510, 564, 627
 alphabet

biography, individuals.
dictionaries, 255
fiction, 2, 3, 4, 28, 29, 65, 118, 213, 236, 278, 337, 381, 383, 397, 434, 516, 517, 538, 600, 604, 652
legends, 111, 112, 113, 121, 143, 178, 186, 219, 220, 221, 399, 498
songs and music, 217
Cowgirls, 166, 510, 613
Coyotes
fiction, 211, 597
legends, 497
Cranes, Whooping. **See** Whooping cranes
Crockett, David, 62, 110, 165, 198, 225, 263, 300, 463, 533, 557, 578
fiction, 15, 180, 257, 385, 440, 442
Cronkite, Walter, 628
Cross-cultural friendship. **See** Friendship, Cross-cultural
Cuban Americans -- fiction, 90, 239
Cultures, Indian and Anglo-American. **See** Indian and Anglo-American cultures
Cultures, Mexican American and Anglo-American. **See** Mexican American and Anglo-American cultures
Cultures, Mexican and Anglo-American. **See** Mexican and Anglo-American cultures
Customs, Social. **See** Social life and customs
Czech Americans -- history, 316

Dallas
fiction, 346, 353, 486
history, 601, 615
Dallas Cowboys (Football team), 126, 163, 415
Death -- fiction, 467, 629
Declaration of Independence (Texas) -- Signers, 7
Denison -- fiction, 351
Denver, John, 336, 439
Depression -- 1929 -- fiction, 550, 623
Description and travel, 280, 372, 540. **See also** use as subentry.
alphabet books, 22
Detective stories. **See** Mystery and detective stories
Dickenson, Susanna, 363
fiction, 405
Dictionaries. **See** Encyclopaedias and dictionaries, and use as subentry.
Didrikson, Babe. **See** Zaharias, Mildred Didrikson
Dinosaurs, 159
Discovery and exploration -- fiction, 37, 64, 137, 234

Dogs -- fiction, 41, 42, 43, 129, 191, 199, 210, 211, 212, 245, 247, 401, 623, 624, 633
Dorsett, Tony, 163
Duval, John Crittenden, 201

East Texas -- fiction, 40, 43, 153, 214, 394, 395, 396, 402, 472, 550, 624
Easter fires. **See** Fredericksburg -- Easter fires
Easter stories, 277, 288
Economic conditions, 36, 144, 230, 612
El Paso -- history, 231, 562
Elementary schools -- fiction, 544
Emancipation Day -- fiction, 570
Empathy -- fiction, 134, 508
Encyclopaedias and dictionaries, 117
Estevan, 37, 64, 560
Ethics, Christian. **See** Christian ethics
Ethnic groups, 6, 63
Expedition, Santa Fe, (1841). **See** Santa Fe Expedition, (1841)
Expeditions, Archaeological. **See** Archaeological expeditions
Exploration. **See** Discovery and exploration
Explorers, 33, 262, 362, 474, 560, 588
 fiction, 37, 64, 137

Family life. **See also** Stepfamilies
 fiction, 31, 131, 141, 172, 174, 200, 209, 348, 544, 629
Fannin, James W., 222
Farm laborers. **See** Agricultural laborers
Farm life -- fiction, 141, 149, 153, 155, 295, 331, 386, 406, 575
Fathers, Unmarried. **See** Unmarried fathers
Fiesta, San Jacinto. **See** San Jacinto Fiesta
Fifteenth birthday celebration. **See** Quinceanera
Fisher County -- fiction, 258
Fishery, Shrimp. **See** Shrimp fishery
Flags -- history, 45, 46, 162
Flowers. **See** Bluebonnets; Wild flowers
Folk poetry, Afro-American, 445
Folk songs, 34. **See also** use as subentry.
Folklore, 111, 112, 113, 120, 121, 143, 151, 178, 185, 186, 192, 193, 219, 220, 221, 242, 277, 288, 342, 352, 375, 381, 392, 399, 497, 498, 511, 537, 552, 635
Folklore, Mexican, 527
Folklore, Mexican American, 10, 240
Football players, 123, 126, 128, 163, 502

Football stories, 77, 78, 80, 81, 82, 83, 84, 100, 101, 105, 106, 309, 441
Fort Saint Louis, 474, 553
Foyt, A. J., 369, 479
Fredericksburg
 Easter fires, 277, 288, 352
 fiction, 559
French Americans
 fiction, 207
 history, 317
Friendship -- fiction, 249
Friendship, Cross-cultural -- fiction, 239, 259, 275, 359, 402, 624, 642, 644
Frontier and pioneer life, 6, 8, 14, 19, 197, 241, 281, 447, 448, 460
 fiction, 44, 65, 145, 149, 155, 171, 204, 206, 207, 208, 209, 266, 286, 287, 295, 296, 299, 306, 351, 377, 389, 390, 402, 432, 438, 442, 444, 469, 480, 559, 605, 606, 637, 644

Galveston
 fiction, 543, 544, 545
 storm, 1900
 fiction, 304
Games, Mexican American, 10
Geese -- fiction, 543
Geese, Wild. **See** Wild geese
Geography, 36, 144, 230
Geology -- West Texas -- fiction, 59
German American artists. **See** Artists, German American
German Americans
 fiction, 11, 173, 295, 296, 350, 559, 605, 606
 history, 318
Ghost stories, 228
Gillett, James B., 241
Girls' stories, 12, 13, 20, 35, 68, 130, 132, 172, 174, 175, 206, 208, 209, 239, 304, 334, 339, 347, 348, 353, 357, 382, 384, 394, 395, 396, 406, 429, 450, 484, 485, 486, 487, 488, 489, 490, 491, 492, 493, 494, 541, 543, 544, 545, 586, 610
Goats -- fiction, 289
Golfers, 332, 416, 459
Goliad, Battle of, (1836), 201, 222
 fiction, 25
Goodnight, Charles, 426
Goras, Domingo Leal -- fiction, 409
Grandfathers -- fiction, 608

Greek Americans -- history, 319
Griffin, John Howard, 267
Groups, Ethnic. **See** Ethnic groups
Gulf Coast **See also** Natural history -- Gulf Coast
   fiction, 5, 122, 154, 156, 265, 348, 349, 382, 471, 649

Hadji Ali. **See** Hi Jolly
Handicapped children. **See** Mentally handicapped children;
   Physically handicapped children
Hardin, John Wesley, 483
Hays, John Coffee, 79
Henry, O., 475
Hi Jolly -- fiction, 157, 343, 366
High school students -- Social Groups -- fiction, 310
Hill, Juan C. C., 311
Hill country
   fiction, 58, 132, 191, 244, 245, 246, 247, 393, 473
   folk
   history, 505
   social life and customs, 272
Hispanics. **See** Mexican Americans
Historic trees, 273
History, 36, 144, 230, 273, 280, 333, 354, 500, 580. **See also** use as
   subentry.
   alphabet
   pictorial
   readers, 6, 55, 63, 109, 114, 162, 176, 506
      Chronological subentries
   to 1846, 19, 197, 342, 443, 530, 546
   drama, 268
   to 1865, 45, 46, 181, 187
   Revolution, (1835-1836), 201, 270, 330, 355, 368, 524, 602, 622
   fiction 23, 25, 26, 27, 115, 119, 145, 171, 188, 296, 364, 367, 403,
      440, 442, 462, 539, 579
   Republic, (1836-1846) -- fiction, 378
   War with Mexico, (1845-1848), 148, 196, 293, 376, 634
   fiction, 24, 116, 638
   Civil War, (1861-1865) -- fiction, 73, 303, 433, 449, 636, 643
History, Natural. **See** Natural history
Horse stealing -- fiction, 227, 433
Horses. **See also** specific breeds.
   fiction, 48, 49, 184, 200, 244, 384, 406, 444, 462, 556, 558, 565, 597,
      632, 633
Houston, Samuel, 99, 125, 253, 264, 301, 338, 356, 373, 374, 422,

456, 478, 554, 653
fiction 539, 583
Houston (City) -- fiction, 172, 174, 175, 429, 470, 535, 618
Houston Oilers (Football team), 128, 502, 532
Hudspeth County -- fiction, 633
Humorous stories, 70, 72, 380
Hurricanes -- fiction, 154, 304

Indian and Anglo-American cultures, 216, 460
Indians. Includes works on one or more tribes. Works on a specific tribe are entered here and also under the name of the tribe.
  biography,
  captivities,
    fiction, 32, 61, 69, 234, 247, 261, 299
  fiction, 5, 37, 48, 49, 71, 216, 359, 595, 624, 642, 644
  history, 50, 229, 320, 504, 581
  legends, 1, 185, 587
  masks, 60
  rites and ceremonies, 60
  social life and customs, 341, 344, 504, 620
    fiction, 513
  wars
  wars,
Industries, 612
Industry and trade, Petroleum. **See** Petroleum industry and trade
Integration, School. **See** School integration
Italian Americans -- history, 321

Jack County -- fiction, 155
Jayhawkers -- fiction, 449
Jews -- history, 322
Johnson, Lyndon Baines, 53, 57, 370, 400, 465, 466, 477, 631
  fiction, 455, 542
Johnson Space Center. **See** LBJ Space Center
Jordan, Barbara, 285, 335, 528
Journalists, 628
Juneteenth. **See** Emancipation Day

Karankawa Indians -- fiction, 5
Kendrick, John Benjamin -- fiction, 236
Kerr County -- fiction, 458
Kidnapping -- fiction, 20, 154, 156, 470
King, Billy -- fiction, 594
Kiowa Indians -- captivities, 302

Subject Index 163

La Salle, Robert Cavelier, 474, 553
Lost mines
 fiction, 549
 legends, 192
Love, Nat, 218
Lungkwitz, Hermann, 616
Lyndon Baines Johnson Ranch. **See** LBJ Ranch
Lyndon Baines Johnson Space Center. **See** LBJ Space Center
 fiction, 234
Laborers, Agricultural. **See** Agricultural laborers
Lafitte, Jean, 252
 fiction, 152
LBJ Ranch -- fiction, 542
LBJ Space Center, 161
Lebanese Americans -- history, 328
Legends. **See** Folklore; and use as subentry.
Legislators, 17, 285, 335, 528
Leprechauns -- fiction, 393, 635
Lipan Indians -- history, 50
Little League baseball -- fiction, 75, 85, 86, 87, 88, 90, 91, 92, 93, 94, 95, 96, 97, 98
Llano Estacado -- fiction, 61, 361
Long, Jane Wilkinson, 251
Longhorns -- fiction, 120, 259, 278, 375, 537
Lost -- fiction, 496

Mackenzie, Ranald Slidell -- fiction, 507
Magicians -- fiction, 468
Man, Prehistoric -- fiction, 582
Masks. **See** Indians -- masks
Mason County -- fiction, 243
May Day -- fiction, 571
Mentally handicapped children -- fiction, 596
Meridian -- fiction, 266
Mexican American and Anglo-American cultures -- fiction, 508
Mexican American folklore. **See** Folklore, Mexican American
Mexican American games. **See** Games, Mexican American
Mexican American nursery rhymes. **See** Nursery rhymes, Mexican American
Mexican Americans. Includes Mexicans in Texas both before and after statehood
 biography, 332, 416, 459
 fiction, 41, 42, 52, 76, 91, 127, 226, 233, 275, 515
 history, 135, 169, 323, 329

social conditions, 453, 645
  fiction, 142, 205
social
Mexican and Anglo-American cultures -- fiction, 638
Mexican folklore. **See** Folklore, Mexican
Midland County -- fiction, 28
Mier Expedition, (1842), 311, 421
Migrant agricultural laborers, 645
  fiction, 142, 590, 619
Military air pilots. **See** Air pilots, Military
Missions, 308. **See also** names of individual missions.
  fiction, 513, 577
Mitchell, Napoleon Bonaparte -- fiction, 593
Mobeetie (Old) -- fiction, 140
Mockingbirds -- fiction, 202
Morgan, Columbus Napoleon -- fiction, 575
Morgan horse -- fiction, 195
Mules -- fiction, 256
Musicians, 336, 439
Mustangers -- fiction, 216, 637, 650
Mustangs -- fiction, 178, 204, 220, 238, 287, 433, 434, 499
Mystery and detective stories, 138, 139, 140, 141, 154, 156, 361, 379, 404, 468, 470, 471, 472, 473, 566, 617
Mythical animals. **See** Animals, Mythical

Natural history, 292, 342
  Gulf Coast, 649
Natural resources, 144
Naval air bases. **See** Air bases, Naval
Negroes. **See** Afro-Americans
New Braunfels -- fiction, 11
New Year -- fiction, 282
North Texas -- fiction, 179, 480
Norwegian Americans -- history, 324
Nunez Cabeza de Vaca, Alvar. **See** Cabeza de Vaca, Alvar Nunez
Nursery rhymes, Mexican American, 10

Offshore oil wells -- fiction, 520
Offshore pipe lines -- fiction, 522
Oil fields -- fiction, 40, 291
Oil wells -- fiction, 279. **See also** Spindletop oil well
Oil wells, Offshore. **See** Offshore oil wells
Oldham County -- fiction, 286

Open range, 193
Orphans -- fiction, 11, 44, 51, 68, 91, 98, 215, 393, 438, 473, 481, 600, 623
Owls -- fiction, 210

Padre Island -- fiction, 566
Painting books, 615
Paleontology -- Mesozoic, 159
Palo Duro Canyon
 description and travel, 124
 fiction, 138, 582
Panhandle -- fiction, 29, 195, 206, 207, 208, 209, 211, 286, 496, 517, 595, 596, 597
Parker, Cynthia Ann, 250
Parker, Quanah, 30, 417
Parodies, 283, 307
Peacocks -- fiction, 177
Pecos 111, 112, 113, 121, 143, 178, 186, 219, 220, 221, 399, 498
Peddlers and peddling -- fiction, 481, 555
Peruna (Football mascot) -- fiction, 531
Peters' Colony -- fiction, 287
Petri, Richard, 616
Petroleum industry and trade -- fiction, 291, 413
Petroleum workers -- fiction, 294
Physically handicapped children -- fiction, 48, 93, 94, 156, 595
Pickett, Bill, 276, 476
Picnicking -- fiction, 541
Pigs -- fiction, 340
Pike, Zebulon Montgomery, 33
Pioneer life. **See** Frontier and pioneer life
Pipe lines, Offshore. **See** Offshore pipe lines
Pirates, 252
 fiction, 152, 428
Players. **See** Football players; Soccer players
Poetry. **See** Folk poetry, Afro-American; and use as subentry.
Polish Americans -- history, 325
Ponies -- fiction, 531
Port Arthur -- fiction, 401
Port Isabel -- fiction, 431
Porter, William Sidney. **See** Henry, O.
Prehistoric man. **See** Man, Prehistoric

Quinceanera, 240

Rabbits -- fiction, 398
Race discrimination. See the name of the racial or ethnic group with subentry, Social conditions.
Racing drivers, Automobile. See Automobile racing drivers
Ranch life, 564. **See also** XIT Ranch
dictionaries, 255
fiction, 12, 13, 35, 51, 89, 107, 130, 131, 132, 136, 179, 210, 211, 238, 266, 282, 289, 339, 383, 384, 397, 414, 437, 458, 516, 517, 558, 565, 585, 604, 626
Ranchers, Sheep. **See** Sheep ranchers
Randall County -- fiction, 28
Range, Open. **See** Open range
Range wars -- fiction, 89
Rayburn, Sam Taliaferro, 17
Readers. **See** History -- readers; Zoology -- readers
Recitations, 371
Reconstruction -- fiction, 575
Red 158
Resources, Natural. **See** Natural resources
Revolution, (1835-1836). **See** History -- Revolution, (1835-1836)
Rio Grande, 170, 345
Rio Grande Valley, 170, 345
 description and travel, 56
 fiction, 127, 240, 450
 social conditions, 645
Rites and ceremonies. **See** Indians -- rites and ceremonies
Road Runner (Bird) -- fiction, 603
Rockport -- history, 599
Rodeo performers, 276, 476, 613
Rodeos, 510, 613
 fiction,
Roosters -- fiction, 248
Rote, Kyle, Jr., 194
Runaway Scrape -- fiction, 145, 296, 390
Rural life -- fiction, 31, 246, 454, 610

San Antonio, 358
 fiction, 13, 41, 42, 52, 205, 306, 392, 404, 473, 514
 social life and customs -- fiction, 409
San Antonio Spurs (Basketball team), 457
San Felipe de Austin
 fiction, 389, 390
 history, 270
San Jacinto, Battle of, (1836), 524

drama, 189
fiction, 27, 104, 145, 167, 168, 403, 525
San Jacinto Fiesta -- fiction, 52
San Juan Baptista Mission -- fiction, 577
Santa Fe Expedition, (1841), 423
School children -- fiction, 515
School integration -- fiction, 618
Schools, Elementary. **See** Elementary schools
Scottish Americans -- fiction, 173
Seabrook -- fiction, 428
Seashore biology, 599, 649
Sequoyah (Cherokee Indian) -- fiction, 359
Shackelford County -- fiction, 44, 516
Sheep ranchers, 281
   fiction, 480
Shelby, Joseph Orville -- fiction, 435
Shreve, Henry Miller, 158
Shrimp fishery -- fiction, 431
Smith County -- fiction, 575
Smuggling -- fiction, 227
Snakes -- fiction, 111
Soccer players, 194
Social adjustment -- fiction, 175, 395
Social groups. **See** College students -- Social groups; High school
   students -- Social groups
Social life and customs, 36. **See also** use as subentry.
Soldiers, Boys as. **See** Boys as soldiers
Songs, 576. **See also** Ballads; Cowboys -- Songs and music; Folk
   songs
South Texas -- fiction, 294, 437, 534, 549
Spanish Americans -- history, 326
Spanish arms and armor. **See** Arms and armor, Spanish
Spindletop oil well -- fiction, 279
Sports stories, 108
Staked Plain. **See** Llano Estacado
State archives. **See** Archives, State
Stepfamilies -- fiction, 94, 488
Stephens County -- history, 281
Stinson, Katherine, 529
Stories. **See** Adventure stories; Baseball stories; Basketball stories;
   Boys' stories; Career stories; Christmas stories; Circus stories;
   Easter stories; Football stories; Ghost stories; Girls' stories;
   Humorous stories; Mystery and detective stories; Sports stories;
   and subentry Legends and stories

Story, Nelson, 627
Stowaways -- fiction, 214
Students. See College students; High school students
Survival, Wilderness. See Wilderness survival
Swensen, Christina Torstensen, 281
Swiss Americans -- history, 327
Syrian Americans -- history, 328

Tascosa
 Boys' Ranch. See Boys' Ranch
 fiction, 361
Taylor, Zachary, 634
Tejas Indians. See Caddo Indians
Tennis -- fiction, 310
Texas Rangers, 8, 14, 79, 235, 241, 290, 410, 436, 625
 fiction, 260, 438, 444, 496
Thanksgiving Day -- fiction, 569
Thompson, Corrie, 599
Tigua Indians -- history, 581
Town life. See City and town life
Trails, 109
Trails, Cattle. See Cattle trails
Trains, Wagon. See Wagon trains
Travel. See Description and travel
Travis, William Barrett, 224, 425
Treasure, Buried. See Buried treasure
Treasure trove. See Buried treasure
Treatment of animals. See Animals, Treatment of
Trees, Historic. See Historic trees
Trevino, Lee, 332, 416, 459
Turkeys -- fiction, 149
Turtles -- fiction, 398

Unmarried fathers -- fiction, 535

Van Zandt County -- history -- fiction, 21
Vasquez de Coronado, Francisco. See Coronado, Francisco
 Vasquez de

Wagon trains -- fiction, 256
Walker, Doak, 123
Wallace, Big Foot, 235, 420, 421
 fiction, 536

War with Mexico, (1845-1848). See History--War with Mexico, (1845-1848)
Wars, Range. See Range wars
Washington County -- fiction, 173
Wayne, Henry Constantine -- fiction, 133
West Texas -- fiction, 35, 69, 131, 136, 184, 216, 282, 384, 386, 406, 412, 414, 629
Wheeler County -- fiction, 139
White, Danny, 126
Whooping cranes, 284, 387, 430
Wild boar -- fiction, 243
Wild flowers, 269, 511, 548, 630. See also Bluebonnets
Wild geese -- fiction, 464
Wilderness survival -- fiction, 61, 213
Wildlife, 182, 598. See also Animals; Birds; Snakes
   fiction, 518
Wolves -- fiction, 640, 644
Women
   biography, 529. See also names of individuals.
   dress. See Costume
Woodcarving -- fiction, 454
Workers, Petroleum. See Petroleum workers

XIT Ranch -- fiction, 89

Zaharias, Mildred Didrikson, 160, 271, 446, 547
Zoology -- readers, 182

TITLE INDEX

A.J. FOYT, **479**
ABCs OF TEXAS WILDFLOWERS, THE, **269**
ABSOLUTELY PERFECT HORSE, THE, **200**
ADVENTURES OF L.A., THE, **183**
AFRO-AMERICAN TEXANS, THE, **312**
AFTER PA WAS SHOT, **20**
AFTER THE ALAMO, **293**
ALAMO SOLDIER, **593**
ALAMO, THE, **419**
ALL ABOUT MARJORY, **172**
AMANDA GOES WEST, **447**
AMANDA GOES WEST, **447**
AMANDA'S NEW LIFE, **448**
AMERICAN CATTLE TRAILS, **503**
AMERICAN COWGIRLS, **166**
ANGELINA, **577**
ANGLO-AMERICAN TEXANS, THE, **313**
ANNUNCIATA AND THE SHEPHERDS, **392**
APPLES ON A STICK, **445**
ARTHUR'S AUSTIN ABC, **305**
AT THE BATTLE OF SAN JACINTO WITH RIP CAVITT, **145**
AUGUSTUS RIDES THE BORDER, **380**

BABE DIDRIKSON, **547**
BABE DIDRIKSON ZAHARIAS, **446**
BALL BOYS ON THE BAY, THE, **265**
BALLAD OF CACTUS JACK, THE, **70**
BALLOON FARM, THE, **573**
BANJO HITTER, **74**

BARBARA JORDAN, **285**
BARBARA JORDAN, **335**
BARBARA JORDAN, THE GREAT LADY FROM TEXAS, **528**
BARTLETTS OF BOX B RANCH, **136**
BATTLE OF THE ALAMO, **463**
BECKONING STAR, **389**
BEEF FOR BEAUREGARD !, **303**
BELGIAN TEXANS, THE, **314**
BEST OF FRIENDS, THE, **38**
BEST TOWN IN THE WORLD, THE, **58**
BIG BAD WOLF IN TEXAS, THE, **307**
BIG FOOT WALLACE OF THE TEXAS RANGERS, **235**
BIG GAME, THE, **75**
BIG THICKET OF TEXAS, THE, **495**
BIGFOOT WALLACE, **420**
BIGFOOT WALLACE AND THE HICKORY NUT BATTLE, **536**
BILL PICKETT, **276**
BILLY BEDAMNED, LONG GONE BY, **65**
BIOGRAPHY OF A WHOOPING CRANE, **284**
BIRTH OF TEXAS, THE, **355**
BIRTHDAY IN TEXAS, **A,** 364
BIRTHDAY KITTENS, **646**
BLACK MUSTANGER, THE, **650**
BLACK PEOPLE WHO MADE THE OLD WEST, **360**
BLAZING HILLS, THE, **277**
BLUE BONNET BEND, **549**
BLUE BONNET'S RANCH PARTY, **334**
BLUEBONNET AT THE ALAMO, **146**
BLUEBONNET OF THE HILL COUNTRY, **147**
BLUEBONNETS FOR LUCINDA, **543**
BLUEBONNETS FOR LUCINDA, **543**
BONZINI! THE TATTOOED MAN, **18**
BOOK OF KNOWLEDGE, VOL. 21: THE BOOK OF TEXAS, THE, **117**
BORROWED BOOTS, **508**
BOY CAPTIVE OF THE TEXAS MIER EXPEDITION, THE, **311**
BOY HUNTERS, THE, **518**
BOY IN THE ALAMO, THE, **167**
BREAKAWAY BACK, **309**
BRONCHO RIDER BOYS WITH THE TEXAS RANGERS, THE, **227**
BUFFALO MOON, **642**
BUSBOYS AT BIG BEND, **275**
BUTTERFLY TREE, THE, **467**

Title Index 173

CABEZA DE VACA, DEFENDER OF THE INDIANS, **362**
CAMEL EXPRESS, **133**
CAMELS WEST, **343**
CAMELS WEST, **343**
CANNON BOY OF THE ALAMO, **594**
CAPTURE OF JOHN WESLEY HARDIN, THE, **483**
CAT HOTEL, **346**
CATHY, **347**
CAVALRY MOUNT, **195**
CHANTICLEER OF WILDERNESS ROAD, **385**
CHICANO ROOTS GO DEEP, **169**
CHILD'S HISTORY OF TEXAS COLORING BOOK, A, **333**
CHILD'S HISTORY OF TEXAS, A, **55**
CHILDREN INDIAN CAPTIVES, **302**
CHINESE TEXANS, THE, **315**
CHINTO, THE CHAPARRAL COCK, **603**
CHOC, THE CHACHALACA, **9**
CHRIS, **294**
CHRISTMAS CARD CAT, THE, **647**
CISSY'S TEXAS PRIDE, **406**
CLAN TEXAS, **173**
CLOVER CREEK, **484**
COMANCHES AND OTHER INDIANS OF TEXAS, **504**
COME COLOR DALLAS, **615**
COME HOME, BILL BAILEY, **632**
COMRADES OF THE CANYONS, **633**
CONFEDERATE FIDDLE, THE, **636**
CORONADO, **262**
CORONADO'S CHILDREN, **192**
COTTON-FARM BOY, **412**
COWBOY ALPHABET FOR GROWNUPS AND YOUNG'UNS TOO, **519**
COWBOY ENCYCLOPEDIA, THE, **255**
COWBOY JAMBOREE, **217**
COWBOY MANIA, **510**
COWBOY ON THE TRAIL, **538**
COWBOY SMALL, **383**
COWBOY'S NITE BEFORE CHRISTMAS, A, 639
COWBOYS, **254**
COWBOYS, **564**
COWBOYS AND CATTLE DRIVES, **150**
COWBOYS AND CATTLE DRIVES, **426**
COWBOYS AND CATTLE TRAILS, **236**

COWHAND GEORGE GOES TO TOWN, **585**
COWHAND GOES TO TOWN, **585**
CROSSROADS AT SAN FELIPE, **270**
CURLY AND THE WILD BOAR, **243**
CURLY OF THE CIRCLE BAR, **28**
CYCLONE, **256**
CYNTHIA ANN PARKER, **250**
CZECH TEXANS, THE, **316**

DALLAS COWBOYS, THE, **415**
DANNIE, **304**
DANNY WHITE, **126**
DAUGHTER OF TEJAS, **513**
DAVID CROCKETT, **15**
DAVY CROCKETT, **62**
DAVY CROCKETT, **180**
DAVY CROCKETT, **198**
DAVY CROCKETT, **225**
DAVY CROCKETT, **257**
DAVY CROCKETT, **300**
DAVY CROCKETT, **533**
DAVY CROCKETT, **578**
DAVY CROCKETT, FRONTIER ADVENTURER, **263**
DAVY CROCKETT, FRONTIER HERO, **110**
DAY AT THE LBJ RANCH, A, **542**
DAY WITH BECKY, A, **648**
DEADLY GAME OF MAGIC, A, **468**
DEATH OF JIMMY LITTLEWOLF, THE, **595**
DEBBY, **348**
DEEP WATER BOY, **431**
DISCOVERIES OF ESTEBAN THE BLACK, THE, **560**
DOAK WALKER, **123**
DOMINO HORSE, THE, **437**
DON COYOTE, **497**
DRIVEN TO WIN, **369**

EARL CAMPBELL, **128**
EARL CAMPBELL, **502**
EARLY IN THE SADDLE, **266**
EARLY TIMES IN TEXAS, **201**
EASTER FIRES, **288**
EDDIE AND GARDENIA, **289**
EDDIE NO-NAME, **215**
EDGE OF TWO WORLDS, **359**

Title Index

EMERALDS ON HER HANDS, **485**
EXPLORING THE BAYOUS, **611**

FAMOUS BABY-SITTER, THE, **52**
FAMOUS TEXANS, **526**
FAMOUS TREES OF TEXAS, **273**
FAR FROM HOME, **550**
FAST BREAK, **76**
FATHER OF TEXAS, **54**
FATHER OF TEXAS, STEPHEN F. AUSTIN, THE, **501**
FIDDLING COWBOY, **516**
FIELD GOAL, **77**
FIFER OF SAN JACINTO, THE, **432**
FIFTY-NINE FOR FREEDOM, **7**
FIGHTING QUARTERBACK, **78**
FIRST ACROSS NORTH AMERICA, **64**
FIRST BOOK OF THE WAR WITH MEXICO, THE, **148**
FIRST BULLDOGGER, THE, **476**
FIRST MAN TO CROSS AMERICA, **588**
FIRST TEXAS RANGER, JACK HAYS, THE, **79**
FISH FRY, **541**
FIVE LITTLE STARRS ON A RANCH, **534**
FLAGS OF TEXAS, THE, **162**
FLYING TO THE MOON AND OTHER STRANGE PLACES, **161**
FOOT PRINTS OF TEXAS HISTORY, **187**
FOOTBALL FEVER, **80**
FOR TEXAS AND FREEDOM, **579**
FOR TEXAS AND FREEDOM, **579**
FOR THE LIBERTY OF TEXAS, **115**
FRENCH TEXANS, THE, **317**
FROM TEXAS TO ILLINOIS, **590**
FURTHER ADVENTURES OF HANK THE COWDOG, THE, **210**

GAIL BORDEN, A RESOURCEFUL BOY, **482**
GALLEONS SAIL WESTWARD, **137**
GASTON DRILLS AN OFFSHORE OIL WELL, **520**
GASTON GOES TO TEXAS, **521**
GASTON LAYS AN OFFSHORE PIPELAND, **522**
GEE WHILLIKINS, **558**
GERMAN ARTISTS OF EARLY TEXAS, **616**
GERMAN TEXANS, THE, **318**
GHOST OF PADRE ISLAND, THE, **566**
GHOST SQUADRON, THE, **452**
GHOST STORIES OF OLD TEXAS, **228**

GIRL OF THE ALAMO, THE, **363**
GLORY HORSE, THE, **403**
GOAL TO GO, **81**
GOLDEN CLOUD IN TEXAS, **565**
GONE TO TEXAS, **651**
GOOD LAND, THE, **206**
GOOD LUCK ARIZONA MAN, **71**
GOODBYE TO THE PURPLE SAGE, **72**
GRACIELA, **453**
GRANDPA HAD A WINDMILL, GRANDMA HAD A CHURN, **331**
GREAT RED RIVER RAFT, THE, **158**
GREATEST CATTLE DRIVE, THE, **627**
GREEK TEXANS, THE, **319**
GRETCHEN AND THE WHITE STEED, **556**
GRIDIRON GLORY, **82**
GROWING UP IN THE HILL COUNTRY, **272**
GULF COAST ADVENTURE, **649**

HACKBERRY JONES, SPLIT END, **83**
HALF-TIME HERO, **84**
HANK THE COWDOG, **211**
HANK THE COWDOG, IT'S A DOG'S LIFE, **212**
HAWK OF HAWK CLAN, **341**
HEAD TO THE WEST, **295**
HEROES OF TEXAS, **16**
HI JOLLY !, **366**
HILLVIEW HOUSE, **486**
HISTORY OF THE SOUTHWEST, **231**
HORSE HUNTERS, THE, **433**
HORSE TALKER, THE, **637**
HORSE WHO LOVED PICNICS, THE, **184**
HOUSE ON PENDLETON BLOCK, THE, **617**
HOUSTON OILERS, THE, **532**
HOW MANY MILES TO SUNDOWN, **66**
HOW THE CRITTERS CREATED TEXAS, **1**
HUNT FOR THE WHOOPING CRANE, THE, **430**

I WANT TO BE A COWBOY, **604**
IF YOU ARE A HUNTER OF FOSSILS, **59**
IF YOU SAY SO, CLAUDE, **469**
IN TEXAS WITH DAVY CROCKETT, **442**
IN TEXAS WITH DAVY CROCKETT, **440**
IN THIS PROUD LAND, **645**

Title Index

INDIAN SADDLE-UP, **48**
INDIAN TEXANS, THE, **320**
INDIANS OF THE SOUTHWEST, **50**
INDIANS WHO LIVED IN TEXAS, **620**
INTEGRATION OF MARY-LARKIN THORNHILL, THE, **618**
ITALIAN TEXANS, THE, **321**

JAMES BOWIE AND HIS FAMOUS KNIFE, **237**
JANE LONG, **251**
JAYHAWKER, THE, **449**
JEAN LAFITTE, **152**
JEWISH TEXANS, THE, **322**
JIM AND ALAN ON A COTTON FARM, **386**
JIM BOWIE, BOY WITH A HUNTING KNIFE, **641**
JIMCO AND HARRY AT THE ROCKING H, **626**
JOE AND ANDY WANT A BOAT, **349**
JOE JACOBY, **623**
JOHN DENVER, **336**
JOHNNY TEXAS ON THE SAN ANTONIO ROAD, **297**
JOHNNY TEXAS:, **296**
JOHNNY TEXAS:, **296**
JUAN AND JUANITA, **61**
JUANA, **32**
JUANITO, **515**
JUST LIKE NANCY, **174**

KARANKAWA BOY, **5**
KATEY, **339**
KENSIL TAKES OVER, **239**
KEY TO DALLAS, THE, **601**
KIDNAPPING OF CHRISTINA LATTIMORE, THE, **470**
KITTENS AND THE CARDINALS, THE, **39**
KYLE ROTE, JR., **194**

L.B.J., **465**
LA SALLE, **553**
LA SALLE AND THE GRAND ENTERPRISE, **474**
LADD OF THE LONE STAR, **119**
LAFITTE, **252**
LANK OF THE LITTLE LEAGUE, **85**
LANTERN IN THE VALLEY, **281**
LANTERNS FOR FIESTA, **233**
LARRY COMES HOME, **86**

LARRY LEADS OFF, 87
LARRY OF LITTLE LEAGUE, 88
LAST OUTLAW, THE, 89
LAVENDER CAT, THE, 393
LBJ, 53
LEE TREVINO, 416
LEE TREVINO, 459
LEGEND OF THE BLUEBONNET, THE, 185
LEOPARD HORSE CANYON, 258
LET'S PRETEND, 568
LET'S PRETEND, 571
LET'S PRETEND, 569
LET'S PRETEND, 567
LET'S PRETEND, 570
LET'S PRETEND, 572
LIFE IN A LOG CABIN ON THE TEXAS FRONTIER, 460
LISTEN TO THE MOCKINGBIRD, 202
LITTLE ANDIRONS, 188
LITTLE ARLISS, 244
LITTLE CLOUD AND THE GREAT PLAINS HUNTERS, 15,000 YEARS AGO, 582
LITTLE DEPUTY, 605
LITTLE DUDE, 155
LITTLE GIRL LOST, 596
LITTLE HAWK AND THE FREE HORSES, 49
LITTLE LEAGUE AMIGO, 90
LITTLE LEAGUE DOUBLE PLAY, 91
LITTLE LEAGUE HEROES, 92
LITTLE LEAGUE LITTLE BROTHER, 93
LITTLE LEAGUE STEPSON, 94
LITTLE LEAGUE VICTORY, 95
LITTLE LEAGUE VISITOR, 96
LITTLE LEAGUE WAY, THE, 97
LITTLE LEAGUER, 98
LITTLE MANUEL, 299
LITTLE MISS CRINOLINE, 606
LITTLE TEJAS, 344
LIVE BOYS, 458
LOBLOLLY FARM, 153
LOG OF A COWBOY, 2
LONE STAR FIGHT, 203
LONE STAR FULLBACK, 441
LONE STAR LEADER, 99

Title Index

LONE STAR OF COURAGE, **367**
LONE STAR REBEL, **73**
LONE STAR RISING, **171**
LONE STAR TOMBOY, **13**
LONESOME END, **100**
LONESOME LONGHORN, **375**
LONG WAY TO WHISKEY CREEK, A, **67**
LONG-LEGGED, LONG-NOSED, LONG MANED WOLF, THE, **640**
LONGHORN, **259**
LONGHORN COWBOY, **164**
LONGHORNS TO ABILENE, **600**
LOOK AT ME! EXPERIENCES OF CHILDREN OF DALLAS, **391**
LOOK TO THE RIVER, **481**
LOS TEJANOS MEXICANOS, **329**
LOST ELEVEN, THE, **101**
LOST GOLD OF THE MONTEZUMAS, THE, **584**
LOST HILL, **31**
LOST LAKES, THE, **496**
LOVE, BID ME WELCOME, **394**
LUKE AND THE VAN ZANDT COUNTY WAR, **21**
LYNDON B. JOHNSON, **57**
LYNDON BAINES JOHNSON, **370**
LYNDON BAINES JOHNSON, **477**

MAGIC FOR MARY M., **40**
MAGIC TRAIN AT SAD MONKEY, THE, **124**
MAGNOLIA HEIGHTS, **487**
MAJOR AND HIS CAMELS, THE, **411**
MAKE WAY FOR LAUREN, **488**
MAN OF THE FAMILY, A, **131**
MANY TEXANS, **563**
MARGARET, **395**
MARY WARE IN TEXAS, **357**
MASCOT PERUNA, **531**
MEETING MISS HANNAH, **379**
MEXICAN TEXANS, THE, **323**
MIDDL'UN, **132**
MIER EXPEDITION, THE, **421**
MONTH OF CHRISTMASES, A, **350**
MOTHER GOOSE ON THE RIO GRANDE, **10**
MOTHER TREE, THE, **629**
MR. JELLYBEAN, **455**
MUSEUM MYSTERY, THE, **138**

MUSTANG ON THE PRAIRIE, **204**
MUSTANGERS, THE, **434**
MY BEACH BUDDIES OF BYGONE DAYS, **599**
MY PARDNER, **213**
MYSTERY CAMP, **428**
MYSTERY OF HURRICANE CASTLE, **471**
MYSTERY OF MCCLELLAN CREEK, THE, **139**
MYSTERY OF OLD MOBEETIE, **140**
MYSTERY OF THE DOUBLE DOUBLE CROSS, THE, **154**
MYSTERY OF THE STOLEN FISH POND, **404**

NAME THE DAY, **489**
NAT LOVE, NEGRO COWBOY, **218**
NAVY WINGS OF GOLD, **591**
NECESSARY NELLIE, **41**
NELLIE AND THE MAYOR'S HAT, **42**
NEW TALL TALES OF PECOS BILL, **219**
NEW TOWN IN TEXAS, **351**
NIGHT BEFORE CHRISTMAS, IN TEXAS, THAT IS, THE, **283**
NO WAY OF KNOWING, **388**
NORTH TO ABILENE, **51**
NORWEGIAN TEXANS, THE, **324**
NOT LIKE THAT, ARMADILLO, **398**

O. HENRY, **475**
OILFIELD BOY, **413**
OLD AZTEC STORY TELLER, THE, **527**
OLD BILL, **387**
OLD BLUE, **278**
OLD WATTLES, **149**
OLD YELLER, **245**
ON STAGE: JOHN DENVER, **439**
ON THE OPEN RANGE, **193**
ON THE STAKED PLAIN, **361**
ORPHANS ON THE GUADALUPE, **11**
OTTO IN TEXAS, **199**
OUR MEXICAN ANCESTORS, VOL. 1, **135**

PANTHER LICK CREEK, **287**
PARADISE CALLED TEXAS, A, **559**
PARTNERS IN THE SADDLE, **517**
PASSAGE TO TEXAS, **614**
PAULINE AND THE PEACOCK, **177**

PECOS BILL, **121**
PECOS BILL, **186**
PECOS BILL, **399**
PECOS BILL AND LIGHTNING, **498**
PECOS BILL AND THE LONG LASSO, **143**
PECOS BILL AND THE MUSTANG, **220**
PECOS BILL AND THE WONDERFUL CLOTHESLINE SNAKE, **111**
PECOS BILL CATCHES A HIDEBEHIND, **112**
PECOS BILL FINDS A HORSE, **178**
PECOS BILL RIDES A TORNADO, **113**
PECOS BILL, TEXAS COWPUNCHER, **221**
PERSONAL HISTORY, A, **407**
PETE, COW-PUNCHER, **29**
PHILIP OF TEXAS, **480**
PICTURE BOOK OF TEXAS, **36**
PICTURE LIFE OF LYNDON BAINES JOHNSON, THE, **631**
PINEY WOODS PEDDLER, THE, **555**
PIONEERING IN TEXAS, **19**
PLAYMAKER, THE, **102**
POLEY MORGAN, **575**
POLISH TEXANS, THE, **325**
POLLYANNA OF MAGIC VALLEY, **450**
PORTRAIT BY SHERYL, **490**
PRAIRIE CHRISTMAS, **523**
PRESIDENT FROM TEXAS, THE, **400**
PROMISE OF JUNE, **491**

QUANAH PARKER, **30**
QUANAH, LEADER OF THE COMANCHE, **417**
QUEST OF THE FOUR, THE, **24**

RABBIT FIRES, **352**
RAGS AND PATCHES, **401**
RAMBLER CLUB ON THE TEXAS BORDER, THE, **561**
RATTLESNAKE RUN, **377**
REAL BOOK ABOUT THE TEXAS RANGERS, THE, **14**
REBOUND, **103**
RECOLLECTION CREEK, **246**
REMEMBER GOLIAD, **222**
REMEMBER THE ALAMO!, **622**
RETREAT TO GLORY, **373**
RETURN TO RAMOS, **142**
REX GOES TO THE RODEO, **589**

RIDE A NORTHBOUND HORSE, **652**
RIDE FOR TEXAS, **435**
RIDIN' THE RAINBOW, **635**
RINGS ON HER FINGERS, **396**
RIO GRANDE, THE, **170**
RIO GRANDE, THE, **345**
RISE OF THE LONE STAR, **197**
ROAD TO GALVESTON, THE, **574**
ROAD TO SAN JACINTO, **525**
RODEO, **613**
RODEO ROUNDUP, **232**
RODRIGO AND ROSALITA, **127**
RONNIE AND THE TEXAS CAMEL, **461**
ROOM TO GROW, **207**

SALLY TAIT, **544**
SAM BASS, **609**
SAM HENDERSON, TEXAS RANGER, **438**
SAM HOUSTON, **125**
SAM HOUSTON, **253**
SAM HOUSTON, **301**
SAM HOUSTON, **422**
SAM HOUSTON, **456**
SAM HOUSTON, **583**
SAM HOUSTON OF TEXAS, **264**
SAM HOUSTON, FIGHTER AND LEADER, **653**
SAM HOUSTON, FRIEND OF THE INDIANS, **478**
SAM HOUSTON, HERO OF TEXAS, **374**
SAM HOUSTON, PATRIOT, **554**
SAM HOUSTON, THE TALLEST TEXAN, **356**
SAM RAYBURN, **17**
SAN ANTONIO SPURS, THE, **457**
SAN ANTONIO, ST. ANTHONY'S TOWN, **358**
SAN JACINTO, **104**
SANCHO OF THE LONG, LONG HORNS, **120**
SANCHO, THE HOMESICK STEER, **537**
SAND IN MY HAND, **122**
SANTA FE EXPEDITION, THE, **423**
SATURDAY HEROES, **105**
SAVAGE SAM, **247**
SCARLET COAT, THE, **234**
SEANCE, THE, **472**
SECRETS INSIDE, **429**

Title Index

SEEING TEXAS, **372**
SERAPHINA TODD, **306**
SHAG CHACOTA, **624**
SHIRLEY TAKES A CHANCE, **610**
SHRINE OF LIBERTY, THE ALAMO, **274**
SIDELINE PASS, **106**
SILVER DOLLAR, THE, **397**
SILVER TIP, **597**
SIX FEET SIX; THE HEROIC STORY OF SAM HOUSTON, **338**
SIX GUN, **260**
SONG OF THE HEART, **492**
SONGS TEXAS SINGS, **576**
SONNY-BOY SIM, **43**
SPANISH TEXANS, THE, **326**
SPECTER, THE, **473**
SPINDLETOP, **279**
SPRING IN THE AIR, **493**
SPRING IN THE AIR, **493**
SPRING IN THE AIR, **493**
STALWART MEN OF EARLY TEXAS, **427**
STARS OVER TEXAS, **6**
STEPHEN F. AUSTIN, **223**
STEPHEN F. AUSTIN, **424**
STOCKY, **44**
STORIES FROM THE HISTORY OF TEXAS, **546**
STORY OF DAVID CROCKETT, THE, **165**
STORY OF LYNDON B. JOHNSON, THE, **466**
STORY OF TEXAS, THE, **621**
STORY OF TEXAS, THE, **500**
STORY OF THE ALAMO, THE, **512**
STORY OF THE ALAMO, THE, **524**
STORY OF THE TEXAS RANGERS, THE, **625**
STOUT RIDER, **107**
STOWAWAY TO TEXAS, **214**
SUN, SAND AND STEEL, **190**
SUNRISE SONG, **240**
SUPER CHAMP! THE STORY OF BABE DIDRIKSON ZAHARIAS, **160**
SUPERMEX, **332**
SUSAN'S YEAR, **353**
SWEET THANG IS MY BLOODHOUND, **129**
SWISS TEXANS, THE, **327**
SYLVAN CITY, **494**
SYRIAN AND LEBANESE TEXANS, THE, **328**

TADPOLE TAYLOR, **378**
TAG-ALONG-TOOLOO, **545**
TAG-ALONG-TOOLOO, **545**
TAGALONG WITH CODY, **507**
TAME THE WILD STALLION, **638**
TEAMWORK, **108**
TED MARSH AND THE ENEMY, **562**
TEJANOS, **226**
TELL US ABOUT TEXAS, **342**
TEN COUSINS, **141**
TEN TALL TEXANS, **368**
TEN TALL TEXANS, **436**
TEN TEXAS TALES, **242**
TEXAN SCOUTS, **25**
TEXAN STAR, **26**
TEXAN TRIUMPH, **27**
TEXANS ! TEJAS TO TODAY, THE, **63**
TEXANS RIDE NORTH, THE, **337**
TEXAS, **144**
TEXAS, **280**
TEXAS, **443**
TEXAS ABC BOOK, THE, **22**
TEXAS AND THE AMERICAN REVOLUTION, **330**
TEXAS AND THE WAR WITH MEXICO, **196**
TEXAS FLAG PRIMER, **45**
TEXAS GEMS, **371**
TEXAS HEROES, **176**
TEXAS HILL COUNTRY, THE, **505**
TEXAS HISTORY MOVIES, **530**
TEXAS IN HISTORY--STORY--LEGEND, **506**
TEXAS IN WORDS AND PICTURES, **230**
TEXAS MISSIONS AND LANDMARKS, **308**
TEXAS NEWS, **580**
TEXAS RANCH BOY, **414**
TEXAS RANGER, THE, **241**
TEXAS RANGERS, THE, **8**
TEXAS RANGERS, THE, **290**
TEXAS RANGERS, THE, **410**
TEXAS STAR, **444**
TEXAS STORIES FOR READING AND ACTING, **189**
TEXAS TALES, **552**
TEXAS TOMBOY, **384**
TEXAS TOMBOY, **384**

TEXAS TRAIL DRIVE, **238**
TEXAS TREASURE, **509**
TEXAS WILD FLOWER LEGENDS, **511**
TEXAS WILD FLOWERS, **548**
TEXAS WILDFLOWERS IN NATURAL COLORS, **630**
TEXAS WILDLIFE, **182**
TEXAS WILDLIFE, **598**
TEXAS YANKEE, **47**
TEXAS--THE GOLDEN LAND, **451**
TEXAS, THE LAND OF THE TEJAS, **354**
THAT SPOTTED SOW, **34**
THAT TERRIBLE NIGHT SANTA GOT LOST IN THE WOODS, **365**
THAT'S ONE ORNERY ORPHAN, **68**
THEIR SHINING HOUR, **405**
THEY PUT ON MASKS, **60**
THEY WERE MADE OF RAWHIDE, **499**
THIS IS TEXAS, **540**
THORNBUSH JUNGLE, **454**
THRILLS ON A TEXAS RANCH, **12**
THUNDER ON THE TENNESSEE, **643**
TIGUAS, THE, **581**
TIME OF ROSIE, THE, **340**
TIME TO BE HUMAN, A, **267**
TONY DORSETT, **163**
TOP HAND OF LONE TREE RANCH, THE, **179**
TOUGHEY, **130**
TRAIL BOSS IN PIGTAILS, **586**
TRAIL DRIVE, **3**
TRAIL DRIVERS, THE, **118**
TRAIL-DRIVING ROOSTER, THE, **248**
TRAILS TO TEXAS, **109**
TRESSA, **35**
TRIP THROUGH THE MAGIC VALLEY OF TEXAS, A, **56**
TURN-OF-THE-CENTURY PARTY, THE, **282**
TURNABOUT SUMMER, **382**
TWELVE LEGENDARY STORIES OF TEXAS, **151**
TWO LITTLE TEXANS, **46**
TWO SIEGES OF THE ALAMO, **23**

UNCLE KRIS AND HIS PETS, **607**
UNCLE KRIS IN HIS WORKSHOP, **608**
UNDER SIX FLAGS, **181**

UNITED STATES IN THE MEXICAN WAR, THE, **376**
UP WITH YOUR BANNER, **390**

VALENTINE FOR CANDY, **175**
VALIANT FEW, THE, **602**
VERY GOOD NEIGHBORS, **205**
VICTORY VOLLEY, **310**

WAIT FOR ME, WATCH FOR ME, EULA BEE, **69**
WALK THE WORLD'S RIM, **37**
WALT DISNEY'S OLD YELLER, **191**
WALTER CRONKITE, **628**
WARPATH, **261**
WAZA WINS AT WINDY GULCH, **157**
WE CAN FLY, **529**
WE WERE THERE AT THE BATTLE OF THE ALAMO, **168**
WE WERE THERE ON THE CHISOLM TRAIL, **592**
WESTWARD THE COURSE OF EMPIRE, **268**
WHAT DO YOU DO IN QUICKSAND?, **535**
WHEN COWBOYS RODE THE CHISHOLM TRAIL, **418**
WHEN THE PINES GREW TALL, **402**
WHEN THE STORM GOD RIDES, **587**
WHITE HARVEST, **619**
WHO ARE THE CHINESE TEXANS?, **408**
WHO STOLE KATHY YOUNG ?, **156**
WHY COWBOYS SING, IN TEXAS, **381**
WHY THE CHISHOLM TRAIL FORKS, **4**
WIDE HORIZON, **208**
WILD BOY, **216**
WILD GEESE CALLING, **464**
WILDCAT, **291**
WILDERNESS PIONEER, **298**
WILLIAM BARRET TRAVIS, **224**
WILLIAM BARRET TRAVIS, **425**
WIND BLOWS FREE, THE, **209**
WINDING TRAIL, THE, **229**
WINGED COLT OF CASA MIA, THE, **134**
WINTER OF THE WOLF, **644**
WISH FOR LUTIE, A, **286**
WITH CROCKETT AND BOWIE, **462**
WITH DOMINGO LEAL IN SAN ANTONIO, **409**
WITH SAM HOUSTON IN TEXAS, **539**
WITH TAYLOR ON THE RIO GRANDE, **116**

WITH THE MAKERS OF TEXAS, **114**
WONDERS OF TEXAS, THE, **612**
WORDS BY HEART, **551**
WRONGHAND, **654**

YANKEE THUNDER, **557**
YEAR OF THE DINOSAUR, THE, **159**
YOUNG HIDALGO, **514**
YOUNG NATURALIST, **292**
YOUNG PRINCE AND THE MAGIC CONE, THE, **249**

ZACH TAYLOR, YOUNG ROUGH AND READY, **634**
ZAHARIAS!, **271**
ZEB PIKE, **33**

Bas les masques !

Nicolas Gerrier

hachette
FRANÇAIS LANGUE ÉTRANGÈRE

Audio

Durée: 118'
Format: MP3

Piste 1	Chapitre 1
Piste 2	Chapitre 2
Piste 3	Chapitre 3
Piste 4	Chapitre 4
Piste 5	Chapitre 5
Piste 6	Chapitre 6
Piste 7	Chapitre 7
Piste 8	Chapitre 8

Rédaction du dossier pédagogique: Nicolas Gerrier

Édition: Atelier des 2 Ormeaux (Christine Delormeau)

Maquette de couverture: Nicolas Piroux

Photos de couverture: poisson: © Shutterstock/Kankitti Chupayoong - masque: Thomas Lother und Volker Thomas, Nürnberg, courtesy of Zemanek-Münster

Maquette intérieure: Sophie Fournier-Villiot (Amarante)

Mise en pages: Atelier des 2 Ormeaux (Franck Delormeau)

Illustrations: Bruno David

Enregistrements: Quali'sons

Comédien: Catherine Creux

ISBN: 978-2-01-401646-8

© HACHETTE LIVRE 2020, 58 rue Jean-Bleuzen, 92178 VANVES CEDEX, France.

Tous les droits de traduction, de reproduction et d'adaptation réservés pour tout pays. La loi du 11 mars 1957 n'autorisant, aux termes des alinéas 2 et 3 de l'article 41, d'une part, que « les copies ou reproductions strictement réservées à l'usage privé du copiste et non destinées à une utilisation collective » et, d'autre part, que « les analyses et les courtes citations » dans un but d'exemple et d'illustration, « toute représentation ou reproduction intégrale ou partielle, faite sans le consentement de l'auteur ou de ses ayants droit ou ayants cause, est illicite » (Alinéa 1 de l'article 40). Cette représentation ou reproduction, par quelque procédé que ce soit, sans autorisation de l'éditeur ou du Centre français de l'exploitation du droit de copie (20, rue des Grands-Augustins, 75006 Paris), constituerait donc une contrefaçon sanctionnée par les articles 425 et suivants du Code pénal.

SOMMAIRE

L'œuvre

Chapitre 1 5
    Un dîner qui finit mal…

Chapitre 2 13
    Agathe Langlois, suspecte numéro 1

Chapitre 3 21
    François Yasaki ment-il ?

Chapitre 4 29
    Que cache Thibault Fontaine ?

Chapitre 5 35
    Perte de mémoire

Chapitre 6 43
    Et si Juliette…

Chapitre 7 49
    Le piège

Chapitre 8 57
    La bonne occasion ?

Activités

Chapitre 1 69

Chapitre 2 71

Chapitre 3 73

Chapitre 4 75

Chapitre 5 77

Chapitre 6 79

Chapitre 7 81

Chapitre 8 83

Activités de synthèse 86

FICHES

Fiche 1 : Le Musée du Quai Branly-Jacques Chirac..................... 88
Fiche 2 : Le Musée des Confluences 90
Fiche 3 : Le Musée des Civilisations (Mucem) 91

CORRIGÉS DES ACTIVITÉS 93

CHAPITRE 1

Un dîner qui finit mal...

Lundi 19 septembre, 21 h 15

Je m'appelle Emma Lorenzo. J'ai cinquante-quatre ans et je suis commandant à l'OCBC, l'Office central de lutte contre le trafic de biens culturels.

Ce soir, j'assiste au dîner annuel de l'association « Les amis du musée du quai Branly – Jacques Chirac ». Le musée est tout près de la tour Eiffel à Paris. Il est spécialisé dans les arts d'Asie, d'Afrique, d'Amérique et d'Océanie. Je suis membre de cette association depuis l'ouverture du musée, en 2006. L'art est ma passion. J'ai fait des études à l'École du Louvre avant de devenir policière.

Je suis assise à une table de dix personnes. Nous attendons le dîner depuis quinze minutes et je relis le menu pour la troisième fois. Mon voisin de gauche s'appelle François Yasaki. Il est le directeur de la plus grande galerie d'art japonais de Paris. Je l'interroge sur l'entrée proposée sur le menu :

— Sashimi de fugu, c'est du poisson cru ?

— Tout à fait, commandant. Vous pouvez le déguster sans crainte.

— Pourquoi dites-vous cela ?

— Vous ne connaissez pas ce poisson ? Ses organes contiennent un poison mortel pour l'homme, la tétrodotoxine. Au Japon, l'empereur n'a pas le droit d'en manger.

— Mais pourquoi on nous le sert dans ce cas ? C'est très dangereux.

CHAPITRE 1

François Yasaki pose la main sur mon avant-bras.

— Ne vous inquiétez pas. Kenji Ono est le meilleur cuisinier japonais ! Il est aussi un très bon ami.

Qui a eu l'idée de servir un poisson mortel à ce dîner ? Sans doute Jean-Charles Latour, le directeur du musée. Je le connais depuis trente ans et, depuis trente ans, il a des idées étranges. Je le cherche des yeux. Jean-Charles est installé à la table d'honneur. Hana Lebosse, la femme du milliardaire Georges Lebosse, est assise à sa droite. Elle est l'invitée d'honneur de cette soirée. Il y a neuf mois, son mari a donné au musée un très ancien masque japonais de théâtre nô[1]. C'était trois semaines avant sa mort.

— Vous connaissez l'âge de Madame Lebosse ?
— Une soixantaine d'années, répond François Yasaki.

Six ans de plus que moi ? Elle en paraît dix de moins. Cette Japonaise est d'une beauté et d'une élégance extraordinaires.

— Vous connaissiez son mari ?
— Je l'ai rencontré plusieurs fois. Lebosse est un nom connu dans le monde des arts asiatiques. Mais vous le savez aussi bien que moi.

— On dit qu'elle veut ouvrir un musée au Japon, c'est vrai ?
— Est-ce un interrogatoire, commandant ?

La question me fait sourire. Je n'ai pas revu François Yasaki depuis un an. À l'époque, j'enquêtais sur des objets volés en vente dans sa galerie. François Yasaki connaît très bien Hana Lebosse, mais il ne veut pas parler d'elle.

Ma voisine de droite, une jeune femme d'une trentaine d'années, me pose deux questions sur mon travail de commandant. Lorsque je lui parle de l'OCBC, elle me fixe longuement.

— Quelque chose ne va pas, Mademoiselle ?

Elle secoue la tête.

---

[1] Le théâtre nô : théâtre traditionnel japonais.

– Non rien, excusez-moi. Mais, tout à l'heure, vous vous êtes présentée comme…

– … membre de l'association des Amis du musée ? Je le suis aussi. C'est la passionnée d'art qui est là ce soir. Ce n'est pas la chasseuse d'œuvres volées. Oubliez le commandant ! Vous êtes aussi membre de l'association ?

Au même instant, une femme de petite taille aux cheveux courts coupés au carré pose ses deux mains sur les épaules de ma voisine.

– Alors, tout va bien ?

Je reconnais Juliette Bourdelle, la conservatrice responsable des collections asiatiques du musée du quai Branly.

– Juliette ! Je t'ai aperçue tout à l'heure, mais tu étais en grande conversation. Je n'ai pas voulu te déranger. Tout est parfait !

Alors que des serveurs commencent à poser les entrées sur les premières tables, j'ajoute :

– Sauf peut-être ce poisson cru…

– Il faut tout goûter dans la vie. Tu vas adorer.

Juliette présente ensuite ma voisine à toute la table :

– Avez-vous fait connaissance avec Agathe Langlois ? Agathe est l'héroïne de la soirée. Mais elle est trop modeste pour le dire. Le masque de Georges Lebosse était dans un très mauvais état. Agathe l'a très bien restauré[2]. Elle a un grand talent.

Les convives félicitent la jeune femme. L'un d'eux ajoute :

– C'est une grande chance d'avoir ce masque au quai Branly. Il a parfaitement sa place dans ce musée !

– Je ne partage pas votre enthousiasme, intervint François Yasaki. Le quai Branly fait un travail magnifique, mais… comment vous dire ? Ce masque appartient à l'histoire du Japon. Sa place n'est pas en France, mais là-bas.

---

2 Restauré : réparé, remis en état.

La remarque de François Yasaki déclenche une conversation animée. Je suis surprise de son opinion, car il vend des objets de toute l'Asie dans sa galerie. Après quelques minutes, Juliette Bourdelle nous quitte :

— Je dois rejoindre ma table. Je vous laisse parler de ce sujet difficile. Agathe, on se voit à quelle heure demain matin dans le bureau de Jean-Charles ?

— À 10 h.

Agathe Langlois a répondu d'un ton sec. L'ambiance entre les deux jeunes femmes n'est pas bonne.

Une dame assise en face d'Agathe lui demande :

— Est-ce que restaurer les objets anciens est une bonne chose ? Ne faut-il pas les laisser dans leur état ? Un masque ancien ne devient-il pas une simple copie de l'original après une restauration ?

Agathe Langlois ne répond pas. Elle se lève et dit :

— Excusez-moi, je dois aller aux toilettes.

Les convives la regardent partir avec surprise. La dame demande à son mari :

— J'ai dit quelque chose de mal ?

Un serveur pose devant moi une assiette de sashimi de fugu. Elle est joliment préparée, mais elle ne me fait pas envie. Je déteste le poisson cru. Lorsqu'Agathe revient dix minutes plus tard, je n'ai rien mangé. Agathe est très nerveuse. Je lui demande si tout va bien. Elle me répond d'un simple mouvement de la tête puis se jette sur son assiette. Elle avale la moitié du poisson en trois bouchées et vide son verre de saké[3] en une seule gorgée.

— Hum, cela fait du bien. Les Japonais sont les meilleurs cuisiniers du monde !

Les autres convives se régalent également. À mon tour d'être courageuse. Je mange deux petites tranches sans les mâcher.

---

3 Le saké : un alcool japonais fait avec du riz.

CHAPITRE 1

Je remarque alors que François Yasaki n'a pas touché à son assiette. N'aime-t-il pas le poisson cru ? Je vais lui poser la question quand Agathe Langlois me dit :

— Commandant, je veux vous montrer quelque chose. J'ai…

Agathe s'arrête de parler et pose les mains sur son ventre.

— Agathe, vous allez bien ?

— Mon ventre me fait terriblement mal.

Trois autres convives se plaignent de respirer avec difficulté. Puis c'est à mon tour de me sentir mal. François Yasaki se lève et crie :

— Il faut un docteur. Vite ! Ces personnes ne vont pas bien.

Puis il ajoute pour tous les invités :

— Arrêtez de manger. Le fugu est empoisonné !

L'ordre fait rapidement le tour des tables. Les invités regardent leur assiette avec terreur. Trois secouristes accourent vers notre table. Je vois un secouriste faire un massage cardiaque à Agathe. Ma vue se trouble ensuite.

— C'est sérieux, appelle le SAMU[4], ordonne le secouriste à sa collègue.

Au même instant, une alarme sonne dans le musée. Les invités ont peur : ils quittent leur table et courent vers les sorties. J'essaye de me lever pour leur dire de rester calmes. Mais mes jambes lâchent. Dans ma chute, ma tête heurte violemment le bord de la table et je m'évanouis.

---

4 SAMU : service d'aide médicale urgente.

Bas les masques !

CHAPITRE 2

Agathe Langlois, suspecte numéro 1

Mardi 20 septembre, 8 h 30

J'ouvre les yeux et reconnais le visage qui me sourit. C'est le lieutenant Samir Lacoste, un collègue de l'OCBC. Nous avons l'habitude de faire équipe tous les deux.

— Eh bien, tu nous as fait peur !

— Je suis où ? Que s'est-il passé ?

Samir me rappelle le dîner de gala, les malaises des convives et l'alarme. Il m'apprend que je suis dans une chambre de l'hôpital européen Georges-Pompidou. L'établissement est près du musée du quai Branly.

— Quelqu'un a prévenu Dany ?

— Ton mari est à la cafétéria. Il n'était pas au dîner avec toi hier soir ?

— Dany dans un musée ? Jamais ! En plus, son équipe préférée de rugby, le Racing 92, avait un match hier soir.

Dany et moi sommes mariés depuis vingt-sept ans. Nous avons des goûts totalement opposés. J'aime l'art et les musées, il aime le sport et les stades. Je ne veux pas quitter la ville, il rêve de vivre à la campagne. J'adore la blanquette de veau et le vin rosé, il dévore des pizzas et boit de la bière. Et, pourtant, nous nous aimons follement ! C'est un mystère pour tous nos amis, notre famille et parfois pour nous-mêmes.

Samir va prévenir une infirmière de mon réveil. Quelques minutes plus tard, un médecin entre dans la chambre.

CHAPITRE 2

— Madame Lorenzo, comment vous sentez-vous ?
— Fatiguée et un peu perdue. Que m'est-il arrivé ?
— Vous avez eu une intoxication à la tétrodotoxine. Mais la dose était faible. Tout va redevenir normal très vite.

Le médecin ajoute :
— Huit personnes sont arrivées hier soir du musée avec le même problème que vous. Vous êtes sept à bien vous porter. Malheureusement, une patiente a fait des réactions très violentes. Il s'agit d'Agathe Langlois. Elle est dans le coma.
— Oh mon Dieu ! Elle va s'en sortir ?
— Il est difficile de répondre pour l'instant. Mais vous devez penser à vous et vous reposer pendant deux jours. Je reviens vous voir dans l'après-midi.

Lorsque nous sommes de nouveau seuls, je demande à Samir :
— Pourquoi parle-t-il de huit personnes ? Il y avait trois cents invités au dîner.
— Il y a eu des problèmes seulement à ta table. C'est une chance, sauf pour ceux qui dînaient avec toi, bien sûr.
— Bien sûr…

Je compte les personnes à ma table : Agathe Langlois, François Yasaki, un couple de quinquagénaires, une place vide à côté d'Agathe, une femme avec une robe rouge trop voyante, deux jeunes hommes accompagnés d'une jeune femme et moi. Cela fait neuf. Pourquoi huit personnes seulement ont fait des réactions au poison ? Samir me donne les noms des personnes intoxiquées.
— Et François Yasaki ? Il était aussi à ma table.

Je me souviens alors : juste avant de me sentir mal, j'ai remarqué que le marchand d'art ne mangeait pas l'entrée. Pourquoi ? Était-il au courant pour le poison ?
— Je ne comprends pas une chose, dis-je. Qu'est-ce qui a déclenché l'alarme ? Ce n'est pas le poison quand même !
— Je ne t'ai pas encore tout dit : on a volé le masque japonais.

Bas les masques !

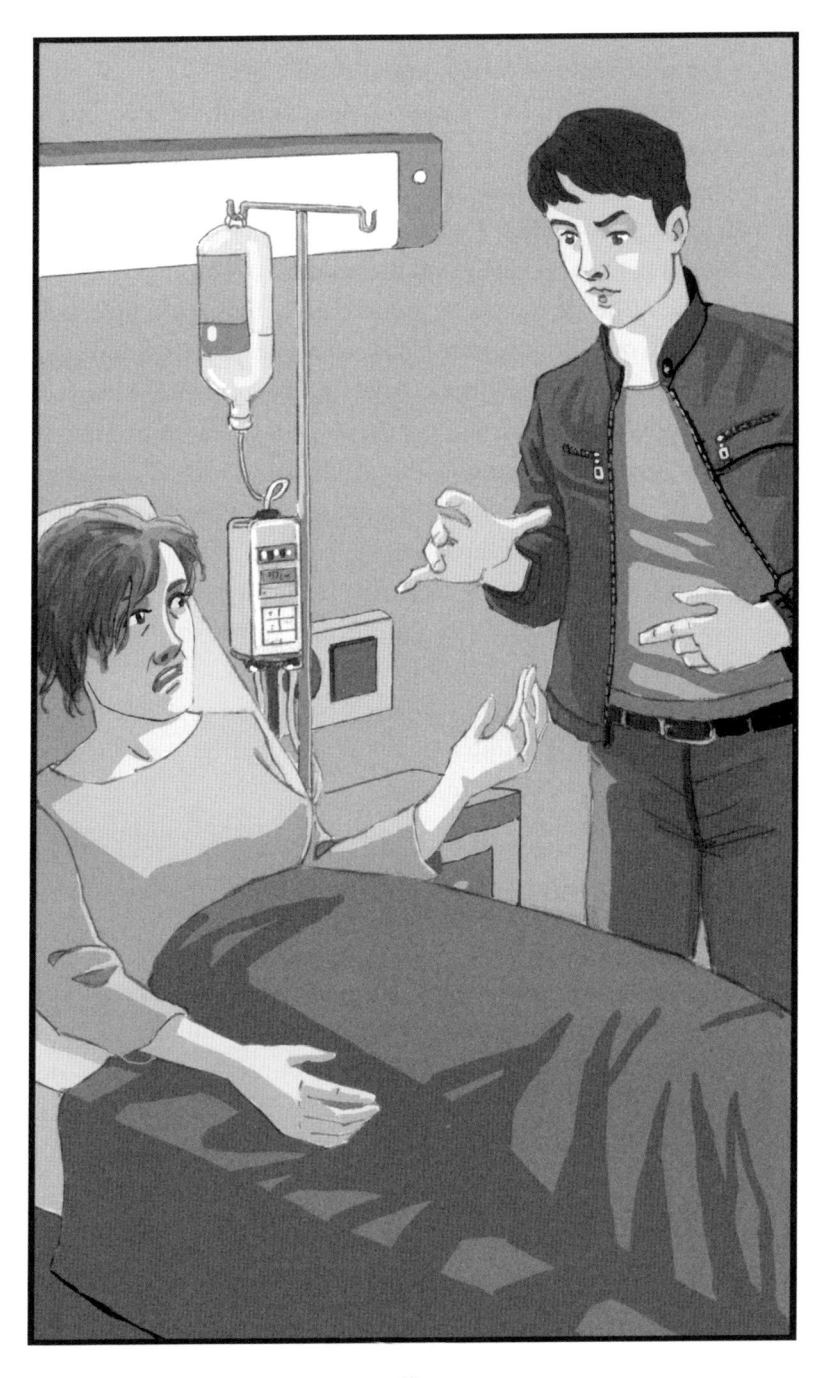

CHAPITRE 2

— Quoi ! Tu me dis ça seulement maintenant ?
— Le médecin m'a dit « pas de choc violent aujourd'hui ». Tu dois te reposer.
— Je me reposerai plus tard ! Attends-moi dehors, j'appelle le patron et je m'habille. J'en ai pour dix minutes. On passera à la cafétéria prévenir Dany et on file au musée.

Une demi-heure plus tard, je suis dans le bureau du directeur du musée du quai Branly, Jean-Charles Latour. Juliette Bourdelle, la conservatrice des collections d'Asie, est aussi présente. Je connais Juliette depuis deux ans. J'ai participé avec elle à un groupe de travail sur la sécurité du musée du quai Branly. Depuis, j'ai assisté à quatre de ses conférences[1]. Nous ne nous voyons pas souvent, mais je l'apprécie beaucoup.

Je les informe des instructions du chef de la police judiciaire :
— Je m'occupe des deux enquêtes : le vol du masque et l'empoisonnement à la tétrodotoxine.
— Ce sont deux tragédies, dit Jean-Charles Latour. Cette pauvre petite Agathe, c'est une fille tellement bien. Pourquoi a-t-on servi du fugu ? Je suis vraiment un idiot !
— Ce n'est pas de ta faute, dit Juliette. Le chef cuisinier a dû faire une erreur.
— Un de mes collègues est en train de l'interroger, dis-je. Parlons pour l'instant du masque. Que s'est-il passé ?

Juliette m'explique le déroulement de la journée d'hier. Le musée était fermé au public comme tous les lundis.

Le matin, Juliette et Agathe ont présenté le masque à des professionnels de l'art. Cela s'est passé de 9 h à midi. Puis, elles ont placé le masque dans une armoire de l'atelier de restauration du musée.

— Vous étiez seulement toutes les deux ?

---

1 Une conférence : présentation d'un sujet devant un public.

— Oui, c'était l'heure du déjeuner. Il n'y avait pas d'autres employés.

— Vous avez respecté toutes les procédures de sécurité ?

— Oui. Agathe n'a pas travaillé hier après-midi sur le masque. Il devait toujours être dans l'armoire au moment du vol.

L'atelier de restauration est un lieu très sécurisé. Seules les personnes avec un badge d'accès peuvent y entrer. Mais cela fait tout de même une trentaine de personnes avec le directeur, les employés, les conservateurs… Le voleur est-il parmi eux ?

Juliette m'accompagne ensuite jusqu'au poste central de sécurité[2].

— Jean-Charles paraît très affecté par les événements, lui dis-je quand nous passons devant les collections africaines.

— Nous aimons tous beaucoup Agathe. Jean-Charles lui a même proposé le poste de Responsable de l'atelier de restauration la semaine dernière. Agathe était très intéressée.

— Elle ne travaille pas actuellement à l'Atelier Fontaine ?

— Si. Mais l'Atelier Fontaine a de grosses difficultés financières. Les relations d'Agathe avec son patron, Thibault Fontaine, ne sont pas bonnes.

— Comment sais-tu cela ?

— Tout se sait dans le petit milieu de l'art.

Laurent Belon, le responsable Sécurité du musée, nous accueille à son PC. Il a l'air épuisé. Il a passé la première partie de la nuit avec la police scientifique et la deuxième partie à regarder les vidéos des caméras de surveillance.

Nous nous installons tous les trois devant un grand écran. Laurent Belon nous rappelle les positions des différentes caméras sur un plan du musée. Puis, il lance la lecture des vidéos.

— J'ai regardé les vidéos depuis l'ouverture des portes

---

[2] Un poste central de sécurité (PC) : une pièce où travaille le personnel qui surveille le musée.

CHAPITRE 2

du musée, à 18 h, jusqu'au déclenchement de l'alarme. Regardez ce qui se passe à 21 h 55 : cette personne se lève de sa table.

Je reconnais ma table et Agathe Langlois.

– Cela doit être l'heure où Agathe Langlois est allée aux toilettes.

– D'accord, dit Laurent Belon d'une voix calme. Par contre, elle ne se dirige pas vers les toilettes. Elle prend les escaliers qui descendent au sous-sol. On la retrouve sur la caméra 43B. Elle prend ce long couloir, passe devant des bureaux de l'administration puis tourne sur la droite. Elle introduit ensuite son badge dans le dispositif placé à gauche de cette porte.

– Elle entre où ?

– Dans l'atelier de restauration, dit Juliette Bourdelle.

Laurent Belon arrête l'image et nous demande de bien nous souvenir du sac qu'Agathe porte à l'épaule. Puis il fait avancer les images de trois minutes. Nous voyons Agathe sortir de l'atelier. Laurent Belon fait un nouvel arrêt sur image.

– Vous voyez son sac ? Il est plus gros. Agathe a pris quelque chose dans l'atelier.

– Le masque ? demande Juliette.

– Je ne sais pas. Mais quand elle ressort… là… Agathe oublie de refermer correctement la porte. C'est ça qui va déclencher l'alarme quinze minutes plus tard.

Je demande à Laurent Belon de repasser la scène où Agathe sort de l'atelier.

– J'ai l'impression qu'Agathe retient la porte. Regardez, elle tend sa main droite vers la porte. Pourquoi fait-elle cela ?

Agathe disparaît ensuite des images pendant plus de trois minutes. Puis on la voit passer entre les tables des invités et rejoindre la sienne. Laurent Belon arrête la lecture.

Agathe Langlois a-t-elle volé le masque ? Pourquoi l'a-t-elle fait lors du dîner de gala ? Voulait-elle déclencher l'alarme en empêchant la porte de l'atelier de se refermer ?

CHAPITRE 3

François Yasaki ment-il ?

Mardi 20 septembre, 14 h 30

Le directeur du musée, Jean-Charles Latour, ne veut pas croire les vidéos. Elles montrent pourtant Agathe Langlois entrer dans l'atelier de restauration pendant le dîner.

– C'est ridicule ! Agathe ne peut pas avoir volé le masque ! Le masque est très connu. Agathe ne pouvait pas le revendre. Que voulait-elle en faire ? Elle voulait l'accrocher dans son salon ? C'est ri-di-cule !

– Elle peut l'avoir volé pour quelqu'un. Les caméras perdent Agathe pendant deux minutes. Cela suffit pour donner le masque à un complice. Celui-ci a pu très facilement quitter le musée après le déclenchement de l'alarme. Elle a laissé la porte de l'atelier de restauration ouverte pour déclencher l'alarme et créer la panique.

Jean-Charles s'énerve :

– Agathe allait devenir la Responsable de l'atelier de restauration. Elle ne pouvait pas commencer son travail par un vol !

Je comprends la réaction de Jean-Charles. Mais les voleurs sont parfois des gens bien avant de passer à l'acte. Jean-Charles a prévenu dès ce matin Thibault Fontaine, le patron d'Agathe. Il est depuis deux semaines à Toulouse pour la restauration d'un tableau dans un château. Il rentre à Paris dans la journée. Je l'interrogerai demain. Je dois commencer par rassembler plus d'informations sur le masque.

CHAPITRE 3

— Jean-Charles, tu connaissais personnellement Georges Lebosse avant son don au musée ?

— Non. Il a fait fortune dans les casinos et les cercles de jeu, ce n'est pas du tout mon univers. Il ne connaissait rien en art. Sa femme s'occupe seule de leur collection d'œuvres d'art.

— Tu la connais, elle ?

— Pas vraiment. Juliette Bourdelle a rencontré les Lebosse plus souvent que moi.

Le directeur émet un petit rire.

— Qu'y a-t-il ?

— Georges Lebosse nous a reçus dans son cercle de jeux du 16e arrondissement de Paris pour la remise du masque. Il nous l'a donné rapidement. Il n'était pas ému. Juste après, il nous a proposé de jouer à la roulette. Le jeu et l'argent étaient plus importants pour lui que l'art.

— Il a acheté le masque au Japon ?

— Pas du tout ! Il appartenait à sa famille depuis le 17e siècle ! Georges Lebosse est un descendant de François Caron, le premier explorateur français au Japon. François Caron parle du masque dans une lettre à sa mère en 1622 ! Georges Lebosse nous a aussi donné ce document extraordinaire. Je vais te dire une chose : Hana Lebosse tenait beaucoup plus à ce masque que son mari. Elle voulait le garder. Mais le masque appartenait à Georges Lebosse, pas à elle.

Après mon entretien avec Jean-Charles, je retrouve le lieutenant Samir Lacoste devant l'entrée du musée. Il me donne des informations sur l'interrogatoire de Kenji Ono.

Le cuisinier ne peut pas expliquer la présence de tétrodotoxine. Il a tout préparé dans les règles de l'art.

Des experts arrivent demain du Japon pour vérifier ses explications.

Les analyses des assiettes de ma table ont donné un résultat très

CHAPITRE 3

intéressant : une seule assiette contenait une dose mortelle, celle d'Agathe Langlois ! L'intoxication n'est donc pas accidentelle. Quelqu'un voulait tuer Agathe.

Vingt minutes plus tard, un taxi me dépose à quelques mètres de la galerie de François Yasaki. Elle s'appelle ZenArt et se trouve rue Charlemagne, dans le quartier du Marais.

Il est 16 h 30 et je n'ai rien mangé depuis hier soir, j'ai très faim. J'entre dans un café à l'angle de la rue Charlemagne et de la rue du Fauconnier et m'installe au comptoir.

— Je sers quoi à la jeune fille ?
— Un jambon beurre[1] et un expresso, c'est possible ?
— Pour vous, tout est possible, mademoiselle ! Un jambon beurre et un expresso, c'est parti !

Je croque dans mon sandwich avec envie. Bien meilleur que le fugu !

Je paye ensuite mes consommations et quitte le café.

Lorsque j'arrive devant la galerie, François Yasaki ferme le rideau de fer qui protège la vitrine de sa boutique. Il a un casque de moto sur la tête et porte un sac de sport en bandoulière.

— Vous fermez déjà ?
— Ah, bonjour commandant, je vais au cinéma avec une amie sur les Champs-Élysées. La séance est dans trente-cinq minutes. Comment vous sentez-vous ?
— Beaucoup mieux. Je peux vous parler juste quelques instants ?

François Yasaki regarde sa montre, soupire et finit par accepter.
— Je vous donne dix minutes.

Il remonte le rideau de fer et nous pénétrons dans sa galerie. Je lui demande directement :
— Avez-vous goûté le sashimi de fugu hier soir ?
— Non.

---

[1] Un jambon beurre : un sandwich de baguette avec du jambon et du beurre.

— Pourquoi ? Vous le saviez empoisonné ?
— Bien sûr que non !

François Yasaki me raconte l'histoire de sa grand-mère. Elle est morte empoisonnée par un fugu lors d'un repas familial. Elle l'avait préparé elle-même ! Depuis, toute sa famille a peur de ce poisson.

Est-ce que je peux vérifier son histoire ?

Je lui demande :

— Vous conseillez Hana Lebosse pour sa collection d'œuvres d'art. Elle n'a pas apprécié le don de son mari au musée du quai Branly. Peut-elle vouloir récupérer le masque ?
— Vous l'accusez de vol ?
— Je vous pose une question.
— Votre métier vous fait voir des voleurs partout. Madame Lebosse pense comme moi : la place du masque est au Japon. Mais je ne lui ai pas conseillé de le voler !

François Yasaki garde un calme parfait.

Joue-t-il un rôle dans le vol du masque ? Si oui, lequel ?

Je lui pose d'autres questions sur les voleurs possibles de ce masque. Mais il répond toujours par :

— Vous connaissez le trafic des œuvres d'art mieux que moi, commandant.

Puis, il me fait remarquer que les dix minutes sont passées.

— Si vous entendez parler du masque ou si on vous propose de l'acheter, pouvez-vous me prévenir ?
— Je n'achète pas d'objets volés, commandant. Vous le savez bien. Mais je vais garder les oreilles et les yeux grands ouverts pour vous.

Je parcours une cinquantaine de mètres dans la rue Charlemagne puis m'arrête. Je regarde vers la galerie ZenArt.

François Yasaki monte sur son scooter.

Me dit-il toute la vérité ?

CHAPITRE 3

Cercle de
Jeux
Du
Trocadéro

Je n'ai pas vérifié le contenu de son sac. Peut-il contenir le masque ?

J'arrête la première voiture qui passe, ouvre la porte et ordonne au conducteur de suivre le scooter.

— On n'est pas au cinéma, Madame, me répond-il interloqué[2].

Je lui montre ma carte de police et dis fermement :

— Suivez-le ou je vous mets en prison !

Ma menace est stupide, mais elle l'impressionne. Le conducteur démarre à toute vitesse.

Quinze minutes plus tard, le scooter s'arrête devant un bel immeuble du 16e arrondissement. Je remercie chaleureusement mon conducteur.

François Yasaki entre dans l'immeuble. Je m'approche de la grande porte en bois et lit sur une plaque dorée : Cercle de jeux du Trocadéro.

Je téléphone à Jean-Charles Latour :

— Bonsoir Emma. Tu as des nouvelles du masque à me donner ?

— Pas encore. Le cercle de jeux de Georges Lebosse dont tu m'as parlé, c'est le Cercle du Trocadéro ?

— Oui, c'est cela. Tu veux jouer à la roulette ?

Que fait François Yasaki ici ? Il avait un rendez-vous sur les Champs-Élysées. Pourquoi m'a-t-il menti ?

---

2 Interloqué : très étonné.

CHAPITRE 4

Que cache Thibault Fontaine ?

Mercredi 21 septembre, 8 h 40

L'Atelier Fontaine est situé quai de la Loire, sur le bassin de la Villette. Je descends du bus 26 à l'arrêt Marché Secrétan. J'ai prévenu Thibault Fontaine de mon passage hier soir par téléphone. La journée est magnifique et les bords du bassin donnent à Paris des airs de vacances.

Je pousse la porte de l'atelier et lance un « Bonjour » bien fort. Un homme d'une quarantaine d'années apparaît au fond de l'atelier.

— Bonjour Madame, je peux vous aider ?

— Bonjour. Je suis le commandant Emma Lorenzo. Nous nous sommes parlé au téléphone hier soir.

— Ah oui. Je suis Thibault Fontaine, très heureux de vous voir.

L'homme est grand et a de longs cheveux noirs attachés en catogan[1]. Sa barbe a de nombreux reflets roux. Il est habillé dans un style décontracté. Il ressemble à un artiste. Mais il a aussi la tête de quelqu'un qui a mal dormi depuis plusieurs jours. Son visage est blanc et il est très nerveux. Je lui demande :

— Vous allez bien ?

— Non, je... vous voulez un café ?

J'accepte volontiers. Thibault Fontaine me conduit dans une cuisine qui occupe le mur du fond de l'atelier. Nous passons devant une grande bibliothèque. Elle est remplie de livres sur l'art,

---

[1] Cheveux en catogan : les cheveux attachés derrière la tête par un ruban.

CHAPITRE 4

les techniques de restauration et les musées du monde entier. J'aperçois aussi plusieurs livres sur la cuisine asiatique, dont trois sur l'art de préparer le poisson cru. Je tourne la couverture de l'un d'eux et lis la dédicace :

Pour Thibault, peut-être un jour, aimeras-tu le poisson cru ?
Agathe.

Thibault Fontaine fouille dans les placards, mais ne trouve pas de café.

— Je suis désolé. Je suis absent depuis deux semaines et personne n'a fait les courses. Je…

— Un verre d'eau sera très bien. Nous pouvons nous asseoir ?

— Oui, bien sûr. Je… je suis désolé, je me sens complètement perdu avec ce drame. Que s'est-il passé au musée ? J'ai lu les journaux, eu Jean-Charles Latour au téléphone et parlé avec un médecin de l'hôpital Georges-Pompidou. Mais je n'arrive pas à comprendre. Il s'agit vraiment d'un empoisonnement au fugu ?

— Oui. Et il est volontaire.

— Mais c'est impossible, qui peut en vouloir à Agathe ?

— C'est ce que nous essayons de trouver.

J'interroge Thibault Fontaine sur son employée, Agathe Langlois. La jeune femme a 32 ans et est célibataire. Elle est fille unique[2] et ses parents sont morts il y a trois ans dans un accident de voiture. Elle vit seule.

— Agathe est passionnée d'art asiatique et se consacre entièrement à son travail. Malheureusement.

— Que voulez-vous dire ?

— Le travail n'est pas tout dans la vie. Notre activité est passionnante, mais elle occupe beaucoup de notre temps. Il ne faut pas oublier notre famille et nos amis.

Je sens de l'amertume[3] dans la réflexion de Thibault Fontaine.

---

2 Être fille unique : être le seul enfant de ses parents.
3 Amertume : tristesse après un échec.

CHAPITRE 4

Il m'apprend qu'il est divorcé depuis trois ans. « À cause du travail » précise-t-il.

— Agathe avait-elle un comportement étrange ces derniers temps ?

— Nous ne nous sommes pas vus depuis un mois environ. Pourquoi me demandez-vous cela ?

— Elle était nerveuse pendant le dîner. La restauration du masque est un beau coup de publicité pour votre atelier. Pourquoi n'êtes-vous pas venu ? La place libre à côté d'Agathe était bien la vôtre ?

— Oui. Mais je suis très occupé en ce moment à Toulouse. Je n'avais pas envie de rouler plus de mille kilomètres à moto juste pour une soirée.

— Le directeur du musée du quai Branly a proposé à Agathe de l'embaucher. Agathe était intéressée. Vous le saviez ?

Thibault Fontaine semble sous le choc.

— Non, pas du tout.

Il parcourt l'atelier de long en large. Il s'arrête puis se remet à marcher. Je lui propose de se rasseoir et lui parle des images des caméras de surveillance.

— C'est absurde. Agathe n'est pas une voleuse.

— Je le crois aussi. Mais elle peut avoir volé le masque pour de l'argent. Par exemple, pour aider un ami qui a des difficultés financières. Parfois, l'occasion se présente et des gens très honnêtes choisissent la mauvaise option.

Thibault regarde dans le vide sans parler. Je décide d'être directe[4] :

— Vous n'avez pas demandé à Agathe de voler le masque pour vous aider, Monsieur Fontaine ? Votre atelier a des difficultés financières, n'est-ce pas ?

---

4   Être directe : parler avec des mots clairs.

Bas les masques !

CHAPITRE 4

— Vous êtes complètement folle ! Bien sûr que non ! Agathe est à l'hôpital entre la vie et la mort et vous venez m'accuser ! Vous n'avez pas honte ?

Il a raison, je suis allée trop loin. Mais il faut savoir secouer les gens pour obtenir des réponses. L'énervement de Thibault Fontaine cache quelque chose. Mais quoi ? Son état psychique m'inquiète. Je lui propose de voir un médecin.

— Non, merci. Je vais rentrer chez moi et prendre des somnifères. J'ai besoin de dormir.

Je laisse à Thibault Fontaine ma carte et lui promets de le tenir au courant de la suite de l'enquête. Je téléphone à Samir. Je lui demande de lancer une recherche sur Thibault Fontaine.

— Je cherche quoi ?

— Je ne sais pas. Tout ce qu'on peut avoir sur lui. Tu cherches sur les réseaux sociaux aussi. Tu fais la même chose pour Agathe Langlois.

Je rentre au musée et fais plusieurs fois le chemin emprunté par Agathe lundi soir entre la table et l'atelier de restauration du musée. Avec le nombre d'invités et de serveurs, elle a pu donner le masque à un complice sans difficulté. Samir me rappelle vers midi.

— Thibault Fontaine est divorcé et a deux enfants. Son nom apparaît dans des revues spécialisées en art. C'est un professionnel reconnu. Un point est intéressant : il est interdit de jeux depuis quatre ans. J'ai téléphoné à son ex-femme. Elle l'a quitté à cause de sa dépendance au jeu. Il a perdu de grosses sommes d'argent. Mais, il y a mieux.

— Quoi ?

— Un radar l'a flashé à 170 km/h.

— Quand et où ?

— Avant-hier sur l'autoroute A6, à trente kilomètres de Paris, en direction de la capitale, à 5 heures de l'après-midi.

Thibault Fontaine n'était pas à Toulouse lundi soir, comme il me l'a dit. Sa femme ne l'a pas quitté à cause du travail, mais du jeu. Il m'a donc menti deux fois. Que cache-t-il ?

CHAPITRE 5

Perte de mémoire

Jeudi 22 septembre, 8 h

La spécialité du lieutenant Samir Lacoste est d'entrer le matin dans mon bureau sans frapper et sans dire bonjour. C'est exactement ce qu'il vient de se passer. Samir a trente ans, il pourrait être mon fils. Je lui rappelle donc, encore une fois, les règles de la politesse. Et lui, encore une fois, me répond :

– Oui, mais cette fois-ci, c'est urgent.

Les matins sont rarement calmes dans nos bureaux. Les trafiquants d'art dorment peu la nuit. Tout est urgent !

– C'est quoi ?

Samir a reçu trois appels de ses indicateurs dans le milieu de l'art. Un mystérieux correspondant leur a proposé un masque japonais.

Un objet volé reste normalement caché durant des semaines, des mois ou des années avant de réapparaître. Si le voleur veut le vendre très vite, c'est qu'il a peur. Mais de quoi a-t-il peur ?

Samir répond à un nouvel appel et parle fort avec son interlocuteur. Je lui fais de grands signes : il doit sortir de mon bureau. C'est aussi une question de politesse.

J'en profite pour téléphoner à François Yasaki. Il s'étonne de mon appel :

– Je connais votre honnêteté, Monsieur Yasaki. Mais vous avez pu entendre des rumeurs. J'imagine que Hana Lebosse,

CHAPITRE 5

par exemple, peut être intéressée pour acheter ce masque et…
— Je vous arrête, commandant. Je ne travaille plus pour Hana Lebosse.

Je déteste quand on me ment.
— Vous êtes pourtant allé mardi soir au Cercle du Trocadéro. C'était pour jouer ou pour rencontrer la propriétaire des lieux ?

François Yasaki reste silencieux.
— Vous êtes encore là, Monsieur Yasaki ?
— Oui, commandant. Vous m'avez suivi ?

Moi aussi, je peux mentir :
— Bien sûr que non. Je me promenais dans le quartier du Trocadéro et je vous ai vu entrer dans cet établissement avec votre sac de sport. Rappelez-moi : le cercle du Trocadéro n'est pas une salle de sport, n'est-ce pas ?

J'entends un grand soupir, puis le galeriste me dit :
— J'étais durant de longues années le proche conseiller de Hana Lebosse. Elle m'a annoncé mardi soir une mauvaise nouvelle : elle ne travaillera plus avec moi. Elle a trouvé un nouveau conseiller.
— Qui est-ce ?
— Je ne connais pas son nom. Je sais simplement que c'est une femme.
— Vous aviez une dernière œuvre pour elle dans votre sac ? Peut-être un masque de théâtre nô ?
— Décidément, quand vous avez une idée dans la tête…

François Yasaki m'apprend qu'il va tous les mardis soir dans une salle de sport.

Je lui en demande le nom et après notre conversation, je téléphone à la salle de sport. Le directeur me confirme la venue de François Yasaki, mardi dernier.

Samir Lacoste fait de nouveau irruption dans mon bureau, toujours sans frapper. Il lit mon énervement sur mon visage.
— Mais c'est urgent ! Thibault Fontaine n'a pas de chance avec

CHAPITRE 5

sa moto. Après le radar le lundi, il a eu un accrochage avec une Datsun le mardi à minuit, dans le 16ᵉ arrondissement.

— Où exactement ?
— 23 avenue Henri Martin, juste devant le Cercle de jeux du Trocadéro.

Que puis-je déduire de cette information ? Tout d'abord, Thibault Fontaine était à Paris lundi soir. Ensuite, il était le mardi soir au Cercle du Trocadéro, c'est-à-dire quelques heures après François Yasaki. Les deux hommes se connaissent-ils ? Ont-ils passé la soirée au Cercle de jeux ensemble ? Pourquoi ?

Mais, j'y pense tout d'un coup : Thibault Fontaine est interdit de jeu, que faisait-il alors au Cercle du Trocadéro ? Est-il venu rencontrer Hana Lebosse ? Lui a-t-il apporté le masque japonais ?

Mon téléphone sonne. C'est l'hôpital Georges-Pompidou. Agathe Langlois est sortie de son coma. C'est une excellente nouvelle, je laisse Samir et file à l'hôpital. Agathe est dans une phase de réveil depuis plusieurs heures. Son état est stable et les médecins sont très optimistes. J'ai la permission de la voir, mais je ne peux pas rester plus de cinq minutes dans sa chambre.

Des appareils électroniques entourent le lit d'Agathe. Ils émettent régulièrement des bips sonores. Je m'approche et serre la main de la jeune femme. Agathe ouvre légèrement les yeux et me sourit. Je reste silencieuse quelques instants puis lui dis :

— Bonjour Agathe. Je suis heureuse de vous voir.
— Qui… êtes… vous ?

Agathe parle avec difficulté. J'ai du mal à la comprendre.

— Emma Lorenzo. Nous étions assises côte à côte lors du dîner au musée du Quai Branly lundi soir.

Agathe ferme les yeux puis les ouvre à nouveau dix secondes plus tard.

— Agathe, vous vouliez me parler de quelque chose lors du dîner. Vous vous souvenez ?

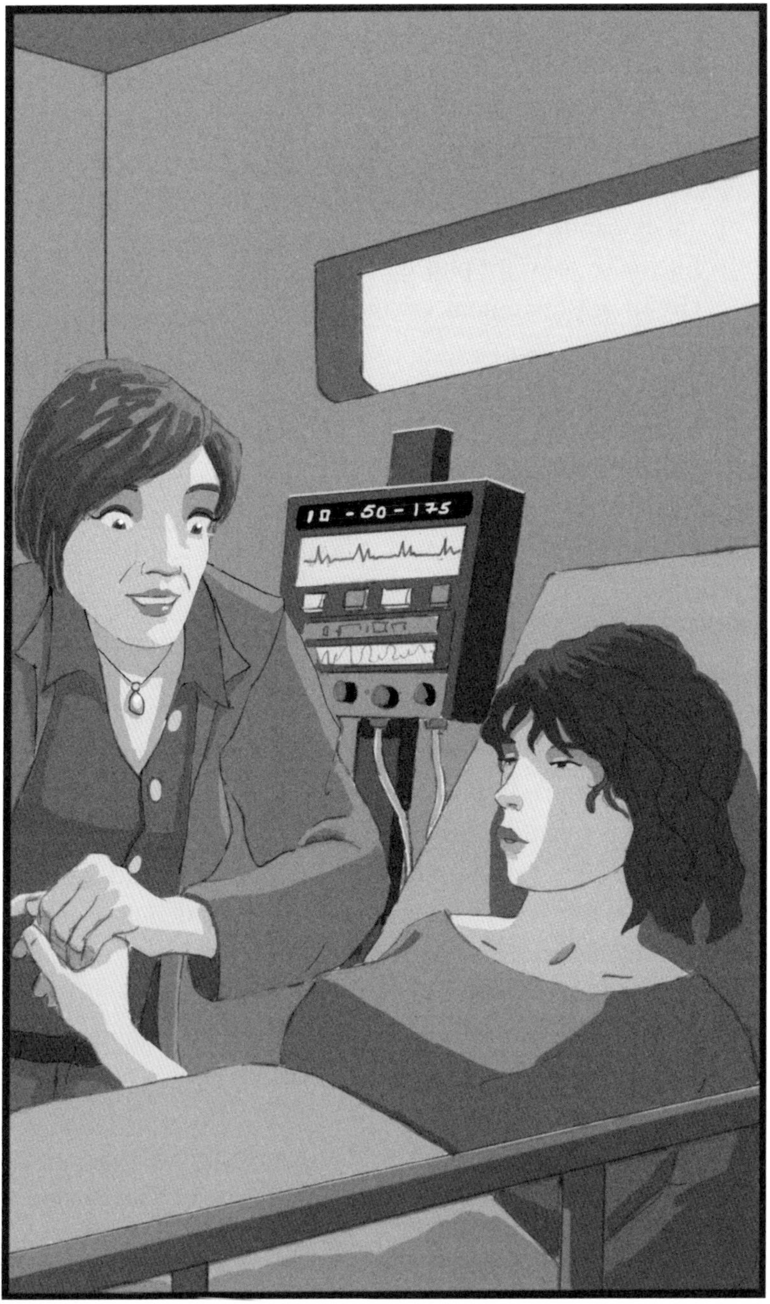

CHAPITRE 5

Son visage se crispe.

— Lun… di… je… ne… sais… pas. Quel… dîner ?

La porte s'ouvre et un médecin entre dans la chambre. Il attrape mon bras et me tire dans le couloir. Il est furieux.

— Je vous ai dit cinq minutes seulement !

Je lui demande de m'excuser.

— Elle ne se souvient plus du dîner. C'est normal ?

— Un empoisonnement est un grand choc pour le corps et l'esprit.

— Elle va retrouver ses souvenirs ?

— Je ne sais pas. Je vous l'ai déjà expliqué au téléphone ce matin. Elle n'aura pas de séquelles physiques[1], mais elle va devoir réapprendre un certain nombre de choses. Elle ne se souvient de rien avant son empoisonnement. Maintenant, il faut la laisser se reposer.

Je n'ai pas parlé avec ce médecin au téléphone. Qui lui a téléphoné en donnant mon nom pour avoir des nouvelles d'Agathe ?

La perte de mémoire d'Agathe est une très mauvaise nouvelle pour mon enquête. De nombreuses questions restent sans réponse. Pourquoi a-t-elle pris le masque ? Qu'en a-t-elle fait ? Que voulait-elle me dire pendant le dîner ?

Je répète plusieurs fois la dernière question. Et là, je me souviens de sa phrase exacte. Je me suis trompée depuis le début. Elle ne voulait pas me « dire » quelque chose. Elle voulait me « montrer » quelque chose. Que voulait-elle me montrer ? Était-ce le masque ? Mais, dans ce cas, Agathe n'a pas de complice. Elle n'a donné le masque à personne. Elle est revenue à notre table avec le masque dans son sac.

Une infirmière m'apprend qu'Agathe est arrivée sans son sac à l'hôpital. Il est donc resté au musée. Je fonce au quai Branly.

---

1 Des séquelles physiques : des problèmes dans son corps qui ne guérissent pas après un accident.

Le musée est fermé au public et ne rouvrira ses portes que demain. Les équipes de nettoyage sont en train de terminer leur travail. Je rejoins le PC de sécurité et interroge Laurent Belon sur le sac d'Agathe. Il me donne la liste des affaires retrouvées après l'évacuation des invités. Le sac n'en fait pas partie. Laurent propose de regarder les vidéos prises après l'évacuation des invités.

Nous nous installons devant les écrans. Je vois les personnes de ma table se sentir mal les unes après les autres.

— Stop ! Là, sous la chaise d'Agathe ! Cette forme, c'est sans doute son sac. Quand allez-vous investir dans des caméras de meilleure définition ?

— Je ne suis pas le directeur du musée. Je peux continuer ?

Après l'évacuation des personnes empoisonnées par le SAMU, nous voyons une silhouette s'approcher de la chaise d'Agathe. Elle s'accroupit et attrape le sac. Elle regarde à l'intérieur et part le sac sous le bras en direction de la sortie. C'est une femme de petite taille aux cheveux courts coupés au carré. Je la reconnais tout de suite : c'est Juliette Bourdelle, la conservatrice des collections d'Asie.

CHAPITRE 6

Et si Juliette...

Jeudi 22 septembre, 17 h

Je sors du PC de sécurité pour me diriger vers le bureau de Jean-Charles Latour, le directeur du musée. Alors que je vais frapper à la porte, son assistante m'interpelle :
— Jean-Charles est en réunion avec Juliette Bourdelle.
— C'est une bonne nouvelle.
Je donne deux grands coups dans la porte, puis entre sans attendre de réponse. Le directeur est assis dans son grand fauteuil de cuir. Il a la tête d'un homme qui vient d'apprendre une mauvaise nouvelle. Juliette se lève de sa chaise et dit :
— Nous avons fini, Jean-Charles, je vais vous laisser tous les deux.
— Le vol du masque ne t'intéresse plus, dis-je à Juliette ?
— Si bien sûr, mais...
Jean-Charles m'explique la situation.
— Juliette vient de m'annoncer son départ. Elle a eu une proposition pour travailler au Centre national des Arts de Tokyo. Je suis très triste, mais je comprends sa décision.
— Et le départ est prévu quand ?
Juliette doit quitter la France dans une semaine. On l'attend le plus tôt possible au Japon.
— Tu vas devoir nous expliquer quelque chose avant ton départ, dis-je à Juliette. Je verrai ensuite si tu peux quitter la France.
Jean-Charles et Juliette sont stupéfaits. Je leur parle de la vidéo

CHAPITRE 6

qui montre Juliette prendre le sac d'Agathe après le déclenchement de l'alarme. Juliette garde son calme et dit :

— C'est vrai, j'ai pris le sac d'Agathe avec le masque. Mais il ne s'agissait pas du vrai masque.

— Il y avait un faux masque ? s'étonne Jean-Charles.

— Agathe a réalisé une copie sans notre autorisation. Elle voulait la vendre pour aider Thibault Fontaine, le directeur de l'atelier où elle travaille. Mais je l'ai découvert. Je lui ai demandé de détruire la copie avant mardi matin.

— Le masque dans le sac d'Agathe était donc une copie. Où est l'original ?

Juliette ne sait pas. Elle suppose qu'Agathe a volé les deux, donné le vrai à un complice et gardé la copie avec elle. Juliette a-t-elle raison ? Dans ce cas, pourquoi Agathe voulait-elle me montrer un faux masque ? Je ne comprends pas.

— Et où est la copie maintenant ? demande Jean-Charles.

— Je l'ai détruite, dit Juliette. Agathe n'avait pas le droit de faire une copie. Je voulais la protéger. C'est pourquoi je ne t'en ai pas parlé.

Juliette dit-elle la vérité ? Je tente un coup de bluff :

— La bonne nouvelle est qu'Agathe se réveille lentement. D'après le médecin, elle va vite retrouver la mémoire.

J'observe attentivement Juliette. Mon information ne la trouble pas. Elle se réjouit même de cette « merveilleuse nouvelle ». Le futur témoignage d'Agathe ne lui fait pas peur. À moins que… Juliette a-t-elle appelé l'hôpital avec mon identité ? Sait-elle qu'Agathe ne retrouvera jamais la mémoire ? Je demande à Juliette de passer le lendemain à l'OCBC pour enregistrer sa déposition. Elle accepte, toujours très décontractée.

— Sans problème. Si vous le permettez, je vais vous laisser. Je suis à vélo aujourd'hui et je suis déjà en retard.

— En vélo, toi ? dit Jean-Charles. Tu n'as plus ta belle voiture de collection ?

— Elle est chez le garagiste, j'ai eu un accrochage l'autre jour.

Juliette nous embrasse et quitte le bureau. Jean-Charles est déçu de son départ pour le Japon. Pour lui, Juliette est une surdouée, à l'immense culture artistique, toujours de bonne humeur et pleine de créativité.

— Elle a toujours des idées, dit-il. D'ailleurs, le dîner franco-japonais, c'est son idée à elle.

— C'était plutôt une mauvaise idée. Je te rappelle que... Attends, elle a eu l'idée de servir du fugu ?

— Oui. Elle est revenue amoureuse du poisson cru d'un voyage au Japon l'été dernier.

Cette information déclenche une vague de questions dans ma tête. Juliette est-elle la nouvelle conseillère de Hana Lebosse ? Hana Lebosse lui a-t-elle trouvé un travail au Japon ? Juliette a-t-elle volé le masque en échange de ces deux emplois ?

Je présente ma théorie à Jean-Charles :

— Et si Juliette...

Il m'écoute et répond :

— Tu connais le proverbe : avec des si, on peut mettre Paris dans une bouteille[1] ! Après Agathe, c'est Juliette la voleuse maintenant ? Ce sera moi le voleur bientôt ?

Je continue à penser à Juliette. Deux éléments dans mon cerveau doivent s'emboîter comme deux pièces de puzzle. Lesquels ?

Je sais ! Je téléphone à Samir.

— Thibault Fontaine a eu son accrochage mardi soir avec une voiture de collection ? C'est bien cela ?

— Oui.

— De quelle marque ?

— Datsun. Une 240 Z, belle voiture.

— Tu peux rechercher le propriétaire ?

---

[1] Avec des si... bouteille : On peut tout faire et tout expliquer avec des suppositions.

CHAPITRE 6

— Je peux. Je te rappelle quand j'ai l'info.
— Non, c'est urgent. Tu me mets en attente, tu cherches et tu me dis.

Je croise les doigts.

— Trouvé ! C'est amusant, c'est Juliette Bourdelle, la conservatrice du quai Branly. Tu vois qui c'est ?

François Yasaki, Thibault Fontaine et Juliette Bourdelle étaient le lendemain du dîner au cercle du Trocadéro ! Tous les trois m'ont caché cette information ! Qu'y faisaient-ils ? Y étaient-ils ensemble ?

— Samir, je te retrouve au bureau dans trente minutes.
— Oh, non ! J'allais partir du bureau. J'ai rendez-vous avec une amie.
— Annule-le. Ce soir les masques vont tomber !

Je retrouve Samir dans son bureau. Je lui demande de m'excuser pour son rendez-vous annulé et annonce fièrement :

— Le point commun entre François Yasaki, Thibault Fontaine et Juliette Bourdelle est le Cercle de jeux du Trocadéro, dont la propriétaire est Hana Lebosse depuis la mort de son mari. Ce n'est pas beau, ça ?
— C'est tout ? Cela ne prouve rien.

Samir est sceptique. Je n'ai pas de preuves, mais seulement des soupçons. Mais on ne place pas des personnes en garde à vue avec des soupçons. Par contre, nous pouvons les convoquer pour les interroger. Samir a aussi des informations à partager :

— Les experts japonais ont rendu leur rapport. Le chef Kenji Ono n'a fait aucune erreur. Il a préparé ses fugus avec la meilleure technique. Par contre, Kenji Ono n'a pas préparé les poissons servis à ta table. Les experts ont examiné avec attention les restes de vos assiettes : le poisson n'est pas coupé avec sa technique très particulière. En plus, les fugus ne proviennent pas du lot apporté spécialement par le chef du Japon !

Bas les masques !

CHAPITRE 6

— Ils arrivent à savoir cela ?
— Je te rappelle que la préparation du fugu est un art chez eux.
— Mais comment ils expliquent l'empoisonnement, alors ?
— Une autre personne a préparé vos assiettes, les a introduites dans le musée et les a fait servir à votre table.

J'essaye de faire le lien entre les informations de Samir et mes quatre suspects. Lequel peut avoir préparé les poissons ? François Yasaki, dont la grand-mère est morte après avoir mangé du fugu ? Thibault Fontaine grâce aux livres de cuisine de sa bibliothèque ? Juliette Bourdelle et sa passion pour la cuisine japonaise ? Ou bien est-ce un travail d'équipe ? Yasaki fournit le fugu importé du Japon par Hana Lebosse, Fontaine le prépare, Bourdelle l'introduit facilement dans le musée.

— J'ai découvert autre chose, dit Samir. Deux serveurs ont eu leur badge d'accès au musée avec une demande de dernière minute, deux heures avant le dîner.
— Qui les a fait venir ?
— Je ne sais pas. Et ces deux serveurs sont introuvables. Ce sont eux qui ont servi les assiettes empoisonnées à ta table.

Samir a fait du bon boulot. Je le félicite. Depuis quatre jours, il travaille comme un fou et il est très fatigué. Je vais avoir besoin de lui pour les interrogatoires des prochains jours. Il doit absolument se reposer avant.

— Voilà ce que nous allons faire, lui dis-je. Je vais relire tous tes documents avec attention.
— Et moi ?
— Toi ? Tu vas passer une bonne soirée. Demain matin, on convoque[2] tout le monde ici et on leur pose des questions. Tu peux encore appeler ton amie ?

---

2 Convoquer : faire venir une personne pour lui poser des questions.

CHAPITRE 7

LE PIÈGE

Jeudi 22 septembre, 23 h 30

La sonnerie de mon téléphone me réveille en sursaut. Oh ! Je me suis endormie sur mon bureau. C'est François Yasaki :

— Commandant, je viens de recevoir un appel d'un type qui se fait appeler François Caron. Il me propose le masque japonais.

— Vous êtes sûr que c'est sérieux ? C'est le nom du propriétaire du masque en 1622 !

— Je sais bien. Mais il m'a envoyé une photo du masque. Il n'y a pas de doute. Il va me rappeler dans deux heures. La transaction doit avoir lieu cette nuit. Je fais quoi ?

— Vous êtes où ?

— Dans ma galerie.

— Vous ne bougez pas, on arrive.

J'appelle Samir. Son amie et lui sortent à l'instant du restaurant. Je lui demande de m'excuser encore une fois, mais j'ai vraiment besoin de lui. J'envoie un message à Dany, mon mari, je vais encore passer une nuit en dehors de chez moi.

Trente minutes plus tard, j'arrive à la galerie ZenArt. Samir est déjà là. Je remercie François Yasaki de nous avoir prévenus.

— Le vendeur a une demande très spéciale, dit-il. Il ne veut pas d'argent. Il veut faire du troc : il veut échanger le masque contre un sabre de samouraï[1] que je possède dans ma galerie.

---
1 Un sabre de samouraï : une arme d'un guerrier japonais.

C'est très étonnant et inhabituel. D'habitude, les voleurs veulent de l'argent. Pourquoi veut-il l'échanger contre un autre objet ?

— Je garde ce sabre dans un coffre spécial, dit François Yasaki. Il a appartenu à Sanada Yukimura, un samouraï mort en 1615. Il est estimé à environ 400 000 euros. Seules quelques personnes connaissent son existence.

— Hana Lebosse fait partie de cette liste ?

François Yasaki me regarde avec un air étonné.

— Oui. Mais vous pensez qu'elle a le masque volé ? Dans ce cas, pourquoi voudrait-elle l'échanger ? Et puis, je lui ai déjà proposé le sabre pour sa collection et elle a toujours refusé.

Je viens de perdre deux de mes suspects, François Yasaki et Hana Lebosse. Que deviennent les autres, Agathe Langlois et Juliette Bourdelle ?

J'ai très faim et demande à Samir d'aller chercher quelque chose à manger. François Yasaki lui donne le nom d'un restaurant asiatique ouvert jusqu'à 2 heures du matin.

L'idée me fait sentir le goût du fugu dans la bouche. Je préfère autre chose.

— Dans ce cas, dit François Yasaki, il y a un restaurant de kebab à cent mètres. Dépêchez-vous, il ferme bientôt.

Manger me fait du bien. J'ai appelé les services spécialisés pour mettre sur écoute le téléphone[2] de la galerie ZenArt et le portable de François Yasaki.

Je convaincs François Yasaki d'accepter l'offre du vendeur. Une équipe d'intervention assistera à l'échange. Le voleur ne pourra pas s'échapper avec son sabre. J'ai déjà prévenu le GIGN[3] d'une opération pour cette nuit.

Cette nuit, nous récupérerons le masque et François Yasaki gardera son sabre.

---

2 Mettre sur écoute un téléphone : écouter les appels au téléphone d'une personne.
3 GIGN : Groupe d'Intervention de la Gendarmerie Nationale.

À 3 h 20 du matin, le téléphone sonne enfin. L'inconnu parle d'une voix étrange. Il refait sa proposition et François Yasaki accepte l'offre. Il fixe un rendez-vous à 4 h du matin dans un ancien supermarché abandonné près de la porte de la Villette. Il envoie par WhatsApp la localisation exacte du rendez-vous.

— Rendez-vous dans quarante minutes, dit-il.

— C'est trop court, proteste Yasaki.

— J'ai un autre acheteur intéressé. Si vous n'êtes pas là dans quarante minutes, tant pis pour vous. Et si je vois un policier dans le coin, je ne vous contacte plus jamais.

La conversation s'arrête. Samir m'informe que l'écoute de l'appel n'a rien donné.

— Qu'est-ce qu'on fait ? dit Yasaki.

— Vous foncez en scooter, dis-je. On vous suit en voiture.

— Et le GIGN ? demande Samir.

— C'est trop court et l'inconnu va les repérer. On va se débrouiller tout seuls.

Je ne suis pas très sûre de moi. Mais, parfois, il ne faut pas trop réfléchir. Je donne quelques instructions à François Yasaki et nous partons.

Nous arrivons à Porte de la Villette à 3 h 30. Nous nous garons à trois cents mètres du supermarché et continuons à pied. Le rendez-vous est dans le parking souterrain.

L'endroit, fermé depuis 2008, est sinistre. Il est devenu aujourd'hui le rendez-vous des artistes du « Street art » et des amateurs d'exploration urbaine. Tout cela sans aucune autorisation bien sûr.

Il fait très sombre dans le parking. Nous éclairons le chemin un minimum avec nos torches. J'aperçois bientôt les phares du scooter de Yasaki. Vingt mètres plus loin, un homme se tient devant les phares d'une moto. Il porte sur le visage un masque japonais de couleur rouge et blanc.

CHAPITRE 7

Nous avançons sans faire de bruit et nous plaçons derrière un poteau. Nous sommes à dix mètres de la scène.

Le vendeur donne des ordres avec des phrases courtes. Les deux hommes marchent l'un vers l'autre. Deux mètres les séparent. Puis, ils avancent encore et échangent leur sac. L'homme vérifie le sabre et dit « Parfait ». François Yasaki vérifie le masque et dit « C'est quoi ce truc en plastique ? »

Le vendeur s'est moqué de nous ! Samir et moi courons vers lui, nos armes pointées dans sa direction :

– Police nationale, pas un geste !

Trois secondes plus tard, je plaque le vendeur au sol.

– Je n'ai rien fait, ce n'est pas moi, je suis innocent. Je ne suis pas armé.

– Enlève ton masque !

Il m'obéit. Les phares du scooter éclairent son visage : c'est Thibault Fontaine, le patron d'Agathe Langlois !

– Thibault ? C'est quoi cette blague ? lui demande François Yasaki.

Je déplace mon arme de Thibault Fontaine vers François Yasaki et leur demande plusieurs fois :

– Vous vous connaissez tous les deux ?

***

Une heure plus tard, nous sommes tous les quatre dans mon bureau de l'OCBC. Thibault Fontaine et François Yasaki nous expliquent leur relation. Ils se sont rencontrés il y a huit mois dans une salle de sport. Ils ont sympathisé et François a invité Thibault à une fête organisée par Hana Lebosse au Cercle du Trocadéro. Bien sûr, Thibault a refusé, car il n'a pas le droit d'entrer dans un établissement de jeux. Mais François Yasaki a réussi à convaincre[4]

---

4   Convaincre : amener une personne à accepter une idée.

Hana Lebosse de le laisser entrer. Thibault Fontaine y est retourné ensuite de nombreuses fois tout seul. Il a rejoué et il a perdu à nouveau une grosse somme d'argent. Il doit aujourd'hui près de cent mille euros au Cercle de jeux.

Hier en fin d'après-midi, Thibault Fontaine a reçu un appel téléphonique d'un inconnu. Il lui a demandé de proposer à François Yasaki d'échanger le masque japonais volé contre un sabre de samouraï.

— Et vous avez accepté cette offre idiote ? dis-je.

— En échange, l'inconnu m'a promis de payer mes dettes au Cercle du Trocadéro. C'était une occasion unique pour moi.

— Vous avez une idée de l'identité de votre correspondant ?

— Non. Mais il connaissait le montant exact de mes dettes.

Je pense bien sûr à un homme de l'entourage de Hana Lebosse[5]. Mais encore une fois, je n'ai pas de preuve. Et pourquoi a-t-elle organisé ce faux échange ?

Je demande aux deux hommes comment ils ont connu la salle de sport où ils se sont rencontrés.

— J'y vais depuis deux ans, dit François Yasaki. Elle est fréquentée par de nombreux Japonais de Paris.

Thibault Fontaine réfléchit.

— Agathe m'a offert une semaine d'essai.

— Pourquoi ? Elle voulait vous remettre en forme ?

— Je ne sais plus. Ah si, quelqu'un du musée du Quai Branly lui avait offert. Mais Agathe déteste le sport. Je ne sais plus qui c'était ?

— Juliette Bourdelle ?

— Ah oui, c'est ça, Juliette Bourdelle.

Bourdelle, Lebosse… encore ! Hana Lebosse a-t-elle organisé le faux échange après ma conversation avec Juliette Bourdelle au

---

[5] L'entourage de Hana Lebosse : les personnes qui vivent ou travaillent avec elle.

Bas les masques !

musée ? Veut-elle me faire perdre du temps ? Cela est possible, mais pourquoi ? Veut-elle permettre à Juliette Bourdelle de s'enfuir pendant ce temps ?

Samir intervient :

— Vous voulez rire ? Devinez le nom du supermarché abandonné de la Villette ? Auchan, Cora, Carrefour ? Non ! c'est Casino.

Nous le regardons sans comprendre.

— Qui dit casino dit aussi jeux, non ? Qui dit jeux, dit Cercle de jeux. Et qui dit Cercle de jeux, dit Hana Lebosse.

Cela ne me fait pas rire. Nous perdons trop de temps. Je dois agir. Il est 5 heures. À partir de 6 heures du matin, la police a le droit de faire une perquisition[6]. Je passe les coups de téléphone pour obtenir l'autorisation.

Dans une heure, on va aller réveiller Hana Lebosse et Juliette Bourdelle.

---

6 Faire une perquisition : Fouiller un lieu privé dans le cadre d'une enquête de police.

CHAPITRE 8

La bonne occasion ?

Vendredi 24 mars, 10 h

Je suis assise dans mon bureau de l'OCBC et regarde le calendrier : le vol du masque japonais au musée du quai Branly a eu lieu il y a six mois.

Les perquisitions du samedi 23 septembre n'ont rien donné. Hana Lebosse était déjà au Japon depuis le mercredi 21 septembre, le lendemain du vol. Juliette Bourdelle n'était pas chez elle. Nous n'avons pas de preuves suffisantes contre ces deux femmes. De son côté, la police japonaise a interrogé Hana Lebosse. Mais la femme d'affaires affirme ne pas avoir proposé de travail à Juliette. Elle n'a, a-t-elle dit, jamais demandé à Juliette de voler le masque.

Depuis le vol, Juliette Bourdelle et le masque sont introuvables.

Samir et moi avons trouvé l'explication de l'empoisonnement d'Agathe. Les caméras de surveillance du musée nous ont aidés à comprendre. Juliette Bourdelle est venue le lundi après-midi au musée, à 14 h. Elle avait avec elle deux glacières[1]. Les gardiens ne les ont pas ouvertes. « On ne contrôle jamais Madame Bourdelle, on la connaît bien, et puis elle est si jolie », a dit l'un d'eux. À l'intérieur se trouvaient les assiettes de sashimis de fugu. À 16 h, Juliette est repartie avec une seule glacière. « Elle avait oublié quelque chose chez elle », a dit le gardien. Dans la glacière, le masque de théâtre nô quittait le musée.

---

1 Une glacière : une caisse qui permet de garder au frais des aliments.

CHAPITRE 8

Je ne comprends pas une chose : pourquoi Juliette Bourdelle et Hana Lebosse voulaient tuer Agathe Langlois ?

Agathe Langlois est maintenant en pleine forme. Sa rééducation s'est parfaitement passée. Par contre, elle n'a pas retrouvé la mémoire. Sa vie avant le lundi 19 septembre à 21 h n'existe plus. Elle a repris son travail à l'atelier Fontaine. Je passe souvent la voir là-bas. Nous déjeunons parfois ensemble. Elle ne prend jamais de sushi.

Son patron, Thibault Fontaine, ne joue plus avec son argent. L'atelier Fontaine a beaucoup de travail et un bel avenir.

Samir ne travaille plus sur l'enquête. J'y consacre un jour par semaine. C'est peu. Mon patron pense que Juliette et le masque sont depuis longtemps au Japon. Mais je ne crois pas. Les douanes surveillent les aéroports, les gares et les ports. Ce n'est pas facile de quitter la France. Pour moi, Hana Lebosse a organisé le départ de Juliette. Elle doit attendre la bonne occasion. Je dois trouver laquelle.

Je suis souvent de mauvaise humeur à cause de cette enquête. Dany, mon mari, essaye de me changer les idées. Il veut m'emmener à des compétitions sportives. Je refuse toujours, mais c'est peut-être une mauvaise idée.

À 10 h 15, Samir Lacoste entre dans mon bureau. Il me parle d'une nouvelle enquête. La sonnerie de mon téléphone l'interrompt. Je parle cinq minutes avec mon mari puis dis à Samir :

— Dany a deux places pour une compétition de sumo[2], ce soir.

— Tu y vas avec lui ?

— Non ! Je ne vais pas regarder des types énormes qui se poussent. Quel président de la République adorait ce sport ?

— Jacques Chirac.

Jacques Chirac, bien sûr. Le président qui est à l'origine du projet du musée du quai Branly. Le musée porte son nom, d'ailleurs.

---

[2] Le sumo : un sport de lutte japonais.

Il faut dire « musée du Quai Branly - Jacques Chirac ».

Je répète plusieurs fois « musée du quai Branly - Jacques Chirac ». Puis, j'ai une idée : cette compétition est-elle l'occasion organisée par Hana Lebosse pour le départ de Juliette Bourdelle ?

Je me connecte sur le web et cherche des informations sur la compétition. Elle rassemble les plus grands sumotoris[3] du Japon. Des associations franco-japonaises sont partenaires de l'événement. Je lis quatre articles sur le sujet et découvre une information très intéressante : une grande réception a eu lieu hier soir avec les sportifs au Cercle du Trocadéro ! Je n'ai plus de doute, c'est bien l'occasion ! J'en parle à mon patron. Mais il n'est pas du même avis que moi. Tant pis, je vais y aller toute seule.

Je rappelle Dany et accepte sa proposition. Il est le plus heureux des hommes.

Le Palais omnisports de Paris-Bercy est rempli. Le spectacle est aussi dans les tribunes. Les spectateurs sont habillés en kimono ou en tenue de samouraï. Des femmes ont le visage peint en blanc, d'autres portent des masques traditionnels japonais.

Dany m'explique les règles de ce sport. Chaque lutteur essaye de faire sortir son adversaire du cercle dessiné au sol. On perd aussi si le corps touche le sol. C'est simple. Dany me prête ses jumelles pour observer les sumotoris. Mais c'est la tribune officielle qui m'intéresse. Juliette Bourdelle y est-elle ?

Pendant la dernière pause, je marche dans les couloirs du Palais omnisports. Je descends plusieurs escaliers et me retrouve dans les vestiaires. Je présente ma carte de police au personnel de sécurité. Je visite plusieurs salles remplies de sacs et de matériel. Je continue ma visite et arrive dans le parking. Des minibus aux vitres noires attendent. Je m'approche de deux chauffeurs. Ils sont en train de vapoter[4].

---

3 Un sumotori : un sportif pratiquant le sumo.
4 Vapoter : fumer avec une cigarette électronique.

CHAPITRE 8

— Bonsoir. Ce sont les bus des athlètes ?

Ils ne répondent pas. Je sors ma carte professionnelle et reformule ma demande :

— Bonsoir, commandant Lorenzo de l'OCBC. Ce sont les minibus de la délégation japonaise ?

— Oui. C'est ça.

— Vous les emmenez à quel hôtel ?

— On va directement à l'aéroport. Ils ont un vol dans la nuit pour Tokyo.

— C'est inhabituel.

— Tout est inhabituel avec eux. Je n'ai jamais vu un vol si tard dans la nuit. On va les déposer directement sur le tarmac[5] de l'aéroport.

— Comment se font l'enregistrement des bagages et le passage en douanes ?

— Tout est déjà réglé, paraît-il. Mais, on ne s'occupe pas de ça.

« Tout est déjà réglé » ? Par qui ? Pourquoi ?

— Il y a d'autres personnes avec les athlètes ? demandais-je.

— Oui, ils sont une cinquantaine. Les minibus sont pour les sumotoris et il y a un bus pour les familles. Certains sportifs sont venus avec leur femme et leurs enfants pour visiter Paris.

— Les familles sont encore à l'hôtel ?

— Non, elles sont ici. Elles attendent dans une grande salle. Vous pouvez y accéder par cette porte.

Je les remercie et me dirige vers la salle. Une vingtaine de femmes et d'enfants attendent leur départ. Ils portent des kimonos. Je montre une nouvelle fois ma carte de police. Ils s'écartent et je la vois. Juliette Bourdelle est assise contre un mur. Elle porte un kimono bleu avec des fleurs. Son visage est peint en blanc et elle a une perruque noire sur la tête.

— Bonsoir Juliette.

---

[5] Le tarmac : Partie de l'aéroport réservée au stationnement et à la circulation des avions.

Bas les masques !

CHAPITRE 8

Juliette se lève d'un bond et se précipite vers la porte. Je la rattrape et la force à se rasseoir. Les femmes et les enfants prennent peur.

— Restez calme, tout va bien. Toi aussi, Juliette. Sinon, je vais devoir employer la force.

— Comment m'as-tu trouvée ? me demande-t-elle.

— Grâce à mon mari.

Elle me regarde étonnée.

— Je dois faire fouiller tous les sacs ou bien tu me dis où est le masque ?

Ses mains serrent un sac à dos posé à côté d'elle.

Je l'arrache.

Le masque et sa copie se trouvent à l'intérieur.

La cachette la plus simple est souvent la meilleure.

— Je ne me sépare jamais d'eux. Agathe est douée, n'est-ce pas ?

L'original et la copie sont en effet magnifiques.

Juliette me semble fatiguée. Je décide d'essayer de la faire parler. Je m'assieds à côté d'elle et lui donne ma version de l'affaire. Elle me sourit et je comprends que Samir et moi avons raison. C'est le moment d'en apprendre plus :

— Pourquoi Agathe a fait une copie ? Elle voulait vraiment la vendre ?

— Ce n'était pas son idée, mais la mienne. Agathe et moi étions les seules à connaître l'existence de la copie. J'ai fait l'échange dans l'armoire de l'atelier le lundi après-midi. La police devait découvrir la copie le lendemain du dîner. Il était alors facile d'accuser du vol l'auteure de la copie. Et, morte, elle ne pouvait pas se défendre. Mon plan était parfait. Mais Agathe est repassée à l'atelier vers 19 h. Elle a découvert l'échange et m'a appelée. J'ai trouvé une excuse et lui ai promis de rendre le masque le mardi matin.

— Pourquoi voulait-elle me montrer la copie pendant le dîner ?

— Elle n'avait plus confiance en moi. Elle a sans doute eu peur d'avoir des ennuis avec la police. Elle t'a trouvée sympathique et a voulu tout te raconter.

— Pourquoi as-tu pris la copie dans le sac d'Agathe ?

— Je devais la remettre dans l'armoire. Mais, après l'alarme, j'ai dû sortir du musée comme tout le monde. Ensuite, ce n'était plus possible de revenir.

Il me reste une chose à comprendre :

— Pourquoi as-tu fait tout cela, Juliette ?

— Hana Lebosse et moi sommes devenues très amies après la mort de son mari.

— Tu as volé un masque et empoisonné une jeune femme pour obtenir un travail avec elle, c'est une étrange amitié.

— Elle rêvait de revoir le masque au Japon. Et, moi, je rêve du Japon depuis mon enfance. Hana m'a proposé de travailler avec elle et dans un très grand musée japonais. J'étais prête à tout faire pour cela.

Juliette m'a raconté toute l'histoire avec calme. Croit-elle encore pouvoir s'enfuir ?

— Ton rêve s'arrête là, Juliette.

— Je ne crois pas. Je pars cette nuit pour le Japon. Hana est une femme organisée et puissante. Elle a tout prévu depuis le début. Ses hommes ne vont pas te laisser m'arrêter.

Juliette essaye de rester calme. Mais sa voix et ses gestes montrent le contraire. Croit-elle encore en l'amitié de Hana Lebosse ?

Juliette crie deux phrases en japonais.

Trois hommes en costumes noirs entrent aussitôt dans la pièce.

Les femmes et les enfants paniquent et sortent de la salle en criant.

Je sors mon arme et saisis Juliette par le bras.

— Je suis Emma Lorenzo, commandant à l'OCBC. Vous ne bougez surtout pas ou bien vous allez avoir des problèmes.

CHAPITRE 8

— Tu perds ton temps, ils ne parlent pas français. Ils ont l'ordre de me protéger. Laisse-moi maintenant, Emma.

Les trois hommes échangent des regards. Juliette leur parle et, rapidement, le ton monte entre eux. Je comprends que quelque chose ne plaît pas du tout à Juliette. La protection de Hana Lebosse est-elle toujours aussi sûre ? L'amitié de la Japonaise pour cette Française est-elle plus forte que sa sécurité ?

La conversation devient très tendue. Puis, tout à coup, Juliette explose :

— Quelle garce[6] ! Tu as raison, Emma, mon rêve est fini.

Je comprends alors que Hana Lebosse ne veut plus la protéger. Je lis dans les yeux de Juliette un grand désespoir. Pendant un court instant, je suis triste pour elle et relâche ma prise. Juliette en profite. Elle me frappe au visage, me pousse violemment par terre et m'arrache le sac à dos. Elle passe devant les trois hommes et s'enfuit en courant. Les trois hommes m'empêchent quelques instants de passer puis s'écartent.

Je me lance à la poursuite de Juliette. Je traverse deux salles et monte trois escaliers avant d'arriver dans le grand hall de la salle de spectacle. La compétition est terminée et les spectateurs se dirigent vers les sorties dans une cohue joyeuse. Où est-elle ? Je regarde de tous les côtés. Mais je ne la vois pas dans cette foule. Que faire ?

Soudain, j'entends une voix derrière moi :

— Tu cherches peut-être cette personne ?

C'est Samir ! À côté de lui, Juliette a les menottes[7] aux poignets.

— Je me suis dit : « Emma va peut-être avoir besoin de moi ».

— Tu es génial ! Je préviens Dany et on se retrouve au bureau.

Je téléphone à Dany et lui donne rendez-vous à notre voiture. Nous nous retrouvons dix minutes plus tard.

---

6 Une garce : mot familier, une femme méchante.
7 Des menottes : deux anneaux reliés par une chaîne qui empêchent le mouvement des bras.

CHAPITRE 8

— Tu étais où ? me demande mon mari. J'étais inquiet.

— J'ai rencontré une vieille amie. Nous avions des choses à nous raconter.

— Tu as quand même vu la fin de la compétition ? Ces sumotoris sont incroyables ! On va dîner quelque part ?

— Je suis désolée, Dany, mais je dois aller à l'OCBC pour une affaire urgente.

Dany est déçu. Mais il ne montre rien. Il sait que ce n'est pas facile d'être le mari d'une policière.

Bas les masques !

Activités

CHAPITRE 1

1 🎵 piste 1 → **Écoutez le chapitre 1. Avez-vous bien compris ? Cochez la bonne réponse.**

1. Emma Lorenzo assiste :
- ☐ a. à l'ouverture d'un musée.
- ☐ b. à l'anniversaire d'un ami.
- ☑ c. au dîner annuel d'une association.

2. Emma est :
- ☐ a. directrice de musée.
- ☑ b. commandant de police.
- ☐ c. directrice d'une galerie d'art.

3. La personne assise à gauche d'Emma est :
- ☐ a. Agathe Langlois.
- ☐ b. Juliette Bourdelle.
- ☑ c. François Yasaki.

4. Le fugu est un poisson dangereux pour l'homme car :
- ☑ a. il contient un poison.
- ☐ b. ses arêtes sont pointues.
- ☐ c. il a de grandes dents.

5. Juliette Langlois a restauré :
- ☐ a. un tableau américain.
- ☑ b. un masque japonais.
- ☐ c. un vase africain.

6. Emma veut dire aux invités de rester calmes, mais :
- ☐ a. elle veut finir son poisson.
- ☐ b. sa voix est cassée.
- ☑ c. elle s'évanouit.

2 Lisez le chapitre. Classez les phrases dans l'ordre de l'histoire.

a. Une alarme sonne dans le musée.
b. La conversation de la table est animée.
c. Un secouriste fait un massage cardiaque à Agathe.
d. Agathe se lève pour aller aux toilettes.
e. Juliette Bourdelle présente Agathe à toute la table.
f. Emma mange deux tranches de sashimis.
g. Emma interroge François Yasaki sur Hana Lebosse.

1	2	3	4	5	6	7
b.	…	…	…	…	…	…

3 Mettez les mots de l'histoire dans l'ordre pour faire des phrases.

1. est / l'ouverture / Emma / de l'association / membre / depuis / du musée.

....

2. galerie d'art japonais / François Yasaki / est / de la plus grande / directeur / de Paris.

....

3. du musée. / Juliette Bourdelle / des collections asiatiques / est / conservatrice

....

4. sur / Agathe / son / pose / ventre. / mains / ses

....

5. vers / Les / courent / les sorties. / invités

....

4 Utilisez la forme « *Il faut* + infinitif » pour exprimer une obligation.

1. Je n'aime pas le poisson cru, mais ……………………………… (goûter l'entrée).

2. Ce masque est très abîmé, ……………………………… (le restaurer).

3. Ils se sentent mal, ... (appeler un médecin).

4. .... (rendre une œuvre) à son pays d'origine ? (forme interrogative)

5. .... (attendre) longtemps l'entrée.

6. L'alarme retentit, ... (sortir) très vite.

5 **Pourquoi Emma doit être courageuse pour manger son entrée ?**

....

....

6 **À votre avis, un masque japonais a-t-il sa place dans un musée en France ?**

....

....

CHAPITRE 2

1 piste 2 → **Écoutez le chapitre 2. Vrai ou faux ? Cochez la bonne réponse. Justifiez lorsque vous pensez que c'est faux.**

	Vrai	Faux
1. Emma se réveille dans une chambre d'hôpital.	☑	☐
2. Samir Lacoste est le mari d'Emma.	☐	☑
3. Agathe Langlois a fait une petite réaction au poison.	☐	☑
4. Tous les convives de la table d'Emma sont à l'hôpital.	☐	☑
5. Agathe et Juliette ont placé le masque dans une armoire vers midi.	☑	☐
6. Sur la vidéo, on voit Agathe entrer dans l'atelier de restauration pendant le dîner.	☑	☐

Justification :

....

....

2 Complétez la grille avec des mots du chapitre et retrouvez le mot qui se cache verticalement.

1. Georges Lebosse a donné un don au musée.
2. Emma et Samir ont l'habitude de faire ensemble.
3. Juliette prend l' ...... qui descend au sous-sol.
4. Jean-Charles Latour a proposé un ...... au musée à Agathe.
5. Emma ne veut pas quitter la ...... mais son mari veut vivre à la campagne.
6. Emma a eu une ...... alimentaire.
7. Agathe retient la ...... de l'atelier.
8. Pour bien observer une vidéo, Laurent Belon fait un arrêt sur ....

Mot mystère :
Juliette est la .... numéro 1.

3 Mettez les lettres dans l'ordre pour retrouver les mots du texte.

1. Y S E E M T R

Emma et son mari ont des goûts très différents. C'est un .... pour leurs amis.

2. O S P R E R E

Emma est fatiguée, elle doit se .... deux jours.

3. S E C O C N E F N E R

Juliette Bourdelle fait des .... sur l'art.

4. I D F L U I C F T E S

L'Atelier Fontaine a de grosses .... financières.

5. M R L A A E

C'est la porte de l'atelier qui déclenche l' ....

4 **Complétez les phrases avec le bon adjectif indéfini : *tout*, *tous*, *toute*, *toutes*.**

1. Emma et Dany sont un mystère pour .... leurs amis.

2. Emma doit rester au lit .... la journée.

3. Juliette et Agathe respectent .... les procédures de sécurité.

4. Le musée est fermé .... les lundis.

5. La police fouille .... le musée.

6. Laurent Belon a vu .... les vidéos.

5 **Pourquoi Emma compte-t-elle les personnes à sa table ?**
....
....

6 **À votre avis, deux personnes en couple peuvent-elles avoir des goûts totalement opposés ?**
....
....

CHAPITRE 3

1 piste 3 → **Écoutez le chapitre 3. Avez-vous bien compris ? Cochez la bonne réponse.**

1. Jean-Charles Latour...
☐ **a.** est d'accord : Agathe est la voleuse.
☐ **b.** s'énerve : c'est ridicule !

2. Georges Lebosse...
☐ **a.** était un grand amateur d'art.
☐ **b.** préférait les jeux à l'art.
3. François Yasaki ne mange pas de poisson cru, car...
☐ **a.** sa grand-mère est morte empoisonnée par du fugu.
☐ **b.** il préfère le fugu cuit.
4. Le conducteur obéit à Emma, car...
☐ **a.** il se croit dans un film policier.
☐ **b.** elle le menace de le mettre en prison.
5. François Yasaki arrête son scooter...
☐ **a.** devant le Cercle de jeux du Trocadéro.
☐ **b.** sur les Champs-Élysées.

2 **Lisez le chapitre. Reliez le début et la fin des phrases.**

1. Les vidéos montrent
2. Emma commence par
3. François Yasaki
4. Au café, Emma
5. La question est :

a. pourquoi François Yasaki ment-il ?
b. va garder les yeux grands ouverts.
c. rassembler des informations sur le masque.
d. Agathe entrer dans l'atelier de restauration.
e. commande un jambon beurre et un expresso.

3 **Complétez le récit de Georges Lebosse avec les mots suivants :**

descendant – cercle – masque – lettre – explorateur – extraordinaire – jouer – famille – siècle

Le .... de théâtre nô appartient à la .... de Georges Lebosse depuis le 17e .... Lebosse est un .... de François Caron, le premier .... français au Japon. François Caron parle du masque dans une .... à sa mère en 1622 ! Nous avons aussi ce document .... Lebosse nous a donné le masque dans son .... de jeux . Juste après, il nous a proposé de .... à la roulette !

4 **Complétez les phrases avec le bon pronom relatif : *qui, que, qu'*.**

1. C'est le masque ...... Georges Lebosse a donné au musée.
2. Yasaki ferme le rideau ...... protège la vitrine de la galerie.
3. Emma mange le sandwich ...... elle a commandé.
4. C'est un inconnu ...... conduit la voiture.
5. Agathe est la personne ...... la policière soupçonne.
6. C'est Juliette ...... a vu le plus les Lebosse.

5 **Pourquoi Emma pense-t-elle qu'on a voulu tuer Agathe ?**

....
....

6 **À votre avis, l'explication de François Yasaki sur sa peur du fugu est-elle claire ?**

....
....

CHAPITRE 4

1 piste 4 → **Écoutez le chapitre 4. Vrai ou faux ? Cochez la bonne réponse. Justifiez lorsque vous pensez que c'est faux.**

	Vrai	Faux
1. Thibault Fontaine ressemble à un artiste.	☐	☐
2. Emma et Thibault boivent un café ensemble.	☐	☐
3. Thibault n'est pas invité au dîner du musée.	☐	☐
4. Emma trouve Thibault en pleine forme.	☐	☐
5. Pour avoir des informations sur Thibault Fontaine, Samir téléphone à sa femme.	☐	☐

Justification :

....
....

2 Complétez la grille avec des mots du chapitre.

1. Thibault et sa femme ne plus ensemble, ils sont ....
2. Paris a des airs de ...... avec ce beau temps.
3. Thibault va prendre des somnifères et ....
4. Agathe n'est pas mariée, elle est ....
5. La barbe de Thibault a des reflets ....
6. Trois livres de la bibliothèque sont sur l'art de cuisiner le ...... cru.
7. Samir cherche sur les ...... sociaux pour trouver des informations.

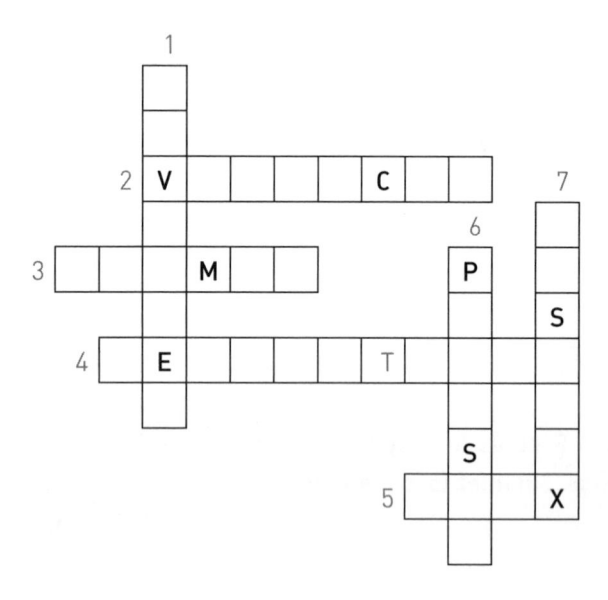

3 Lisez le chapitre. Soulignez la forme correcte.

Thibault Fontaine est *petit / grand* et a de *longs /courts* cheveux noirs. Il est habillé dans un style *strict / décontracté*. Il est *divorcé / marié* et a deux enfants. Son *prénom / nom* apparaît dans des revues *spécialisées / généralistes*. C'est un *amateur / professionnel* reconnu. Il est *permis / interdit* de jeux. *Son ex-femme / Sa future femme* l'a quitté à cause du *travail / jeu*.

4 Conjuguez les verbes pronominaux au présent.

1. Nous .... (se parler) au téléphone.
2. Que .... (se passer) ?
3. Vous .... (s'arrêter) de parler.
4. Je .... (se demander) pourquoi il ment.
5. Ils .... (s'asseoir) sur le canapé.
6. Tu .... (s'accuser) du vol ?

5 Pourquoi Thibault Fontaine a-t-il divorcé ?
....
....

6 À votre avis, Emma va-t-elle trop loin quand elle décide d'être directe ?
....
....

CHAPITRE 5

1 Lisez le chapitre 5. Avez-vous bien compris ? Cochez la bonne réponse.

1. Samir Lacoste entre dans le bureau d'Emma sans frapper, car :
☐ a. il a quelque chose d'urgent à dire.
☐ b. Il est mal élevé.
☐ c. Il veut lui faire une blague.

2. Depuis mardi soir, François Yasaki :
☐ a. a perdu la mémoire.
☐ b. fait du sport.
☐ c. n'est plus le conseiller de Hana Lebosse.

3. Emma Lorenzo se souvient de la phrase exacte, Agathe voulait :
☐ a. lui parler de ses vacances.
☐ b. lui montrer quelque chose.
☐ c. lui dire quelque chose.

4. Le médecin est furieux, car :
☐ **a.** Agathe s'est levée de son lit.
☐ **b.** Emma téléphone trop souvent à l'hôpital.
☐ **c.** Emma reste trop longtemps dans la chambre d'Agathe.

5. Sur la vidéo, Emma voit Juliette Bourdelle :
☐ **a.** terminer les assiettes de fugu.
☐ **b.** prendre le sac d'Agathe.
☐ **c.** faire un massage cardiaque à Agathe.

2 piste 5 → **Écoutez le chapitre 5. Qui dit quoi ? Associez chaque personnage à sa phrase.**

1. Emma Lorenzo
2. Samir Lacoste
3. François Yasaki
4. Agathe Langlois

a. Je ne travaille plus pour Hana Lebosse.
b. Le Cercle du Trocadéro n'est pas une salle de sport, n'est-ce pas ?
c. Décidément, quand vous avez une idée dans la tête...
d. Thibault Fontaine a eu un accrochage avec une Datsun le mardi à minuit.
e. Qui ... êtes... vous ?
f. Elle va retrouver ses souvenirs ?

3 **Complétez les phrases avec le bon adjectif interrogatif :** *quel, quels, quelle, quelles.*

1. « .... dîner ? » demande Agathe à Emma.
2. .... excuse va trouver François Yasaki ?
3. .... appareils électroniques entourent le lit d'Agathe ?
4. .... images montrent Juliette prendre le sac d'Agathe ?
5. .... objet voulait montrer Agathe à Emma ?

4 **Pourquoi la perte de mémoire d'Agathe est une mauvaise nouvelle pour l'enquête ?**

....
....

5 À votre avis, pourquoi est-ce terrible de perdre la mémoire ?

....

....

CHAPITRE 6

1 🎧 piste 6 → **Écoutez le chapitre 6. Aidez-vous des phrases pour trouver dans la grille les mots du chapitre.**

1. Ils sont venus du Japon pour interroger le cuisinier.
2. Emma n'attend pas celle de Jean-Charles pour entrer dans le bureau.
3. Agathe en a réalisé une du masque.
4. Emma dit qu'Agathe va retrouver la sienne.
5. Agathe, Juliette, François et Thibault : cela en fait quatre pour Emma.
6. Emma pense que Samir en a fait du bon depuis quatre jours.
7. « Avec des si, on peut mettre Paris en bouteille » en est un.
8. Juliette a-t-elle volé le masque pour les obtenir ?

X	E	P	R	O	V	E	R	B	E
M	X	S	U	S	P	E	C	T	S
E	P	V	U	V	R	S	B	D	E
M	E	S	U	C	V	T	O	E	M
O	R	T	X	O	Z	N	U	G	P
I	T	U	C	P	A	L	L	J	L
R	S	R	D	I	E	L	O	H	O
E	I	T	S	E	F	L	T	A	I
R	E	P	O	N	S	E	T	P	S

2 Lisez le chapitre. Associez les questions aux réponses.

1. Pourquoi Emma est contente d'apprendre que Juliette est dans le bureau du directeur ?
2. Qu'est-ce qu'il y avait dans le sac d'Agathe ?
3. Qui a eu l'idée du dîner franco-japonais ?
4. Pourquoi Juliette Bourdelle est-elle à vélo aujourd'hui ?
5. Où Juliette part-elle travailler?

a. C'est Juliette Bourdelle.
b. Au Japon.
c. Une copie du masque de théâtre nô.
d. Elle veut lui demander pourquoi elle a pris le sac d'Agathe.
e. Sa voiture est chez le garagiste.

1	2	3	4	5
………	………	………	………	………

3 Imaginez la suite de ces phrases et faites des hypothèses comme dans l'exemple.

1. Si Juliette est coupable, …………………………………… .
   → Si Juliette et coupable, Emma va l'arrêter.
2. Si le masque dans le sac est une copie, …………………………… .
3. Si Emma dit qu'Agathe se souvient du dîner, ………………………… .
4. Si Samir a un rendez-vous, ………………………………… .
5. Si le chef ne fait pas fait d'erreur, ……………………………… .
6. Si Samir peut appeler son amie, ……………………………… .

4 Pourquoi Juliette n'a pas peur de la mémoire d'Agathe ?
…………………………………………………………………………
…………………………………………………………………………

5 Avez-vous envie de goûter du sashimi de fugu ?
…………………………………………………………………………
…………………………………………………………………………

CHAPITRE 7

1 🎧 piste 7 → **Écoutez le chapitre 7 et répondez aux questions.**

1. Où se trouve François Yasaki quand il téléphone à Emma Lorenzo ?
....
2. Le vendeur du masque veut-il de l'argent ?
....
3. Pourquoi Emma ne veut pas manger un repas asiatique ?
....
4. Où Thibault Fontaine et François Yasaki se sont-ils connus ?
....
5. Qu'est-ce que la police a le droit de faire à partir de 6 h du matin ?
....

2 **Lisez le chapitre 7. Qui peut dire quoi ? Associez chaque personnage à sa phrase.**

1. Emma Lorenzo
2. François Yasaki
3. Thibault Fontaine
4. Samir Lacoste

a. Ce sabre est ma plus belle œuvre d'art.
b. Pourquoi m'a-t-on dit de faire l'échange dans cet endroit ?
c. Dans une heure, on va réveiller Hana Lebosse.
d. Pourquoi ma cheffe n'appelle pas le GIGN ?
e. Je dois d'abord avoir les autorisations avant la perquisition.
f. J'espère qu'il n'a pas prévenu la police.
g. Qu'est-ce que c'est que ce masque ?
h. Casino ? Est-ce une blague ? Je vais leur raconter !

3 Transformez les phrases à la forme négative.

1. Partez de votre galerie.

→ ....

2. Enlève ton masque.

→ ....

3. Dépêchez-vous.

→ ....

4. Fais-le.

→ ....

5. Donne-lui le sabre.

→ ....

6. Arrêtez.

→ ....

4 Barrez ce qui est faux pour chaque personnage.

1. François Yasaki : il possède un sabre ancien – il a un scooter – il achète le masque 40 000 euros.
2. Emma Lorenzo : elle appelle le GIGN – elle va en voiture au supermarché – elle a une arme.
3. Thibault Fontaine : il connaît Yasaki – il a volé le masque – il a des dettes de jeu.
4. Samir Lacoste : il a dîné au restaurant – il court avec son arme – il va acheter des sushis.

5 Pourquoi Thibault Fontaine a-t-il accepté de faire cet échange ?

....

....

6 « L'exploration urbaine » est-elle une activité pour vous ? Faites des recherches sur Internet si vous ne la connaissez pas.

....

....

CHAPITRE 8

1 🔘 piste 8 → **Écoutez le chapitre 8. Vrai ou faux ? Cochez la bonne réponse. Justifiez lorsque vous pensez que c'est faux.**

	Vrai	Faux
1. Agathe Langlois est toujours dans le coma.	☐	☐
2. Emma travaille seule sur l'enquête.	☐	☐
3. Emma et Dany vont voir une compétition de judo.	☐	☐
4. Juliette Bourdelle est habillée à la japonaise.	☐	☐
5. Juliette essaye de s'enfuir.	☐	☐
6. Après la compétition, Emma et Dany vont dîner ensemble.	☐	☐

Justification :

....
....
....
....

2 **Trouvez dans le chapitre 8 des phrases synonymes des phrases suivantes.**

1. Les perquisitions n'ont pas permis de résoudre l'affaire.

....

2. Agathe Langlois est guérie.

....

3. Mon patron ne pense pas la même chose que moi.

....

4. Tout est déjà fait.

....

5. Dany cache ce qu'il pense.

....

3 Complétez la grille avec des mots du chapitre.

1. Un grand nombre de personnes.
2. Elles permettent de trouver un coupable.
3. C'est un tableau avec les jours de la semaine.
4. Le contraire de l' « arrivée ».
5. Juliette les a aux poignets.
6. Elle peut être bonne ou mauvaise.
7. Le féminin d' « auteur ».

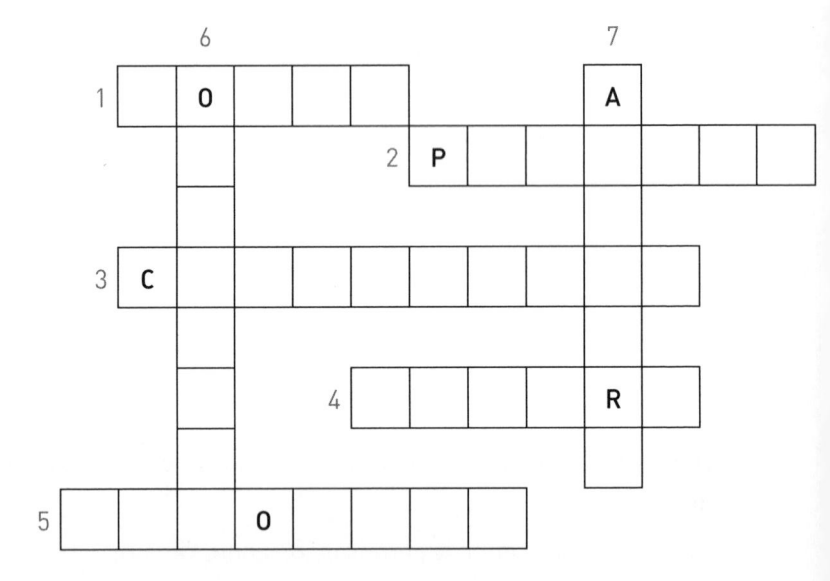

4 Conjuguez les verbes au passé composé.

1. Les images .... (aider) Emma et Samir à comprendre le vol.
2. Les gardiens .... (ne pas ouvrir) les glacières.
3. Comment..(trouver) Juliette ? (2ᵉ personne du singulier)
4. J' .... (faire) l'échange moi-même.
5. Nous .... (devenir) amies.
6. Vous .... (promettre) de me protéger.

5 **Corrigez les erreurs soulignées dans la version du vol du masque.**

Juliette Bourdelle est venue le lundi après-midi au <u>Palais omnisports</u> (..................). Elle avait avec elle <u>trois valises</u> (....................). Les <u>directeurs</u> (..........................) ne les contrôlent pas. À l'intérieur se trouvaient les <u>verres de saké</u> (.........................). À 16 h, elle est repartie avec <u>trois glacières</u> (.......................) . Dans la glacière, le <u>sabre du samouraï</u> (..............................) quittait le musée. Mais pourquoi Juliette <u>Fontaine</u> (..................) et <u>Emma</u> (............) Lebosse voulaient <u>sauver</u> (..............) Agathe Langlois ?

6 **Répondez aux questions.**

1. Qui ne travaille plus sur l'enquête, Samir ou Emma ?

....

2. Qui reprend son travail à l'atelier Fontaine, Juliette ou Agathe ?

....

3. Qui ne joue plus avec son argent, Yasaki ou Fontaine ?

....

4. Qui espère prendre un avion vers le Japon, Juliette ou Emma ?

....

5. Qui est déçu de ne pas dîner avec Emma, Dany ou Samir ?

....

7 **Pourquoi Dany est le plus heureux des hommes quand Emma accepte sa proposition ?**

....
....

8 **À votre avis, pourquoi Hana Lebosse laisse tomber Juliette Bourdelle ?**

....
....

ACTIVITÉS DE SYNTHÈSE

1 **Classez les titres dans l'ordre de l'histoire. Puis proposez votre propre titre pour chaque chapitre.**

☐ a. La bonne occasion ?

....

☐ b. Agathe Langlois, suspecte numéro 1

....

☐ c. Et si Juliette…

....

☐ d. Un dîner qui finit mal…

....

☐ e. Le piège

....

☐ f. Que cache Thibault Fontaine ?

....

☐ g. François Yasaki ment-il ?

....

☐ h. Perte de mémoire

....

2 **Associez chaque personnage aux bonnes informations.**

1. Emma Lorenzo
2. Samir Lacoste
3. Agathe Langlois
4. François Yasaki
5. Thibault Fontaine
6. Juliette Bourdelle

a. Elle rêve de vivre au Japon.
b. Il a perdu beaucoup d'argent aux jeux.
c. Pour lui, la place du masque est au Japon.
d. Elle est une restauratrice d'art très douée.
e. Il entre toujours sans frapper dans le bureau de sa cheffe.
f. Elle est passionnée d'art et chasseuse d'œuvres volées.

3 Classez les scènes dans l'ordre de l'histoire.

☐ a. François Yasaki entre dans l'immeuble du Cercle de jeux du Trocadéro.

☐ b. Juliette Bourdelle annonce son départ pour le Japon.

☐ c. Emma interroge Thibault Fontaine dans son atelier près du bassin de la Villette.

☐ d. Thibault Fontaine et François Yasaki ont rendez-vous dans un ancien supermarché.

☐ e. Emma arrête Juliette avant son départ pour le Japon.

☐ f. Emma rend visite à Agathe à l'hôpital : elle a perdu la mémoire !

☐ g. Un masque japonais est volé au musée du Quai Branly.

4 Qui dit quoi ? Associez une phrase à chaque personnage.

1. Emma Lorenzo
2. Samir Lacoste
3. François Yasaki
4. Juliette Bourdelle

a. Oui, mais cette fois-ci c'est urgent.
b. Kenji Ono est le meilleur cuisinier japonais ! Il est aussi un très bon ami.
c. Je suis désolée, Dany, mais je dois aller à l'OCBC pour une affaire urgente.
d. Quelle garce ! Tu as raison, Emma, mon rêve est fini.

5 À votre avis, quelles sont les qualités indispensables à Emma Lorenzo pour faire son métier ?

....
....

6 Selon vous, est-il pardonnable de faire des choses illégales pour réaliser son rêve ?

....
....

FICHE 1 — LE MUSÉE DU QUAI BRANLY-JACQUES CHIRAC

Le musée

Le musée du Quai Branly à Paris se trouve sur les bords de la Seine, à quelques pas de la tour Eiffel. Il présente des œuvres des civilisations d'Afrique, d'Asie, d'Amérique et d'Océanie. Le bâtiment principal a la forme d'un pont et repose sur des pilotis. C'est l'architecte français Jean Nouvel qui l'a imaginé. Le visiteur découvre tout d'abord l'un des plus grands murs végétaux du monde avec 22 000 plantes de 376 espèces de tous les continents. Puis il pénètre dans un jardin sauvage protégé par un grand mur de verre. À l'intérieur du musée, une installation vidéo, « The River », conduit aux collections : 16 000 noms de lieux et de peuples du monde coulent sur le sol comme de l'eau. Depuis son ouverture en 2006, le musée accueille plus d'un million de visiteurs par an.

1 Lisez le texte. Avez-vous bien compris ? Choisissez la bonne réponse.

1. Le musée du Quai Branly se trouve près :
- ☐ a. de la tour Eiffel.
- ☐ b. de l'Opéra de Paris.

2. Le musée présente des œuvres :
- ☐ a. européennes.
- ☐ b. non européennes.

3. Le musée a la forme :
- ☐ a. d'un pont.
- ☐ b. d'un bateau.

4. Une installation vidéo présente des :
- ☐ a. photos de personnes.
- ☐ b. noms de lieux et de peuples.

5. L'année d'ouverture du musée est :
- ☐ a. 2006.
- ☐ b. 2019.

Les œuvres du musée

Le musée compte plus de 300 000 pièces. Ce sont des œuvres d'art, mais aussi des objets de tous les jours ou servant aux cérémonies religieuses.
Il y a des sculptures, des masques, des vêtements, des peintures, des photos, des tissus…
L'emblème du musée est une petite statue de femme mexicaine de la culture Chupicuaro. Elle vient du Mexique et date de plus de 2 300 ans.
Au centre du musée, une tour de verre présente sur six étages 10 000 instruments de musique.

2 Lisez le texte. Vrai ou faux ? Cochez la bonne réponse. Justifiez lorsque vous pensez que c'est faux.

	vrai	faux
1. Les pièces du musée sont toutes des œuvres d'art.	☐	☐
2. Le musée présente plus de 300 000 pièces.	☐	☐
3. On peut admirer des photos dans ce musée.	☐	☐
4. L'emblème est un masque japonais.	☐	☐
5. Les instruments de musique occupent une tour de verre.	☐	☐

Justification :

....
....
....

3 Soulignez l'intrus dans ces propositions sur le musée du Quai Branly.

1. Jean Nouvel – Tour Eiffel – Paris – ouverture en 2016.
2. Afrique – Asie – Europe – Amérique – Océanie.
3. 100 000 pièces – œuvres d'art – objets de tous les jours – objets religieux.
4. Emblème – tableau – femme mexicaine – 2 300 ans.

FICHE 2 — LE MUSÉE DES CIVILISATIONS (MUCEM)

Le musée

Le Musée des civilisations de l'Europe et de la Méditerranée (Mucem) se trouve à l'entrée du port de Marseille, face à la Méditerranée. Comme le musée du Quai Branly, c'est un « musée de société », c'est-à-dire qu'il s'intéresse au développement des sociétés. C'est pourquoi on trouve de très nombreux objets de la vie quotidienne à côté des œuvres d'art. Un des bâtiments présente les étapes du développement des civilisations de la Méditerranée jusqu'à aujourd'hui. Des conférences et des expositions temporaires sensibilisent les visiteurs sur l'actualité et le futur de ces civilisations. Les visiteurs peuvent admirer la ville et la mer depuis le fort Saint-Jean (un monument du 12e siècle). Autour du fort, le Jardin des migrations rassemble des plantes de toutes les rives de la Méditerranée.

1 **Lisez le texte. Répondez aux questions.**

1. Dans quelle ville se trouve le Mucem ?

   ....

2. Le musée est face à quelle mer ?

   ....

3. Que présente le musée en plus des œuvres d'art ?

   ....

4. Le musée s'intéresse-t-il seulement au passé des civilisations de la Méditerranée ?

   ....

5. Qu'y a-t-il autour du fort Saint-Jean ?

   ....

2 **Quelle est la caractéristique d'un « musée de société » ?**

....
....

FICHE 3 — LE MUSÉE DES CONFLUENCES

Le musée

Le musée des Confluences se trouve à Lyon, au point de rencontre des deux fleuves de la ville, le Rhône et la Saône. Trois espaces à l'architecture très moderne composent le musée : le Cristal, le Nuage et le Socle. Le musée présente plus de deux millions d'objets, aussi différents que des fossiles, le satellite russe Spoutnik 2 ou des masques de théâtre nô. C'est une sorte de cabinet de curiosités[1] du 21e siècle. Un « parcours permanent » permet de découvrir les origines et l'avenir de l'humanité. Il présente la place de l'homme dans le monde vivant, ainsi que la diversité des cultures. Depuis son ouverture en 2014, le musée a reçu plus de trois millions de visiteurs.

[1] Un cabinet de curiosités : au 16e et 17e siècles, pièce où on exposait des objets rares et curieux.

1 Lisez le texte. Associez les phrases.

1. Le musée des Confluences....
2. Le musée est ouvert...
3. À côté du satellite Spoutnik, on peut...
4. Le parcours permanent permet de découvrir...
5. L'architecture du bâtiment est...

a. ...aussi admirer des masques de théâtre nô.
b. ...se trouve à Lyon.
c. ...très moderne.
d. ...les origines et l'avenir de l'humanité.
e. ...depuis 2014.

1	2	3	4	5
....	....	....	....	....

2 Pourquoi le musée des Confluences est un « cabinet de curiosités » du 21e siècle ?

....
....

CORRIGÉS

CHAPITRE 1

1. 1. c - 2. b - 3. c - 4. a - 5. b - 6. c

2. Ordre des phrases : 1. g - 2. e - 3. b - 4. d - 5. f - 6. c - 7. a

3. 1. Emma est membre de l'association depuis l'ouverture du musée.
2. François Yasaki est directeur de la plus grande galerie d'art japonais de Paris.
3. Juliette Bourdelle est conservatrice des collections asiatiques du musée.
4. Agathe pose ses mains sur son ventre.
5. Les invités courent vers les sorties.

4. 1. …il faut goûter l'entrée.
2. …il faut le restaurer.
3. …il faut appeler un médecin.
4. Faut-il rendre…
5. Il faut attendre…
6. …il faut sortir très vite.

5. Car elle déteste le poisson cru et que François Yasaki lui a parlé du poison du fugu.

6. Production libre.

CHAPITRE 2

1. 1. Vrai.
2. Faux. C'est son collègue à l'OCBC.
3. Faux. Elle est dans le coma.
4. Faux. François Yasaki n'a pas mangé de poisson.
5. Vrai.
6. Vrai.

2. 1. masque
2. équipe
3. escalier
4. poste
5. ville
6. intoxication
7. porte
8. image
Mot mystère : suspecte

3. 1. mystère
2. reposer
3. conférences
4. difficultés
5. alarme

4. 1. tous
2. toute
3. toutes
4. tous
5. tout
6. toutes

5. Le médecin parle de huit personnes intoxiquées, et Samir dit qu'il y a eu des problèmes seulement à sa table. Elle veut vérifier combien de personnes dînaient à la même table qu'elle.

6. Production libre.

CHAPITRE 3

1. 1. b - 2. b - 3. a - 4. b - 5. a.

2. 1. d - 2. c - 3. b - 4. e - 5. a.

3. masque, famille, siècle, descendant, explorateur, lettre, extraordinaire, cercle, jouer

4. 1. que
2. qui
3. qu'
4. qui
5. que
6. qui

5. Car seule la dose de poison dans son assiette était mortelle.

6. Production libre.

CHAPITRE 4

1. 1. Vrai.
2. Faux. Il n'y a plus de café dans l'atelier.
3. Faux. Il n'y est pas allé, car il était à Toulouse.
4. Faux. Elle a peur de son état psychique.
5. Vrai.

2. 1. divorcés
2. vacances
3. dormir
4. célibataire
5. roux
6. poisson
7. réseaux

3. grand, longs, décontracté, divorcé, nom, spécialisées, professionnel, interdit, ex-femme, jeu.

4. 1. Nous nous parlons…
2. Que se passe-t-il ?
3. Vous vous arrêtez…
4. Je me demande…
5. Ils s'assoient…
6. Tu t'accuses…

5. Sa femme l'a quitté, car il perdait de grosses sommes d'argent au jeu.

6. Production libre.

CHAPITRE 5

1. 1. a - 2. c - 3. b - 4. c - 5. b

2. 1. Emma Lorenzo : b, f
2. Samir Lacoste : d
3. François Yasaki : a, c
4. Agathe Langlois : e

3. 1. quel
2. quelle
3. quels
4. quelles
5. quel

4. Agathe est la suspecte numéro 1. Elle ne peut plus expliquer pourquoi elle est allée dans l'atelier de restauration lors du dîner.

5 Production libre.

CHAPITRE 6

1 1. experts
2. réponse
3. copie
4. mémoire
5. suspects
6. boulot
7. proverbe
8. emplois

2 1. d - 2. c - 3. a - 4. e - 5. b

3 2. Si le masque dans le sac est une copie, l'original est ailleurs.
3. Si Emma dit qu'Agathe se souvient du dîner, comment va réagir Juliette ?
4. Si Samir a un rendez-vous, il ne peut pas retrouver Emma au bureau.
5. Si le chef n'a pas fait d'erreur, une autre personne a préparé le poisson.
6. Si Samir peut appeler son amie, il peut annuler leur rendez-vous.

4 Juliette est peut-être innocente. Elle n'a donc pas à avoir peur. Si elle est coupable, alors elle a appelé l'hôpital et sait qu'Emma ment.

5 Production libre.

CHAPITRE 7

1 1. Il est dans sa galerie.
2. Non, il veut l'échanger contre un sabre de samouraï.
3. L'idée lui donne le goût du fugu dans la bouche et donc un mauvais souvenir.
4. Dans une salle de sport.
5. Elle peut faire des perquisitions.

2 1. Emma Lorenzo : c, e
2. François Yasaki : a, g
3. Thibault Fontaine : b, f
4. Samir Lacoste : d, h

3 1. Ne partez pas de votre galerie.
2. N'enlève pas ton masque.
3. Ne vous dépêchez pas.
4. Ne le fais pas.
5. Ne lui donne pas le sabre.
6. N'arrêtez pas.

4 1. il achète le masque 40 000 euros.
2. elle appelle le GIGN.
3. il a volé le masque.
4. il va acheter des sushis.

5 On lui offre en échange d'effacer ses dettes de jeu.

6 Production libre.

CHAPITRE 8

1 1. Faux. Elle est en pleine forme.
2. Vrai.
3. Faux. C'est du sumo.
4. Vrai.
5. Vrai.
6. Faux. Emma doit aller à l'OCBC.

2 1. Les perquisitions n'ont rien donné.
2. Agathe Langlois est maintenant en pleine forme.
3. Mais il n'est pas du même avis que moi.
4. Tout est déjà réglé.
5. Mais il ne montre rien.

3 1. foule
2. preuves
3. calendrier
4. départ
5. menottes
6. occasion
7. auteure

4 1. ont aidé
2. n'ont pas ouvert
3. as-tu trouvé
4. ai fait
5. sommes devenues
6. avez promis

5 musée - deux glaciares - gardiens - les assiettes de fugu - une seule glacière - masque de théâtre nô - Bourdelle - Hana - tuer

6 1. Samir ne travaille plus sur l'enquête.
2. Agathe reprend son travail à l'atelier Fontaine.
3. Fontaine ne joue plus avec son argent.
4. Juliette espère prendre un avion vers le Japon.
5. Dany est déçu de ne pas dîner avec Emma.

7 Il essaye de lui changer les idées depuis six mois, mais elle n'accepte jamais de l'accompagner.

8 Production libre.

ACTIVITÉS DE SYNTHÈSE

1 1. d - 2. b - 3. g - 4. f - 5. h - 6. c - 7. e - 8. a
Production libre.

2 1. Emma Lorenzo : f
2. Samir Lacoste : e
3. Agathe Langlois : d
4. François Yasaki : c
5. Thibault Fontaine : b
6. Juliette Bourdelle : a

3 1. g - 2. a - 3. c - 4. f - 5. b - 6. d - 7. e

4 1. c - 2. a - 3. b - 4. d

5 Production libre

6 Production libre.

FICHE 1

1. 1. a - 2. b - 3. a - 4. b - 5. a

2. 1. Faux. Il y a aussi des objets de tous les jours.
2. Vrai.
3. Vrai.
4. Faux. C'est une statue mexicaine.
5. Vrai.

3. 1. ouverture en 2016
2. Europe
3. 100 000 pièces
4. tableau

FICHE 2

1. 1. Marseille.
2. La Méditerranée.
3. Il présente des objets de la vie quotidienne.
4. Non, il s'intéresse aussi à l'actualité et au futur.
5. Il y a un jardin.

2. Il présente des objets de la vie quotidienne à côté des œuvres d'art.

FICHE 3

1. 1. b - 2. e - 3. a - 4. d - 5. c

2. Car il présente des objets très différents, rares et curieux.

Achevé d'imprimer en juin 2020 en France par Chirat - N° 202006.0061
Dépôt légal : juin 2020 - Édition 01 - 42/7702/4